The Englishman's House, From A Cottage To A Mansion: A Practical Guide To Members Of Building Societies, And All Interested In Selecting Or Building A House...

Charles James Richardson

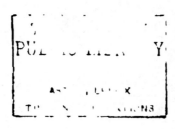
Richards

3-Mfg.

HOUSES MADE PICTURESQUE.

THE
ENGLISHMAN'S HOUSE

FROM

A COTTAGE TO A MANSION.

A

PRACTICAL GUIDE TO MEMBERS OF BUILDING SOCIETIES, AND ALL
INTERESTED IN SELECTING OR BUILDING A HOUSE.

BY

C. J. RICHARDSON, ARCHITECT,

AUTHOR OF "OLD ENGLISH MANSIONS," ETC.

Second Edition, Corrected and Enlarged, with nearly 600 Illustrations.

LONDON :
JOHN CAMDEN HOTTEN, 74 & 75, PICCADILLY.

[1871]

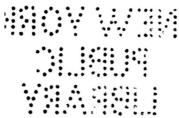
LONDON :
SAVILL, EDWARDS AND CO., PRINTERS, CHANDOS STREET,
COVENT GARDEN.

PREFACE.

SEVERAL years ago the author of this volume published a small work on the Warming and Ventilation of Buildings, which was very favourably received by the Public, but is now out of print. He afterwards wrote various other works illustrating the Architecture of England during the reigns of Queen Elizabeth and James I., with one volume on Ornamental Designs. These had an extensive sale, and are now, like the first small volume, out of print. His last publication was a small pamphlet, entitled, " The Smoke Nuisance and its Remedy, with remarks on Liquid Fuel," the subject of which, at least so far as regards an improved construction for the domestic chimney flue, is continued in the present volume.

The present volume consists of numerous plans, &c., for Cottages, Villas, and small and large Mansions, most of which have been carried into execution. They are carefully selected from a large collection of similar subjects, the result of many years' professional practice, and it is hoped that they may be favourably received.

21, CARLISLE TERRACE, KENSINGTON, W.
December, 1870.

CONTENTS.

INTRODUCTORY CHAPTER

ON THE

PICTURESQUE IN RELATION

TO

ARCHITECTURE.

Grecian Temple.

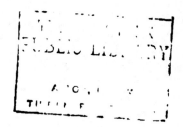

INTRODUCTION.

I T has been said that a definition of the picturesque in respect to architecture, or indeed any branch of the fine arts, is scarcely possible. The most able writers on the subject have failed to convey an adequate and popular idea. In fact the term has so great and extensive an application as to forbid exact definition. The architect usually considers that if his building look well when seen by moonlight, or through the medium of a foggy or dull atmosphere, it is picturesque, and he is satisfied. Blenheim Castle and Castle Howard have always been pointed out as eminent examples of the picturesque in buildings. But this quality varies with every change of situation and circumstance under which it can be conceived.

The entrance to the Acropolis of Athens, with its noble equestrian statues in the foreground, the steps between them, and the beautiful temples rising at different heights behind, giving a varied outline, the

whole probably delicately coloured, must have been
picturesque in the highest degree. The Temple of
the Winds and the Monument of Lysicrates were
equally examples of the picturesque. Yet although
great efforts were made on the publication of Athenian
Stuart's volumes to introduce pure Grecian architecture here, it has obtained no hold with us. St.
Pancras Church, and St. Stephen's, Camden Town, are
probably the last specimens in our metropolis. The
delicate mouldings of the one are destroyed by the
roughness of the climate, and the beautiful figures
of the Caryatidæ in the other are covered with
soot.

There is no doubt that the Roman temples were as
picturesque and as varied in outline as the Grecian
buildings of which they were studies, but none remain
sufficiently perfect to illustrate them. In their original, entire state, with the surfaces and colour smooth
and even, either in painting or reality they were beautiful; in ruins, there is no denying they are highly
picturesque. Observe the process by which time, the
great author of such changes works, first by means of
weather stains, partial incrustations, mosses, &c., which
simultaneously take off the uniformity of surface and
of colour, giving a degree of roughness, and variety of
tint. Then the various accidents of weather loosen
the stones themselves: they tumble in irregular masses

Roman Temple in Ruins.

upon what was perhaps smooth turf or pavement, or nicely trimmed walks and shrubberies, now mixed and overgrown with wild plants and creepers that crawl over and shoot among the falling ruins. Sedums, wall-flowers, and other plants that bear drought, find nourishment in the decayed cement from which the stones have been detached; birds convey their food into the chinks, and yew, elder, and other berried plants project from the sides; while the ivy mantles over other parts, and crowns the top. The even, regular lines of the doors and windows are broken, and through their ivy-fringed openings is displayed in a highly broken and picturesque manner that striking image described by Virgil:

"Apparet domus intus, et atria longa patescunt
Apparent Priami et veterum penetralia regum."

The first view given in this volume attempts to show the picturesque effect of the Grecian Temple in its complete state, the attendants having just retired from some display or ceremony; the second, the front of a Roman Temple in its noble remains.

To the Greeks we owe all the general principles and forms of classic art, but they have been modified to modern ideas and tastes, and, it may be added, to suit also the various climates of the countries where they have been adopted.

However much the occupations of our countrymen may partake of the commercial character, the mental qualities requisite to such pursuits have not been so displayed as to exclude a taste for art. Where, for example, can be found superior specimens of art-choice than exist in their mansions, villas, or cottage-ornées, their picture and sculpture galleries, or the museums and other collections of those whose business pursuits have been the cause of their prosperity.

An essential element of success in every branch of progress is involved in tasteful selection. Without considering those classes who by successful efforts of their ancestry have been placed beyond the pale of want (either artificial or real), a large proportion of our population may be ranked as having advanced morally, socially, and commercially by that intuition which characterizes our national progress. It takes as its basis nature and nature's products. It eliminates from these not only pecuniary benefits that in a commercial point of view may occur, but associating the useful with the beautiful (the sense of the latter having been gained during intervals of quiet thought as a relief from the incessant requirements of business engagements), a tendency to embody the picturesque, especially in regard to architecture, arises. We have no hesitation in assigning to this cause the production of some of the most pictu-

resque architectural erections which grace our country,
—that render English homes an example, and prove
that, while the main element of our national prosperity
is making money, we are not insensible to the benefi-
cent influences resulting from the cultivation of refined
taste.

It would be interesting as an object of careful inquiry, if there existed sufficient data for the purpose, to
trace each of the many steps that have occurred between
the birth of architecture and its present condition. The
early history of mankind had as its locality climates
which favoured the construction and use of the *crudest*
contrivances, intended only to meet the few wants of
shelter and occasional domestic privacy. The first condition of man's existence, either in this primitive or
modern state, is that of roving or wandering tribes.
Instances of this are found in the early inhabitants of
Asia Minor, and adjacent countries, and at the present
day the same habit is maintained in Central Asia,
Arabia, and many parts of America. As soon as the
sustenance afforded for their cattle is consumed in one
district a migration is made to another. Gradually,
however, centres of trade sprung up where commodi-
ties could be bartered for live stock. Men thus became
massed together in villages and towns. Quitting a
semi-savage condition, they built permanent residences
in place of the tent. At first these, like the log-hut

of the modern Canadian, were only sufficient for the most common necessities of life. In course of time, however, the spirit of emulation, the growth of riches, and the germination of man's natural taste for the beautiful, led to artificial wants, which were soon converted into necessities of life. This called out the study of art on the part of the few for the benefit of the many. Systems of art in all its branches gradually developed themselves. By the study of the beauties of nature such systems gradually progressed in purity of style, and produced designs that eventually were appreciated by the common people, in a greater or less degree, according to the capabilities of each individual. Architecture and the other fine arts thus, by slow but sure degrees, began to gain a hold on popular taste, and step by step they arrived at the state of perfection of which we now boast.

It will be evident that whilst the primary objects of architecture were simply those of meeting the immediate necessities of life, its ultimate purpose was only attained when it became an art, cultivated by refined taste, an educated eye, and encouraged by the growth of civilization and commerce. It thus advanced from a state of barbarism into one in which it was connected with all the highest developments of the moral and mental qualities of mankind, but especially with the æsthetic aspirations of our nature.

Incidentally but necessarily connected with the general progress of architecture is the great variety of styles that has been invented. The whole of these are modifications of some one or more primaries. No two individuals acquire the same mental impression by viewing one object; each of their impressions is tinted by the mental characteristics of the individual. It is, therefore, from this cause that so many varieties of style have originated from one first model. An illustration of this is afforded in the Gothic, which in different hands has been greatly divided and modified in its details. This style, which at first was of exclusive application only, has subsequently become most extensively in use for purposes that at first sight it would have been judged as quite unfit for.

The style of architecture just referred to is remarkable for its picturesque character, and may fitly be adduced as an ensample of that quality in the absence of an exact definition of the term.

An able writer criticising Gothic buildings, remarks that the outline of the summit presents a great variety of forms of turrets and pinnacles, some open, some fretted and variously enriched. But even where there is an exact correspondence of parts, it is often disguised by an appearance of splendid confusion and irregularity.

In the doors and windows of Gothic Churches, the

pointed arch has as much variety as any regular figure can well have; the eye, too, is less strongly conducted, than by the parallel lines in the Grecian style, from the top of one aperture to that of another; and every person must be struck with the extreme richness and intricacy of some of the principal windows of our cathedrals and ruined abbeys. In these last is displayed the triumph of the picturesque, and their charms to a painter's eye are often so great as to rival those which arise from the chaste ornaments and the noble and elegant simplicity of Grecian architecture.

These remarks will explain to a certain degree the nature of the picturesque in regard to architecture, so far at least as the general principles are involved. But in the more minute points, other questions and relations arise, to which the attention of the reader will be fully drawn in the descriptive text and illustrations of this work.

The comparative value of Grecian and Gothic architecture, as practically adopted in the erection of ornamental dwellings, is well discussed by an eminent architect in the following remarks, slightly modified from the original. He observes that the two are better distinguished by an attention to their general effects, than to the minute parts peculiar to each. It is in architecture as in painting—beauty depends on

light and shade, and they are caused by the openings
or projections in the surface.   If these tend to produce
horizontal lines, the building must be deemed Grecian,
however whimsically the doors and windows may be
constructed.   If, on the contrary, the shadows give a
preference to perpendicular lines, the general character
of the building will be Gothic.   This is evident from
the large houses built in Queen Elizabeth's reign,
where Grecian columns were introduced.   Yet they
are always considered as Gothic buildings.

In our modern Grecian architecture large cornices
are repeated, with windows ranged perfectly in the
same line, and these lines often more strongly marked
by a horizontal fascia.   There are few breaks of any
great depth; and if there be a portico, the shadow
made by the columns is very trifling compared with
that broad horizontal shadow proceeding from the soffit
(that is, the under side of the heads of apertures,
architraves, and the corona of cornices).   The only
ornament its roof will admit, is either a flat pediment
departing very little from the horizontal, or a dome
still rising from a horizontal base.

But in these remarks attention is chiefly drawn to
the general architectural effect of style, independent
of concomitant circumstances.   Yet it is hardly necessary to do more than call on the experience of any
man of taste to show that position, adjacent scenery,

and other "accidental" or "incidental" matters will modify the special effect of any style in regard to the picturesque, and also those of a general character. A Gothic erection in a confined situation will lose most of its beauties, while one of a Grecian character may be specially suitable. In choosing, therefore, any design for the erection of a new building, or alterations in one already in existence, respect should be had to the natural character of the surrounding country, the aspects in regard to the sun and prevalent winds, the extent of the estate or grounds on which the building is to be erected, the views from the various apartments, the character of wood, plain, or other adjacent tree-scenery, and last, but of equal or greater importance, questions in reference to domestic comfort and convenience, drainage and dry soil, supply of water, and a variety of details, most of which will at once suggest themselves. In many cases the choice of site is necessarily fixed by previous purchase or inheritance of the land, yet in such cases chances are left for a judicious selection in regard to some of the conditions above mentioned. But when the purchase has to be effected, *all* the conditions should be kept in mind, and, if possible, completely satisfied. Such details should form the subject of minute inquiry, and they are here only named for the purpose of showing how the choice of the best style, in regard either to general beauty or picturesque effect, should be decided on with mature attention to all the circumstances of the case.

Most of the old mansions, &c., of this country and many parts of Continental Europe, have been erected in situations that were then immediately, and at little cost, available for the purpose. At one time the choice of such situation depended on careful attention to the special circumstances of those who erected the building. Thus it is found, generally, that the banks of the rivers, as affording ready and cheap means of carriage by the stream, were mostly chosen. Hence our abbeys, monasteries, &c., are frequently found in such localities. Baronial castles were usually erected on hills, the height of which tended to the security of the owners against sudden incursions of their foes. From the varied character of English topography has arisen that great variety of picturesque beauty that distinguishes the ruins which abound in almost every county throughout the length and breadth of the land; such ruins, architecturally considered in relation to the surrounding circumstances of wood, vale, hill and dale, have become subjects of study and suggestion to modern architects, and models, constantly adopted at the present time, in certain details, for producing new designs. In the selection of these, or of any other style, however, Burke has laid down, in his essay on

"The Sublime and Beautiful," an excellent rule: "A true artist should put a generous deceit on the spectators, and effect the noblest designs by easy methods. Designs that are vast only by their dimensions, are always the sign of a common and low imagination. The work of art can be great but as it deceives; to be otherwise is the prerogative of nature only."

It will thus be seen, that to obtain the highest effect of the picturesque in architecture requires an educated eye, a refined taste, great experience, but especially a keen perception of all the conditions, on the fulfilment of which the most successful result can be obtained. In all there is a natural love of unity and effect. Montesquieu, in his dissertation on *Taste*, observes: "Wherever symmetry is useful to the soul, and may assist her functions, it is agreeable to her; but wherever it is useless, it becomes distasteful, because it takes away variety. Therefore things that are seen in succession ought to have variety, for our soul has no difficulty in seeing them; those on the contrary, that we see at one glance, ought to have symmetry. Thus at one glance we see the front of a building, a parterre, a temple. In such things there is always a symmetry which pleases the soul by the facility it gives her of taking in the whole object at once."

The numerous dissertations, essays, &c., that have been produced on the subjects that have here been treated on in a discursive manner only, are a sufficient proof of the difficulty which exists in acquiring, applying, and affording an accurate and ample description of all the conditions necessary to picturesque architecture; they also in some measure explain the reason of the grotesque, and even offensive results that obtrude on refined taste in the productions of builders who are utterly deficient of artistic taste and knowledge in carrying out their objects. A general, and in part a historic view of architecture may serve to show how success has been attained in many cases, and the evils that should be avoided as leading to failure in effect of the general and special features of an erection.

In the cursory view of the history of architecture already given, it has been shown that the earliest efforts of the art were simply directed to satisfy the simple wants of man, without any regard being had to taste. It was not until riches began to accumulate in a few hands that taste in architecture was developed, and by the few examples thus produced the taste of society at large was educed, refined, and extended.

Omitting then any inquiry into the architecture of our earth's aborigines, which was evidently of the rudest character, reference may first be made to early architectural attempts in Asia. It has been ingeniously observed by M. Pair, that the Chinese imitated a tent as the model of their system, a result that undoubtedly arose from the fact that the first Tartar tribes were nomadic or wandering in their nature. It has also been remarked that a bird's-eye view of a Chinese city at once suggests the idea of a fixed camp. In southern and south-western Asia may be found, on the other hand, the remains of extensive architectural productions in caves, such as that of the Pagoda Elephanta, from which many have argued that subterraneous dwellings were amongst the earliest; but it is evident that such could only be made in places where stone existed in masses, as a basis of the country. In a plain and sandy district, and in alluvial soil generally, such could not possibly have been produced. There is not the least doubt that the conditions of climate have in all cases determined the early character of each national system. In both hot and cold countries caves would naturally have been sought as affording shelter from the two extremes of heat and cold. Recent geological discoveries have brought to light the fact that the remains of human and quadruped bones have been found together in such situations, the human inhabitants having most probaby been the predecessors of the beasts of prey, as also of the fowls of the air. It has been suggested too that the forest tree having formerly served for shelter, might have suggested the floral character of columns, and the use of floral decoration generally at their summit.

c

In respect to these "natural" and consequently primitive "systems" of architecture, Billington has made the following judicious remarks: — "Those people or nations who lived by the chase (and in the same class the Ichthyophagi, or fish-eaters, are included) could not for a great length of time have built themselves shelters. The long courses the hunters made prevented them from watching their property, which must have comprised [but] few articles; and they found it more convenient to make hollows in the rocks for their dwellings, or to profit by those which nature offered them in its caverns. It was the same with those who lived by fishing; passing a sedentary life on the sea shores, the sides of rivers, or the borders of the lakes, they always made themselves such abodes, or took advantage of those already formed by nature. The little industry which this mode of life required, and the natural idleness which followed it, was sufficient to induce them to prefer the dwellings presented by nature, to those of art. This fact is proved by experience at the present day, as these descriptions of persons continue to adopt the same plan of life in countries where the arts of civilization have not extended their beneficial influence. The pastors or shepherds, as they were inhabitants of plains during a great portion of the year, could not make use of the retreats hollowed and prepared in the mountains and rocks by the hand of nature; being obliged to seek change of pasture, and thus lead an ambulatory life, it was requisite to have dwellings or shelters that could be carried with them wherever they went, and hence originated the use of tents. But the active operations of agriculture requiring a definite situation, necessity suggested the propriety of building solid and fixed abodes. The agriculturist then, living on his own grounds, and in the enjoyment of his property, had to store his provisions; it was therefore necessary to have a habitation at once commodious, safe, healthful, and extensive; and the wood hut with its roof was soon erected."

The same author considers that there is not the least certainty of this primitive wooden construction, with its inclined roof, having been the universal model of all nations, but especially in regard to Egypt and China. The peculiarities of the early Chinese style of architecture have been already named, and with the persistent continuity in one course yet prevalent, that style is still preserved. But the Grecian style was evidently founded on the rude model, and the ingenuity of that nation eventually led to the transference of material from wood to stone.

At the present day the Orders of Grecian architecture are fundamental to the principles of modern art in numerous varieties of detail; they have survived the prejudices, fancies, and dicta of various schools of art, although, as already shown, the Gothic and other systems have become formidable competitors, and in many cases, especially in regard to the picturesque, efficient, elegant, and ornamental substitutes. The taste for the latter characteristic has led to an increased adoption, for example, of the Italian style, which in many respects resembles the Grecian, but differs from it especially in lightness of detail, with greater variety. The author just quoted traces the origin of the Doric Order of the Greeks to a primary adaptation of the trunks of trees as external supports of the wooden dwelling, seeing in them the foreshadowing of the column designative of that order. " As trees are of greater circumference at their lower extremities, and diminish in rising, the diminution of the column was suggested by them . . . These timbers (as supports) consisting of trunks of trees planted in the ground, offered not as yet the idea of bases and pedestals, as is seen in the Doric Order, which is without base. But in the course of time the inconvenience of this method was perceived, as it exposed the wood to rot, and to remedy this inconvenience pieces of wood were placed under each support to give it a better foundation, and to protect it from humidity. This practice may be traced in some of the ancient edifices in which the columns have no other base than a block of stone. But afterwards, the number of pieces of wood employed for the base was increased, in order to give greater elevation to the supports, or to effect better security against the effects of humidity. From this multiplication of blocks as footings, sprung the *torus* and other mouldings of the base, an origin far more probable than that of ligaments of iron, as imagined by Scamozzi and others. It is also more conformable to the nature of capitals, in which it is known that the same proceeding was employed. After beginning with a simple abacus, several others were afterwards added, which were enlarged, as they rose, one above another, in such a manner that as the base was to the column a kind of footing on which it rested more solidly, so the capital made a head more capable of receiving and supporting the weight and form of the architrave, a large beam placed horizontally on perpendicular supports, and destined to receive the covering of the whole edifice."

The author goes on, in a similarly ingenious manner, to prove the derivation, from nature, of the Orders of Grecian architecture. He ascribes the form of the roof as having necessarily suggested that of the pediment. On this point he quotes the remark of Cicero: "It is not to pleasure that we are indebted for the pediment of the Capitol and those of our temples: necessity suggested the form for the better draining off the water; nevertheless, its beauty is so very great, and it is become so necessary for edifices, that if a Capitol were to be built in Olympus, where it was never known to rain, it would, notwithstanding, be necessary to give it a pediment."

The preceding remarks and ingenious theory amply justify the opinion already suggested, that nature must be the foundation of every true principle of art. Assuming, as we are compelled to do, that the Grecian style as a whole was original, the only perfect model that could have been selected was that afforded by natural objects, in all of which are found the most perfect results, derived from few means but answering an infinity of ends. It will be remembered that the construction of the Eddystone lighthouse was based in regard to durability, and resistance to the force of the waves, on those properties which are possessed by any kind of tree exposed to the full force of the tempest. " Nature ought to be the basis of all imitation."

Proceeding from the teachings of nature, the Greeks learned gradually to introduce new types, consistent in the main with the original mode, but of great variety in detail. By further refinement of this, but close adherence to the facts or the analogies of nature, the Grecian art became developed in the invention of other Orders, the names of which are sufficiently known to all interested in architecture. Limited space prevents our entering into a class of analyses of the characteristics of each. Little doubt exists of the Doric Order having been the first produced, and following it were the Ionic, Corinthian, Composite, and Tuscan, which constitute the five Orders in general of architecture.

Perhaps the best epoch of ancient architecture was that during which, subsequent to the battle of Marathon, the Greeks commenced to rebuild the remains of Persian buildings, and to re-construct Athens. The ruins of this period yet with us, attest the advance which Grecian architectural art had attained. The ingenuity and refinement of Greek art gradually spread to Rome, the Romans adopting the Doric Order under the modification known as the Tuscan. The art having been introduced into Etruria by the Pelasgi, under the celebrated Augustus Rome attained that magnificence which has ever since rendered its name famous as a seat of the arts. Amongst the great erections of this period was the Pantheon, one of the grandest efforts of genius that the world has yet known. Under subsequent emperors architecture also progressed, and the name of Trajan is identified with the erection of triumphal arches, &c., the ruins of which still receive the admiration of every qualified judge in art.

The removal of the seat of Roman government to

Byzantium led to the decadence of art at Rome, which was completed by the incursions of the Visigoths. Eventually the Gothic style arose, phœnix-like, from the ruins of Grecian and Roman art, and obtained a place that has rendered it ever since one of the most favourite styles of architecture.

Just as under the heathens, the art had been chiefly promoted by erections for religious purposes, so when the Christians began to obtain the ascendancy, the erection of churches led to a similar result. From the fourth to the seventh century some magnificent buildings of this kind were erected. At the commencement of the eleventh century the church of St. Mark at Venice attested the wonderful progress which architecture had made, and it continued to progress during the next two or three centuries, being confined chiefly, however, to Italy. But the Gothic style, suited to a northern clime, never obtained full hold there; Italy cannot boast of a single pure Gothic edifice. Gradually the new style spread over Europe. The cathedral at Strasbourg, the Louvre at Paris, suggested improvements in our own country at Windsor Castle, Oxford, &c., all indicated the rapid extension of the Gothic style or its modifications. But in numerous instances the taste that was exhibited showed a decadence from the simplicity and grandeur of the Grecian and Latin styles. In respect to the latter, indeed, the materials of the new erections were obtained from the ruins of the ancient edifices, the columns, &c. there found, being pressed into the service, in any manner, of the new school of architects.

Towards the middle of the fifteenth century a revival in architectural art took place, especially under Brunelleschi. The patronage of the Medici added a stimulus to the progress thus initiated. Improvements were introduced in the erection of private residences in most parts of Western Europe, the art having in its best form been chiefly till then directed to building edifices for religious purposes alone. In the sixteenth century architecture in Rome attained a perfection nearly equal to that it had formerly enjoyed under the Cæsars, especially during the Augustan age. Private and public buildings were erected of great magnificence, yet of simplicity of form combined with grandeur. Under Viguola architecture attained great excellence. Michael Angelo was appointed architect of St. Peter's at Rome about the middle of the sixteenth century, and the mention of his name alone is sufficient to call to mind the extent and value of his labours in the art. In the seventeenth century, about the year 1620, Inigo Jones was engaged in repairing St. Paul's Cathedral in London, and subsequently produced designs for the Royal Palace at Whitehall in the reign of Charles I. Greenwich and Chelsea Hospitals, and other noted buildings, were designed about this period. In France and other continental countries architecture attained great perfection at this period, both in respect to public and private buildings. Among the most eminent architects of a period somewhat nearer to our own time, was Sir Christopher Wren, whose St. Paul's Cathedral serves as a monument to the great genius of that eminent man. This era may, comparatively speaking, be considered as the commencement of the modern style of English church architecture, inasmuch as several productions of Wren are still used for the purposes to which they were first applied, having undergone little or no change since their completion.

Such is a brief, and necessarily very imperfect résumé of the progress of architecture. The styles of Eastern Europe, ancient Mexico, and many others have not been described, because unnecessary, in this Introduction, which has only for its object to call general attention to the causes which have led to the present state of the art. Like all others it has been the subject of alternating prosperity and adversity. At one time fostered by men eminent in their profession, and by those whose means permitted them to lavish riches on magnificent piles, fountains, villas, &c.; and at others, degraded by its students, and neglected by those who should have been its patrons.

In all branches of architecture direct reference

should be had to the objects for which the building is intended. An eminent architect, already quoted, has well set forth this essential point in the following remarks :—" The art of characterizing, that is to say, of rendering evident by material forms the intellectual qualities and moral ideas required to express in edifices, or to make known by the harmony and suitableness of all the constituent parts that enter into their composition the use for which they are intended, is perhaps of all the secrets of architecture the most difficult to develope or to attain. This happy talent of conceiving and of communicating the conception in the physiognomy suitable to each edifice; this sure and delicate discernment, which exhibits the distinguishing parts of such edifices, that at first appear susceptible of no characteristic distinctions; this judicious employment of the different styles which are as the tones of architecture; this skilful application of the signs which the art employs to affect the sight and understanding; this exquisite feeling, which errs neither in the just disposition of the masses and employment of the details, nor in the just dispensation of richness and simplicity, and which is able to combine true expression of character with the harmonious accord of all the qualities susceptible of being represented by architecture—all this requisite talent, which study perfects, but does not produce, is a gift possessed by few. This suitable ex-

pression presents itself under two relations, the one
appertaining to architecture in general, and the other
to edifices in particular.   The first consists in the
expression of the qualities or intellectual ideas which
are the results of the art metaphysically considered ;
the second, in the true indication of the uses for which
edifices are designed, that is, in considering architecture
as a certain mode of expressing or painting.   This
expression, according to the nature of the buildings
and edifices, may be produced by the gradation of
richness and greatness proportionate to the nature and
the object for which they are erected ; by the indication of the moral qualities attached to each edifice,
the manner of expressing which is beyond the reach
of rules ; by the general and particular form of architecture ; by the species of the construction and the
quality of the materials that may be employed in the
execution ; and lastly, by the resources of decoration."
In these remarks will be found a highly valuable *précis*
of the excellence to which the art of the architect
should be directed, and the means that must be adopted
to obtain pleasing and successful results.

The erection of country mansions, villas, and other
residences, has of late years been greatly stimulated
in our country.   The enormous annually accumulated
savings of the commercial portion of the community
have induced a large amount of capital to be invested

in such objects. In regard to questions of taste and decoration, it should be borne in mind that but very little extra cost is incurred in building a residence in a pleasing and picturesque style than in one having not the least pretension to architectural beauty. In our earlier remarks on the nature of the picturesque the *general principles* of obtaining that effect have been pointed out. In the following pages the special details are amply descanted on, and illustrated by designs, drawings, &c. It is the object of every department of constructive skill at the present day, to endeavour to obtain the best possible result by the least possible expenditure of material, and thus taste actually causes economy rather than increased expense. Tons of heavy and unsightly materials are now replaced by hundredweights of decorative, and yet substantial, masonry and iron work. A number of modern elegant erections, affording accommodation equal in extent, but vastly superior in quality, are now made at an expenditure of stone or brick less by one-third in quantity than was employed in many old houses ; those in High Street, Edinburgh, by way of example. The result has been arrived at by the joint aid of science and art, the former giving data as to the strength of the material, and the latter directing its disposal. The peculiar character of English scenery is exactly adapted for giving a picturesque character

to villa residences, provided the latter are designed
and erected in accordance with the principles of sound
taste.   Surely he who would spend money in building
a house, in which all or most of the remainder of his
days are to be spent, will not grudge making that
dwelling the subject of decoration or ornamental art,
by which its aspect shall at all times be suggestive of
pleasure rather than of aversion or disgust.   It has
been said that most individuals, by long association
together, acquire a mutuality of tastes and even phy-
sical resemblance.   It cannot be denied that even
inanimate objects, such as our dwellings, furniture,
landscapes, gardens, and other such surroundings,
have a parallel effect on us.   Hence the wisdom of
using all the means which architectural art places at
our disposal.   Errors in this respect often proceed
from thoughtlessness, if not from want of refined
taste.   An instance may suffice to show how much
such matters should be attended to in the choice of a
site and other conditions.   A retired manufacturer
erected a mansion at a cost exceeding fifty thousand
pounds, and had never paid any heed to the fact that
the most prominent object seen from his dining-room
window was the cemetery of the adjacent town! Soon
this became unbearable, and the house has been comparatively deserted by the family, caused by an over-
sight that the least consideration would have remedied.

The designs given in the following pages have for their object to suggest the most approved, tasteful, and effective plans for the mansion, the villa, or cottage, and great care has been devoted to their production. Whilst a residence must necessarily be kept within a cost suitable to the means of the proprietor, by judicious care of the professional man, possessed of a competent knowledge, a little money may go a long way in the decorative art. Many of the drawings are devoted to the minor but not less effective portions of the house. Congruity in detail inside the dwelling is equally required with symmetry, beauty, or picturesque character of the exterior. Want of judgment in this point may speedily convert the most elegant building into little better than a repository for gewgaws, selected without taste and arranged without skill. It is impossible for *every* man to become his own architect; but it is possible, in most cases, for all who have the means, to select such a design as shall best comport with their taste, leaving the working out of details to the architect. But a remote possibility exists of an unprofessional being able even to state what he requires, and should he ask an architect for a design or plan, it is more than likely that the latter would fail to please. When, however, a variety of designs is placed before the eye of any intelligent person the act of selection becomes easy. Although

no single plan may succeed, a combination may suggest
itself, and the architect can then readily work on
something like a sound foundation, and with the hope
of success.   This work is intended to supply such
requirements.

Again, in building a house, or in effecting alterations in an old one, points apparently of minor, but
really of great importance, require attention. A badly
constructed chimney will make the whole house miserable, independent of the injury done to furniture,
decorations, &c., and the destruction of paint and
paperhangings.   A defective drainage may render
that which was intended to be an abode of peace,
plenty, and happiness, a living charnel-house, or the
door to the grave !   A question of vital importance is
that of ventilation.   These apparently minor questions
can therefore scarcely be exaggerated in their value,
for neglect of them will render nugatory the best external efforts of the architect.   Hence they have
hereafter full attention, in their practical details, directed to them.

On the general principles of ventilation the following remarks may be of value to all who propose to
erect new dwellings, or alter those already inhabited.
In all houses, and in fact every building divided into
stories, a ready means of ventilation may be insured,
or rather always exists.   This is presented in the

opening formed by the staircase. Into this general opening communications can be made into, and from, each apartment by apertures placed in some convenient position in each room. The grand law on which ventilation depends is, that hot air, being lighter than cool air, has a universal tendency to rise, whilst cold air takes the lowest part of a house or apartment. It hence follows, that if a supply of cold air be admitted by an opening at the lower part of a house, and it becomes heated within the house, it will have a tendency to rise to the roof; and if a sufficient opening be there provided, it will escape into the open air. Consequently a constant current may thus be obtained in any dwelling, sufficient to give a supply of pure air and to remove that which has been vitiated by breathing, the combustion of fires, and other causes. The heavy atmosphere of this country requires assistance to make this grand law operative; to cause the air of a room to move as readily as it is required, forced ventilation becomes necessary. The English fireplace provides this; and to that it owes, with us, its extreme popularity. A constant current of air from the room is heated and passed up the chimney flue, and this draws in a corresponding supply of cold air, and proper and convenient apertures should be left to permit this to enter. The fireplace forces attention to the necessity; if sufficient fresh air be not provided for it the smoke enters the room and drives the occupants out. Notwithstanding the attention that has been paid to the stove and its flue, we are still sadly behindhand in a proper construction of them. The flues could be so arranged that a building might be enabled, using a figurative expression, to breathe, whenever its principal flue, that of the kitchen fireplace, was in action; a construction to effect this will be illustrated in the text. In conclusion on this point, it may be added that nothing is more essential to the health and comfort of a house than that it should be thoroughly and constantly ventilated, and if any portion is to be particularized, it should be the sleeping apartments.

Another question which, to a certain extent, should influence the arrangement of a house of any pretensions in respect to size, is that of the method of warming it. The preference, or rather prejudice, in favour of fireplaces is so great, that a revolution of the nation in political matters could be more easily brought about than the abolition of the fire-grate; but it is well known that at least three-fourths of the coal consumed is wasted in the attempt to heat the room to an equable and pleasant temperature. But by such means the result cannot be arrived at. In front of, and close to the fire, the temperature is excessive, while the backs of the sitters facing in are suffering from cold. An equalized temperature in rooms is obtained abroad.

In Russia, a plan is adopted of heating the rooms by means of the walls, the latter being double, and so arranged that they act as flues to a furnace situated at the lower part of the building. By this method every part of the room acquires, simultaneously, an equable temperature. There need be no draught, simply because the air is not drawn in one direction more than in another. From every side a gentle current of warm air arises. This method cannot be adopted here; it would not suit for English houses where coal is used as fuel; the interstices of the double wall would soon be filled with soot. The same effect is produced in a far more elegant way, by means of warm-water pipes passed round the room; by this simple process the staircase and passages and the sides of a room distant from the fireplace are made of equal temperature—one, or at most two furnaces, burning coke and making no smoke, if placed in a cellar outside an extensive building, can render the whole interior, from attic to ground-floor of equal temperature, and not prevent the action of the fireplace, or its agreeable presence in our homes. In the British Museum, where warming apparatus is used, the temperature of the whole is kept uniformly the same, that is, 65° Fah., even throughout the most severe weather, independent of the common fireplace. No greater change is required in any part of our buildings

D 2

than in the latter; not that it requires to be removed, but a change to prevent its waste of heat and its contaminating the outside air with the soot and blacks from its coal fuel; the lower fireplaces in a building should warm or air the upper rooms, and no soot or blacks should be allowed to leave the flues. A construction for this purpose will be shown in the ensuing pages, as well as one for warming an entire building and a conservatory.

An opposite effect to that of warming is frequently desirable in our houses; and to ensure this the position of the site of the house must be considered. It is evident that a room having a south-western aspect must of all others be the warmest, whether in winter or summer, simply because that aspect is most exposed to the influence of the sun's rays. On the other hand, rooms having a north-easterly aspect must necessarily be the coolest, because, except during the earliest part of midsummer mornings, say from 2 to 4 A.M., the sun's rays cannot reach them. It is, therefore, in the power of those who have the requisite resources, to construct a house in such a manner that warm rooms can be provided for winter use, and cool for alleviating the heat of summer. It is by no means an uncommon occurrence to find a large dinner-party assembled in the heat of summer in a room that has been exposed to the sun's rays during the afternoon. Frequently in such cases, owing to the number of persons present, the heat of the viands, lights, &c., the temperature rises above 80°, a circumstance prejudicial to health, enjoyment, and the vivacity of social intercourse, that might have been entirely avoided had the dining-room been placed in a northern aspect. These are points well worthy of attention in constructing a newly-designed dwelling. It unfortunately happens, in many cases, that the supposed exigencies of architectural arrangement must have priority of all other considerations. Yet the architect who wilfully opposes such modifications of his plan for the purpose of conducing to general comfort is shortsighted. His object ought to be to build a house *to be lived in,* and not *to be looked at* alone.

A few remarks on some of the general principles that should lead to a choice of site, situation, and other matters, may not be without advantage. Whatever inducement a plot of ground for building purposes may possess, the great question which has first to be solved is that of *health.* A clayey soil, bog, marsh, or stagnant water; a low level; an undrained or badly drained surface; a moist atmosphere, or exposure to the chill north and east winds, are all objections that a question of price should never be pitted against. Popular knowledge on sanitary subjects is now so extensively diffused that healthy localities are always of ready sale, while those of an opposite character are frequently unsold in the market, and consequently may be had at a low price, but are never really cheap. Nothing can counterbalance the value of a healthy locality, for in the end one of an opposite character becomes far more costly. The timbers of the building fall rapidly into decay, and require renewal ; the decorative portion, internally and externally, becomes faded ; doors and windows cease to fit and work accurately ; the iron work becomes rusted and requires frequent renewal of paint or other protecting coat ; and the same may be remarked in regard to the fences of the estate.

The position of the residence in regard to the sun at different periods of the year is also an important matter. If it stands with each front north and south, the north front will have comparatively little sun, except during summer time ; and if the position be north-east and south-west respectively, the cold bitter winds of winter will be severely felt, whilst from the fact that the greater portion of the year the rainy quarter of the wind is south-west, that front or back of the house will be continually exposed to its influence. Consequently, frontages to the south-east and north-west are to be preferred in all cases, when possible, as such position ensures to both sides the greatest average of sun, heat, and light, and protection from the north-east wind of winter or the south-west of the rainy season. Comparatively little attention has been paid to the influence of light on health and its effects on the mind, in the construction of modern dwelling-houses. An excess is easily avoided by blinds and other contrivances; but if the architectural features of the building be such as to exclude the light, an opposite remedy is impossible. Abundant access of light tends to set off all the internal decorations of the house, and spreads a cheerfulness of appearance that is always highly prized. It gives brilliancy of outline and detail to coloured decorations, and, to use a common phrase, is the best possible " set-off" that the architect or decorator can desire. As already pointed out, the effect of light and shade, in regard to architecture, is a condition of success in respect to the picturesque.

It is always desirable that a house should be placed on an eminence; it becomes thus a prominent object, and its qualities are the more readily perceived. A gradual ascent to the house by the walks or drive adds much to the general effect. The walks are thus constantly drained, and preserve longer a neat appearance, a matter which is of much importance in setting off the advantages of situation, site, &c. In respect to questions of health also, this is of great advantage, as the waste matter of the household more readily falls away by its own gravity, and is thus quickly removed; which if left stagnant would be productive of harm to the inmates.

Abundant access of fresh air is of great importance to health in a residence; unnecessary exposure to wind being at the same time to be avoided. Hence to place a residence in the centre of a close array of trees is not desirable; not only is the access of air, light, and heat prevented, but there is always a tendency induced to dampness in the house. In an open, airy, and well drained situation, the effects of even long-continued wet are soon dispelled, but when all sides of a house are surrounded closely by trees, an opposite result is induced, and, in comparatively dry situations, many evils of a damp one ultimately ensue.

One of our earliest English writers on building, Thomas Fuller (1633), speaking of the choice of situation for a new structure, says: "*Chiefly choose a wholesome air,* for air is a dish one feeds on every minute, and therefore it need be good. Wherefore, great men (who may build where they please, as poor men where they can) if herein they prefer their profit above their health, I refer them to their physicians to make them pay for it accordingly." And as to light, he continues: "*Light (God's eldest daughter!) is a principal beauty in a building,* yet it shines not alike from all parts of heaven. An east window welcomes the infant beams of the sun before they are of strength to do any harm, and is offensive to none but a sluggard. A south window, in summer, is a chimney with a fire in it, and needs the screen of a curtain. In a west window, in summer time, towards night, the sun grows low and ever familiar, with more light than delight. A north window is best for butteries and cellars, where the beer will not be sour for the sun's smiling on it. Thorough lights are best for rooms of entertainment, and windows on one side for dormitories." And he tells us, " *a pleasant prospect is to be respected.* A medley view, such as of water and land at Greenwich, best entertains the eyes, refreshing the wearied beholder with exchange of objects. Yet," he adds, " I know a more profitable prospect—where the owner can only see his own land round about."

Having thus disposed of some of the most important points that should be kept in mind when choosing the site of a house, and of such other conditions as affect its picturesque and sanitary character, a small space may be devoted to the consideration of its internal decoration.

On this point there is no disputing about tastes, but to this may be added that the absence of taste is by no means uncommon. Having fixed on the style of house, the next question for decision, in respect to

its general effect, should be that of its internal decoration.   Congruity of design should exist between the
two, for if an opposite course be adopted, a vulgarity
will be introduced that will be highly displeasing to
good taste.   On the other hand, a slavish adherence
to uniformity of internal with external character
might produce so severe an adherence to system as to
exclude the benefits that arise from judiciously chosen
contrast.   What has before been remarked in regard
to the exterior, applies equally to the interior of a
house—each should have in its general effect an
agreement in appearance to its objects.   In an antique apartment the light character of modern furni·
ture would be evidently out of place, and *vice
versâ*.

It is evidently impossible to direct attention to more
than a few elements of success that may be arrived at
in internal decoration.   Independently of this, each
person has his own views on the matter, that would be
sure in the end to overrule any exact principles, or at
least greatly modify them.   The following observations
however are offered suggestively.

The facility with which the most beautiful designs
in painting, &c. are transferred to paper for paper
hangings, has brought these into very extensive use
for decorative purposes.   Formerly the best patterns
were produced in France alone, but of late years the

British manufactures have rivalled the Continental. The pattern in respect to size, colour, design, &c., should be so chosen as to be in accordance with the amount of light, the size, and other conditions of the room. A large pattern in a small room is equally out of place with the reverse condition. A light pattern again in a dark room, although advantageous in alleviating sombreness, is also incongruous. The general effect of a room on a spectator is thus largely influenced by these points, and consequently they should be carefully attended to. Frequently paint is preferred for covering walls of apartments, and where many pictures are introduced this may be advantageously employed, because the paintings alleviate the monotonous effect that would otherwise ensue. Painted walls are liable to injury by peeling off in places, especially where likely to meet with blows from furniture, &c. In damp weather, from the absorption of heat they generally become not only wet, but frequently stream with water. If the apartment is "smoky," lines of sooty hue soon follow, and the room acquires a dirty appearance. This is avoided by the use of paper, which prevents the abstraction of heat and the consequent deposition of water. Beautiful effects may be produced by graining and other devices which are too well known to require enumeration. When flock paper on walls becomes dirty and requires renewing, if painted it looks extremely well, a diaper ornamental surface being produced by such means.

The mantel-piece of a room adds to or detracts from its general effect. In a well lighted apartment, with light furniture, white marble is decidedly preferable. Whereas serpentine, black, or coloured marbles, grey and even red granite, may all agree in rooms but moderately lighted.

The cornice and ceiling decorations equally require adaptation to the character of the apartment. For these purposes beautiful designs have been suggested and employed. The material of which they are usually made is so plastic as to be capable of receiving and retaining the most intricate forms conducive to elegance and beauty. In some rooms such add greatly to the general effect, while in others, especially with painted walls, plain mouldings seem most appropriate.

A profusion of gold or gilding displays want of taste. A glaring example of this might be pointed out—a white marble mantel-piece supported by gilt angels five feet high, which "graces" the drawing-room of a mansion in one part of this country. The outer room is a gorgeous display of gold, silver, and vulgarity. It serves, however, index-like, to point out at once the riches and "taste" of the owner. On the other hand, paintings and engravings in gilt frames have an excellent effect in setting off a room, provided that their size is in accordance with that of the apartment.

Stained deals, varnished, afford a good material for panelling, and for covering the walls of rooms. We have in our eye a dining-room thus fitted which has an effect approaching to some of the oaken fittings of olden times. The material is cheap and durable, whilst the surface can always be renewed in its freshness by a new coat of varnish. It has been largely adopted in churches for pews and other fittings, with the best possible results.

The minor objects of decoration, such as handles, finger-plates, bell-pulls, &c., &c., can only be here named. In many instances designs are given in the following pages, suggesting the most suitable either for indoor or outdoor use, according to the character of the room or entrance for which they are intended.

So much for the picturesque exterior and tasteful interior of a house; a few words however may be said in respect to its immediate surroundings, such as the lawns, gardens, pleasure grounds, &c.

The most picturesque villa would be a nonentity in a wrong situation. It would be opposed to what is usually called the " fitness of things;" a phrase that expresses much meaning without an exact definition. Hence "landscape gardening" has become an almost necessary adjunct to the art of architecture. An unframed picture has possibly every merit that the painter's art can bestow on it, yet it lacks that finish which the exterior confers on it. So the well laid-out garden, the vista at its extremity, the carefully arranged parterre, the judicious management of floral culture, especially with regard to colour; neatly arranged walks, and many other exterior matters of detail, add to, enhance, and occasionally become indispensable adjuncts to the picturesque.

We give two examples of picturesque accessories to garden architecture; the first rather belongs to the secluded wood, to some sequestered spot of sylvan shade, whence rises a spring which tradition may designate as that of some beautiful nymph; where the limpid crystal flows in gentle, yet ceaseless streams, conveying " health to the sick and solace to the swain." The last, a vignette at the end of this chapter, is the representation of a ruined fountain, designed in 1820 by one of the best teachers of drawing England ever possessed, the late C. J. M. Whichelo. The architect may suggest the addition of a garden, but it is no part of his business to supply the details; these rather belong to the horticulturist. Yet these should not be forgotten; a complete whole is always made up of minute parts, and by these littles an entirety of effect is produced, just as their individual importance is not lost sight of.

The Nymph's Fountain.

In conclusion, it has been attempted in this introductory essay to enable the unprofessional reader to become acquainted with the general principles, and some practical details that should guide him in the selection of a site, and the erection of an elegant, convenient, and pleasant house, both externally and internally. So far as architecture and decorative art can aid such objects, the special details involved have to be perused in the text of this work. Fundamental ideas of such subjects have alone been here treated. A hope may be expressed that any suggestion or advice hitherto offered may not, in all cases, be without value. It is not given to all men to know all things. By the experience of others we gain fresh views of old ideas, invest them with new clothing, and in fact make out of that which is past, the material for something new. We rest on the apparently obsolete for suggestive ideas of improvement. Although the fashion of this world passeth away, yet as a dissolving view it reproduces itself in other forms, which, by the contrast of apparent novelty, and real or supposed merits, gain, either temporarily or permanently, the applause of mankind.

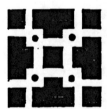 

Old English Garden Plots.

Garden Fountain in Ruins.

DESIGN *No.* 1.

A GARDENER'S COTTAGE.

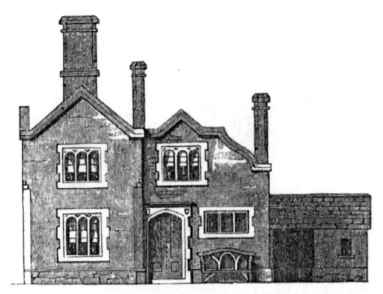

Front elevation.

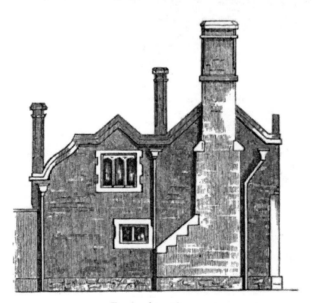

Back elevation.

SOME examples of designs for small cottages will be first given in this volume. There are few domestic

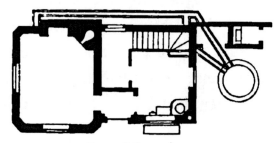

Ground-floor plan.

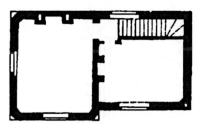

Plan of upper floor.

E 2

structures that have received within the last fifty years a greater share of attention than the English Cottage, especially that designed for the occupation of the labourer. Each detail has received much care; thus, whether its walls should be solid or formed in two thicknesses, as most conducive to warmth and comfort; whether they should be of thin brick or of solid

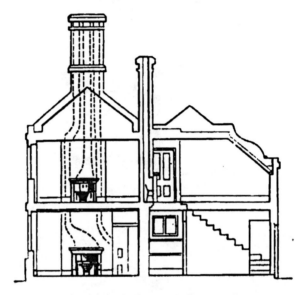

Section through length of building.

thick concrete; the best kind of roof covering, and indeed all such questions, have been fully discussed.

Besides this, the calculation of cost has been of importance; they are required to return a rent that will pay 5 per cent. on the outlay, and to gain their picturesque appearance has generally been sacrificed.

The cottage examples in this volume have been erected on estates where the only aim was to render them substantial and lasting structures, expense being a matter of minor importance. Their picturesque appearance being in every case insisted on.

Before entering into any description of the designs, it must be pointed out that the plans, with the excep-

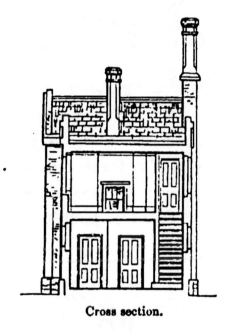

Cross section.

tion only of a few at the end of the volume, are all drawn to the same scale, that of 20 feet to the inch, and that the elevations and sections are to a scale of 15 feet to the inch.

The details and the vignettes, one of which is mostly given between each example, are of various scales suited to each separate subject.

The cottage design shown in the plate, and which forms the first example in this series, was erected on a nobleman's estate in the country, for the use of a favourite gardener, a married man without children,

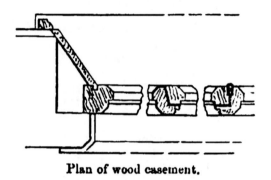

Plan of wood casement.

and the accommodation afforded was all that he required. It consisted of a lower room fifteen feet by twelve, fitted with a small cottage oven; a scullery ten feet by ten feet, and a larder; the upper floor

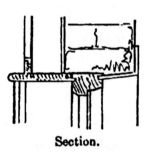

Section.

contained one room of the same size as the lower, and one fourteen feet by ten feet. The building was constructed in a very superior way. It was erected in red brick with compo dressings round the door and windows. The illustrations represent the front and back elevations; and sections through the length and breadth of the cottage, with details of the wood casements, and a plan and section of the cottage oven.

Cottage oven.

A view of a cottage slightly different in design, but having rooms of the same size with similar accommodation, is given. This was intended for the same estate.

The vignette is an elevation of two lead pipes designed for an Elizabethan building in the country,

DESIGN No. 2.

A SMALL COTTAGE OR LODGE.

Perspective view.

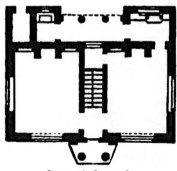

Ground-floor plan.

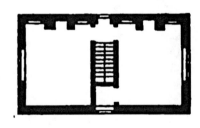

Upper plan.

THIS small building forms the outer lodge to a country park. It is finished in all its parts so as to

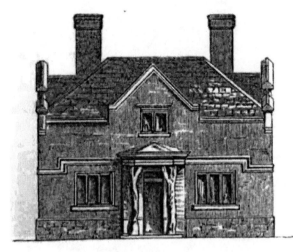

Elevation of front.

correspond in style and details with the old family mansion, and being a prominent object, standing in a cheerful position, each side was made pleasing. It is

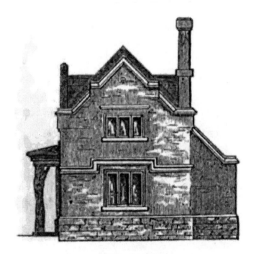

Side elevation.

so placed that the sun during its daily course shines on all the exterior walls.   Cottages should have no

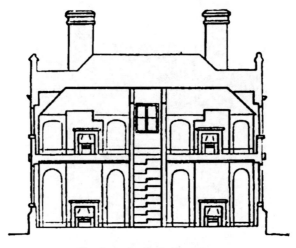

Section through length.

dark corners, the sun should find entrance at all the windows whenever it is bright; the interior is then warm and cheerful. If the plan of a building is either

Cross section.

a square or a parallelogram, and it is placed on the ground so that one of its diagonal lines runs due north and south, the advantage of sunlight at all the openings is obtained, and this has been pointed out by several writers on the subject. The ground plan shows the general arrangement of the interior. The parlour and kitchen are both of the same size (14 feet by 11 feet); it has a small scullery, an open outside porch, and a place for coals; the larder with its win-

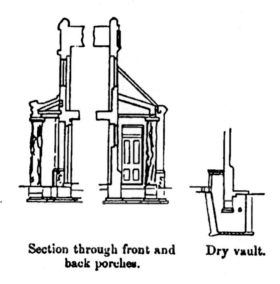

Section through front and back porches.   Dry vault.

dow is under the staircase. The latter is a cottage staircase, occupying only half the usual space. The plan of the upper floor shows two rooms of the same size as those on the lower floor, with the compact reduced form of the staircase. The plate gives the front and side elevations of the building; sections through its length and breadth, and through the two porches back and front, and the dry vault of closet, are given.

The water from the scullery sink is discharged into the dry vault. The staircase, of which a section is given, occupies exactly half the space of a staircase on the ordinary plan. The width is three feet, each step rising in two heights of 6 inches. It is necessary that such a contrivance should have plenty of light. These staircases were first used in France. Loudon, in his "Encyclopædia of Cottage, Farm, and Villa Architecture," gives a representation of one, and remarks that the celebrated American, Jefferson, when

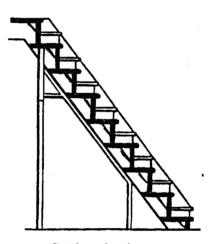

Section of staircase.

A staircase.

making a tour in that country, was so struck with the contrivance, that he noted it in his journal, which was published with his correspondence. A perspective view of one of these staircases is annexed.

A staircase of this description, if made four feet in width, might take up only one-third the usual space : it would be very applicable to offices and warehouses where room cannot be spared, and where staircases little better than ladders are used, but in such cases a baluster and hand-rail should be placed between each second step, to prevent persons falling.

The " Builder" of November, 1843, gave two views of an ingenious double spiral staircase then exhibiting at a manufactory in Berners Street, Commercial Road. It was described as extremely simple, the object being to provide for ascent and descent without chance of meeting or collision. It consisted of a deal or other board of suitable thickness 6 feet long and 12 inches wide, forming a double *tread*, and the *riser* crossed, as it were from corner to corner, except as arranged to form a *newel* in the centre, of about five inches in diameter. The staircase had twenty-two risers, and took one complete turn round.

Plaster ornament for a ceiling.

DESIGN No. 3.

A PICTURESQUE COTTAGE.

Perspective view.

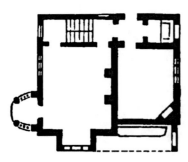

Ground-floor plan.

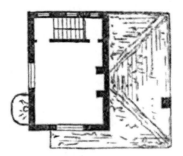

Upper floor.

THIS design for a peasant's cottage possesses no architectural feature beyond what could be given to

Elevation of front.

it by any common country village carpenter.   It was made from the recollection of one at Blaise Hamlet,

Side front.

near Blaise Castle, in Gloucestershire, the seat of John I. Harford, Esq., to whom the hamlet belonged.   This was celebrated for having about a dozen of these small picturesque structures, apparently put up by the owner of the estate. Nearly the whole of them were provided with rustic seats under a projecting roof, as well as with a pigeon-house at the gable. This was called Vine Cottage; there were besides Sweet Briar Cottage, Rose Cottage, Diamond Cottage, Dial Cottage, Jessamine Cottage, Circular Cottage, and Oak Cottage. Views of all of them were first published at Bristol by Mr. Western.

Section.

There are numerous similar hamlets and villages in England, some having the cottages, schoolhouses, literary meeting room, and even the village pump, all in picturesque form, and generally architectural in character. The plan given here is probably not like that of the cottage at the hamlet. It illustrates one room, size 13 ft. by 12 ft., a scullery 12 ft. by 9 ft., and larder under the stairs. The latter are shown with the double-rise step. The upper plan shows one room of the same size as that below, and a closet. The scullery on the ground floor is large enough to form a sleeping room for boys, or to make a small living room. The height of the lower room is 9 feet 6 inches. The section shows the general form and fittings of the rooms. The plate below the plans gives an elevation of the front, showing the rustic seat and the side of the entrance porch, the gable of the cottage formed into a pigeon-house, together with the side front of the cottage and its entrance porch. The small window at the side is intended to light the first steps of the stairs; a small shed for wood or coals is placed at the back. Such a cottage could be built and finished complete at a cost of about one hundred and ten pounds.

Plaster frieze for drawing-room.

F

DESIGN *No.* 4.

A DOUBLE COTTAGE.

Perspective view.

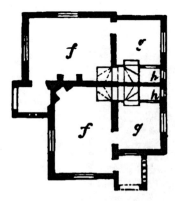

Ground plan.

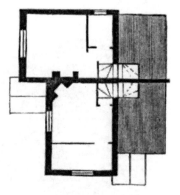

Upper plan.

THESE cottages were intended to be attached to some ornamental grounds which were very carefully attended to ; and as the building formed a promi-

Elevation of front.

nent object, it was rendered architectural and pleasing in character. In plan the cottages are large

Section.

F 2

and roomy, and they are of the cheapest kind.
If constructed in plain brickwork, without the
ornamental gable on the porch, the pair could
not have cost more than 250*l*., and at that sum
they have been estimated for by a London builder.
Each cottage has one living-room on the ground

floor, *ff*, of the size of 14 feet by 10 feet, with a
scullery, *g g*, attached, size 10 feet by 6 feet 6 inches,
and a small larder and staircase.

The latter, with ten risers, leads to the upper
floor, in which are one large and one small room.
The plate gives the ground plan, and the plan of

the upper floor. The closets are in the yard attached to the cottages, but not shown in the plan.

The plate gives an elevation of one of the fronts, and a section, taken through the living-room and scullery: a portion of the ornamental gable is illustrated in the previous page.

The vignette represents an ornamental escutcheon and handle, in brass, for an inner entrance-hall door. The drawing is one-third of the full size.

A DOUBLE COTTAGE AND VILLAGE SUNDAY SCHOOL.

Perspective view.

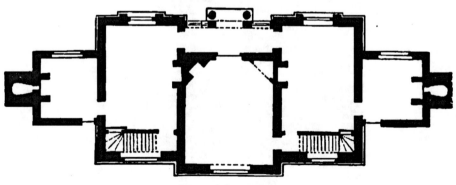

Ground-floor plan.

THIS building was intended to be placed in a village of one of the midland counties, nearly all the buildings in the village being of picturesque character. It was the property of a gentleman who was erecting a large Elizabethan mansion in the neighbourhood; the design is for a double cottage and Sunday school; the latter being under the direction of the clergyman of the parish.

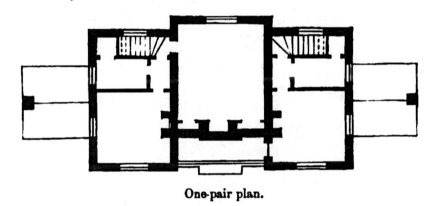

One-pair plan.

The porch was decorated to give it importance, and form a shelter for the clergyman in passing from one school to the other. One part was intended for boys and the other for girls. The chimneys of the building were grouped together in the centre so as to form a prominent object; they were copied from a very fine ancient example, then existing at a farm-house near Ashford, in Kent.

The illustration gives a view of the front, and the plans. Each of the two principal rooms was 16 feet 6 inches by 13 feet 6 inches, with a scullery on the side 10 feet square, and having a good oven; the larder was under the stairs.   The rooms above were

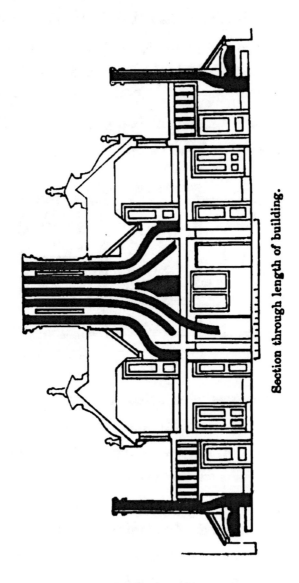

Section through length of building.

of the same size as those below.   One of the cottages had the centre room below as well as that above arranged so that one had four rooms and the other two; but this could be changed at any time, to provide each cottage with three living rooms each. A

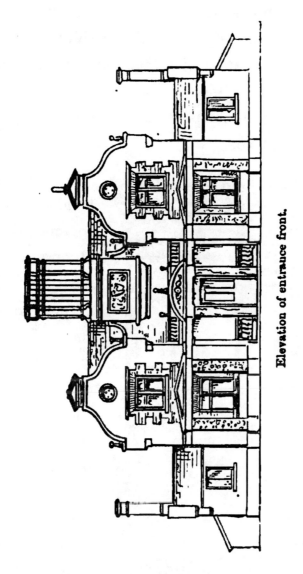

Elevation of entrance front.

section through the length of the building and the chimney stack is given in the previous page, and an elevation of the front is given above.

The building was to be constructed with sound stock bricks, and red brick rusticated facing round the upper windows; the finishing of the gables with their small pediments was of cut red bricks. Small compo finials crowned the whole.

Finial.

Finial.

Elevation of chimney stack.

The porch had trunks of trees for columns, the entablature and pediment were formed of cut bricks and compo facing; the pilasters on each side of the lower windows were of cut squared flint, peculiar to the county, the whole resting on a plinth of rough country stone. A wooden balustrade of simple pattern surmounted the porch, extending on each side of the columns. These latter resting on a stone slab. The chimney stack is shown, and its plan, on the previous page.

The old stack from Ashford, with the plan at its base, and capping, is also illustrated.

Plan.

These representations of the two chimney stacks,

Elevation of a chimney stack at a farm-house, Ashford, Kent.

ancient and modern, are drawn to the same scale, so that the difference between the present and old mode

of treatment may be seen.   The large flues of the old
example permitted the then mode of sweeping, by
discharging a culverin up the flue.   The occupants

Plan of capping.

of the dwelling could not then have cared much for
return smoke in their rooms ; which in these large
flues, with coal as fuel, must have been considerable,

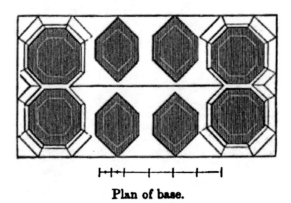

Plan of base.

and could only be obviated or prevented by the
numerous cold draughts of air permitted to pass
through the interior of the building.

The plan of this building was adapted from a very favourite one of the late Sir John Soane. He erected it at Wimpole, in Cambridgeshire, for the Earl of Hardwicke, in 1794. It had a very plain exterior, and the roof was covered with thatch, a very common mode with architects at that time, but now objected to from the serious evil of its harbouring numerous insects—indeed at times they render the building almost untenantable. The walls of the cottages at Wimpole were built in Pisé, or with clay and fine gravel, properly prepared and beaten down in a mould. Each wall was three feet in thickness, the fireplaces and chimneys were of brick. Every opening was covered with strong wood lintels, the whole width of the walls, and two feet longer than their respective openings.

The walls stood on brick foundations two feet above the ground. The cost of the construction was about 450l. Design No. 5 could not now be constructed for less than 630l.

It may be here remarked that nothing certain can be advanced about the cost of a building until the situation and local circumstances are fully known and considered. In the absence of these no estimates can be given with that accuracy which every gentleman wishes for, and ought to be possessed of, before he begins building.

DESIGN No. 6.

A HUNTSMAN'S LODGE OR COTTAGE.

Perspective view.

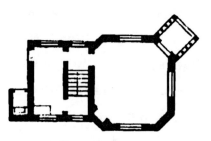

Ground plan.

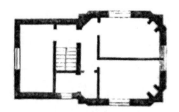

Upper plan.

THIS edifice was erected in the neighbourhood of some thick plantations in a sporting district. It was constructed of brick, with a wooden porch; the facing bricks of the walls being of a light-yellow colour, with red bricks round the windows; and the whole of the cornices and the four chimneys were of cut red brick. The building seen from among the trees looks

Front elevation.

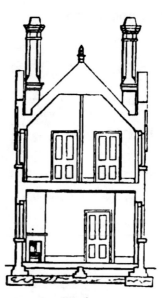

Section.

very pleasing. The ground plan shows a front room 13 feet square, with a small scullery behind; the larder is under the stairs, which have the double riser, and a window is placed both at the bottom as well as at the upper part of the staircase, to give plenty of light. The upper plan shows three bedrooms, each about 10 feet by 6, and a small bed

closet for children, the closet having a ventilator in
the chimney at the angle.   These chimneys, instead
of being grouped together in the centre of the structure, occupy the four corners—an expensive form of
erection, but one that gives more room in the interior.
The elevation of the front is given in the plate, and
the section by its side; the small figure below shows
the different courses of cut bricks forming the pediment and cornice.

These were carefully executed,
and had a good effect. The first
figure likewise illustrates the
oak finial on the top of the roof.
A chimney-piece in one of the
upper rooms had a quaint carving in the centre of a
fox's head, a subject appropriate to the pursuits of
the occupant of the cottage.

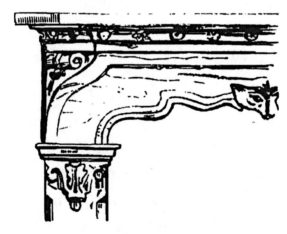

The chimney-piece, and the fox's head on a larger

scale, are here represented. The gateway seen at the side of the building in the view was formed by the workmen out of various old fragments; it leads to a yard in which are various sheds and out-buildings.

This vignette affords a specimen of ornamental iron railing intended for exterior work, and suitable for any situation in which such may be required, in consequence of the neatness of its pattern.

G

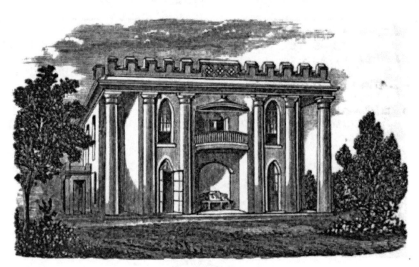

Rose Hill Villa.

THE CONCRETE CONSTRUCTION FOR BUILDING COTTAGES.

CONSIDERABLE pains have been taken for the last fifty years to discover the best and cheapest method of building cottages; bricks, stones, wood, mud, plaster, and lately straw and bitumen, have all been selected. Sound bricks and good building stones, well incorporated with mortar of a good and binding quality, will last for centuries; while those of mud, clay, plaster, or concrete are continually becoming out of repair, and therefore ought never to be introduced where sound construction is desired, and better materials can be procured. In our moist climate, unless great pains are taken in compounding such materials as clay or concrete, in constructing walls, and in protecting these against the effects of the weather, they will soon decay. Mud walls, however, made perfectly in the common manner, of clay well tempered and mixed with sharp sand, will last very many years.

The preceding view represents Rose Hill Villa, near Stockbridge, Hampshire. It is probably the largest and most important specimen of such a construction in England, and comprises dining and drawing-rooms, each 20 feet by 18 feet, morning-room, housekeeper's-room, kitchen, back kitchen, pantry, excellent cellars and all requisite offices; five very superior bedrooms, two dressing-rooms, a water-closet on the landing and ground floor, and five servants' bedrooms. It has a double coach-house, harness-room, and stabling for four or six horses, and in the outhouses a four-roomed cottage for the coachman.

This villa was formerly in the occupation of Fothergill Cooke, Esq.,* the inventor of the Electric Telegraph, and is now the residence of Sir Augustus Webster, Bart.

The building is constructed of chalk concrete, and has stood the test of forty years' exposure without any signs of decay. Mr. James Flitcroft sent in 1843 a view of the villa to the "Builder," and thus

---

* Now Sir William Fothergill Cooke,—October, 1869.

described the construction of such houses in the locality:—The walls are carried above the ground two and sometimes three feet to prevent the damp from rising to the mud, which if wetted would scale off by the action of frost. The kind of earth used is fine chalk, dug from the surface; if timely notice of any building will permit, it is best dug in winter, that the frost may act upon it. Buildings formed of this material can be erected only iu dry warm weather. The workmen in preparing this chalk for use put about a cartload of it together, throw water over it, and tread it with their feet, turn it over, again tread and turn it, until it begins to bind something like loamy clay; then let it soak a little while, when it is ready for use. The waller is able to put on a layer of about fifteen inches; he begins at one corner and goes round the building, putting one layer on another, taking care that the lower one is sufficiently dry to bear the upper. In buildings of two stories high, the walls are generally eighteen inches thick. When the walls are got up five or six feet, and pretty dry, the quoins are plumbed, and the walls dressed down a little, in order that the waller may see what he is about. A small short spade is the best tool for this purpose, with short handle and rather bent. The work is then proceeded with as before, until it is raised up to the square of the building, when the

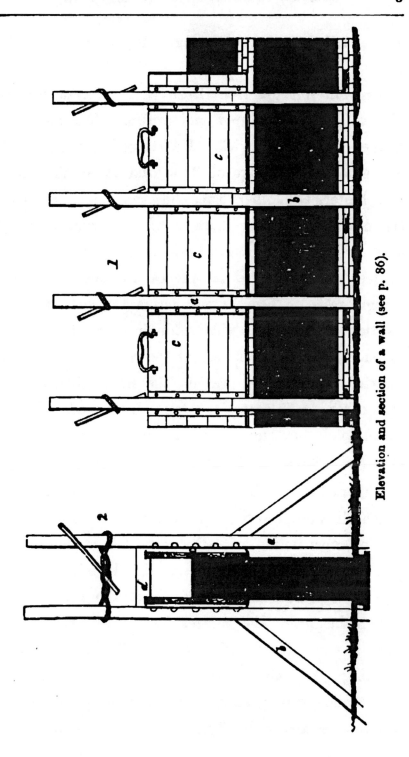

Elevation and section of a wall (see p. 86).

walls get their general dressing, ready to receive their coating.

Mr. Flitcroft describes Rose Hill Villa as coated with stone, lime-coloured and drawn. The columns of the villa are of brick. He states that there are several other buildings of this kind at Stockbridge, Winchester, and other places in the neighbourhood. He describes a better method of constructing such walls by the use of a moveable trough or box about 12 feet in length by 18 inches in depth. This trough rests on bearers put across the wall, with a mortice at each end wide enough apart to receive the sides, and the thickness of the wall; in these are inserted uprights to prevent the sides giving way, with others to go across the top. This mode of construction is however very ancient, and when done on a large scale the primitive method is still pursued.

This method is shown in the preceding engraving, which gives an elevation and section of a wall in process of construction, with the posts, *b b,* the moveable planking, *c c,* and cross pieces, *d.* It will be seen that three courses of bricks are put about every five feet in height. The figures here given are copied from a very old French work on Architecture and Building; they also show the manner in which roof construction was attempted with slabs of the same material, as shown in figs. 1 and 2: the building is

supposed to be square, as shown by the dotted lines
a, b, c, d.

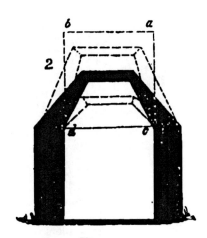

Fig. 1.   Fig. 2.

The plan, elevation, and section given below
represent a small tomb wholly formed of concrete
slabs, the door alone being excepted. This little

Elevation.   Section.

building forms really a solid concrete monolithic edifice.

The entrance door.

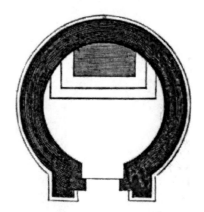

Plan.

A very common method of forming partitions, and even roofs in some of the agricultural districts in Hampshire, is first to put them up with strong wattle hurdles. They are double the size of the common hurdle, and made of a thicker material. When in their place, they are plastered over with concrete, and made about four inches in thickness; they very often require repair. It is said that concrete walls are subject to contraction and expansion, and speedily show vertical cracks at intervals, which in our damp climate would soon permit the wet to enter. There can be no question as to its strength as a building material, as some experiments conducted by the Institute of British Architects gave the following results—viz., " Concrete composed of two parts of lime, thirty-six parts of sand, and five parts of cement, can resist a crushing weight of four tons to the square inch, being twice the strength of Portland stone, eight times the strength of Bath stone, and sixteen times the strength of brickwork."

In constructing cottages with concrete everything depends upon the goodness of the cement and the care with which it is used. The occupiers of these cottages are frequently their own operators; the work is generally too speedily performed, and the consequence is that the fruits of their labour are in most instances of but short duration.

For obvious reasons it is necessary that the greatest economy should be observed in the construction of peasants' cottages, and for these reasons the apartments should always be on the ground floor, which will render it unnecessary to build them more than eight or nine feet high. Where mud walls are introduced, the lower they are made the better, in which case they should be made to batir on the outside so as to resist the pressure of the roof, the covering of which should project as much as possible, to throw off the wet and protect the walls. The chimney flues in these clay and concrete walls are formed of drain-pipes, which answer admirably. These humble dwellings should be paved with brick-on-edge paving laid on sand, which is much warmer, and more conducive to health than any sort of rough flagging, plaster, mud, or concrete floor. The latter, although much cheaper, can never be made to look clean. Foundations of clay or concrete walls should be of brick a few courses above the surface, and the walls when dry should be covered with a thick coat of plaster consisting of lime and sand, or what is still better, a coating of good Portland cement. This ought constantly to be kept perfect, as everything depends upon the goodness of the work. Concrete improperly mixed is not so strong as brickwork, but is mere rubbish; but when perfectly done it hardens with age, becoming like stone, impervious both to wet and frost.

Materials can be found in every locality. One of the principal constructors using such, Mr. Tall, who works with an excellently contrived apparatus, thus describes them:—"Clay, which may be burnt into ballast easily and cheaply, and is a most superior material for concrete; gravel, stone, crushed slag from furnaces, smith's clinkers, oyster-shells, broken glass, crockery, or any hard and durable substance. Where sandstone or any flat stone is to be found, walls can be built even cheaper than of gravel concrete, as a labourer can break the stone." He gives the proportions of materials used in houses then being constructed at Gravesend, as follows:

	£	s.	d.
7 yards of burrs from brickfield, at 5s. . . .	1	15	0
7 yards of gravel stone, at 3s.	1	1	0
1 yard of Portland cement, 16 bushels to the cubic yard, at 2s.	1	12	0
Labour, at 2s. per cube yard	1	10	0
Total	£5	18	0

Three cubic yards of concrete will build 60 yards of 9-inch work, at a fraction under 1s. 11d. per yard.

Concrete cottages have been built at Setting, in Kent, under Mr. Adkins, architect, that cost only 105l. per pair; the ground floor contained two rooms, with the usual larder and closets, and the upper floor three rooms and a cupboard; these cottages had gabled fronts and were picturesque in character. It would be an extra expense over the common method to construct floors and roofing of concrete; the advantage to be gained would be their fire-proof character.

In superior buildings the high tenacious power of good cement is repeatedly, it may be said commonly taken advantage of in the construction of roofs. These are formed by cementing plain tiles, and they have considerable strength. Roofs of 12 feet span, constructed in segmental form, rising three feet, and only of three plain tiles in thickness, successfully resist great pressure, and are durable in a very superior degree; but they require to be well tied in, and formed between iron girders connected together with iron tie rods, otherwise they sink and force out the walls. Roofs of cemented tiles have been constructed from 30 to 40 feet span, and have been found to answer well; hoop-iron bond, laid at intervals between the tiles, is a great advantage. The tenacious power of good cement was proved in a very high degree a few years ago by Mr. Brunel, in the construction of two semi-arches built of brick, springing from a pier or abutment 14 feet in height. One extended 50 feet in length, the other 38; the rise of the arches was 10 feet, the width only 4 feet 6 inches; a weight of about 40 tons was suspended to the extremity of the shorter arch without breaking it.

The result of this test proved that arches of 200 feet or 300 feet span, and probably more, might be constructed in the same manner at very moderate expense, without centering. Iron-hoop bond is said to nearly double the strength or holding-power of the cement. Flat experimental beams have been constructed of brick and cement, with hoop-iron bond laid horizontally between the joints or courses of the brickwork, which have given equally extraordinary results.

Concrete for walling was extensively used in England at the beginning of the present century; it got into bad repute through failure of a river wall at Woolwich, where it was either badly done, some mistake was made, or it was unsuited to the position. The wall was constructed of blocks of concrete cast in moulds, and submitted to pressure while setting; a coating of fine stuff being applied for the sake of appearance, ample time having been allowed for the blocks to set and harden before use. The blocks were 1 foot 6 inches high, the binders and stretchers in the course being each 2 feet 6 inches long, the bed of the former being 2 feet, and of the latter 1 foot; the wall was built upon piles, its height above the piles being 24 feet; the thickness at bottom was 9 feet, at top 5 feet, with a batir in front of 3 feet in 22.

The face of the wall was composed of blocks, as described, and rough concrete thrown in to complete its thickness, and that of the counterforts. After a frost it was found that this wall was seriously damaged, hardly a single block having escaped, and in many cases their whole face had peeled off to the depth of half an inch. The discharge of a drain from a height of 6 or 8 feet had worn away the lower courses to the depth of some inches. On a like wall at Chatham, similar but much more severe effects were produced.

The failure of this wall, costing about 80,000l., was a serious matter, and for several years after architects looked upon concrete as being so much uneatable hasty pudding, considering that it was only beneficial when confined in a trench for foundations. Sir Robert Smirke used it in the foundations of the Penitentiary, Millbank, and Sir John Soane in 1830 used it in the foundations of the new State Paper Office (now pulled down) in St. James's Park. Here the ground had to be excavated to a depth of 22 feet before arriving at a gravelly stratum; at each high tide the Thames filled the trenches with water, which remained in considerable quantity; as this was pumped out, the adjoining party walls of the buildings in Duke-street cracked so completely that they had to be taken down. The trenches were first filled to the height of two feet with broken stones and bricks from the old buildings, and then dry lime and clean river sand, with a large quantity of small broken granite stones, were thrown in from the height above. A body of concrete 8 feet in width by a thickness of 3 feet was thus formed; the water ceased to enter the trenches, and the building was commenced.

Mr. G. Godwin, the editor of the " Builder," in an essay on concrete which gained the first prize given by the Royal Institution of British Architects, appears to have been the first to suggest its use in walls above ground; and for these Portland cement concrete, when properly prepared, is without question an admirable material.

A garden gate—plan and elevation.

In France it is used to a very great extent, in numerous bridges, and several miles of large sewers. A church (that at Vésinet, near Paris, of mediæval architecture), constructed entirely with iron and this concrete, is completely fireproof. In England a considerable length of sewer has been constructed of concrete at Sidmouth, under the direction of Mr. Phillips; and near London, between the Kensington and Gloucester Road stations of the Metropolitan Railway, a very large handsome bridge, rusticated, and in design similar to, and in every respect in appearance a stone bridge. From some alteration required in the railway, it has been removed.

This mode of construction is now being practically tested in the north of England, at Church Bank, Alnmouth, in its complete form, in a cottage built entirely of concrete, having three rooms, scullery, and other conveniences. The material used in the building, as we are told by the "Builder," is Portland cement and gravel from the sea-shore. The foundation is in sand, 6 inches thick and 18 inches wide; in this there is a base course, and above, the walls are 9 inches in thickness. Part of the erection is two stories in height. The roofs are all flat, and are constructed entirely of concrete and old wire rope. The ceilings are divided into panels by ribs at right angles, and require no plastering. A wall on the upper floor is supported by a concrete beam with a 13-feet span; and a large cistern is formed under the roof of the pantry for rain water. The sides of the cistern forming the walls of the bedroom will test severely the impermeability of the material. No wood is used except for doors, and no iron except five shillings' worth of old wire rope. This is said to be an experiment made by the Duke of Northumberland.

Another experimental cottage has been constructed under Mr. Edwin Chadwick's superintendence at East Sheen near Mortlake. In this the walls are formed of light iron framework filled with compressed straw, bitumen, and concrete. The thickness of each wall complete is only about three and a half inches. The floors are of bitumen and concrete, covered with ordinary deal boards; the roof has the same construction as the walls. These, inside, may be either left rough or finely smoothed, without additional cost. In the former case it is said they resemble the ordinary "dashes" of stuccoed cottages; in the latter they appear as if coated with Roman cement, after the fashion of villas and town houses.

If a construction of this kind can be made durable it possesses superior advantages to every other. In England both stone and brick are great absorbents of moisture, causing the occupants of the houses to be afflicted by rheumatism and other undesirable ailments.

Any building material that is non-absorbent of moisture is a great desideratum yet unsatisfied.

An elevation of a design for a garden gate and balustrade to be formed of concrete blocks is given in Design No. 7. It was originally intended for the entrance to an old house in Berkshire.

The vignette beneath is a Swiss pattern of open woodwork used by the author as balustrading. The construction is too simple to require explanation.

DESIGN No. 8.

A PARK LODGE.

Front elevation.

THE entrance lodge to a country park may be considered as a superior kind of cottage; it is

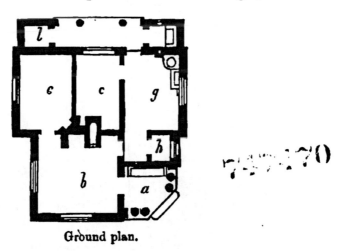

Ground plan.

often occupied by some favourite domestic or other attaché of the family. It is usually placed in a prominent position, dressed with surrounding trees, and with the accompanying gates, posts, and rails. Considerable attention is always paid to the lodge. An

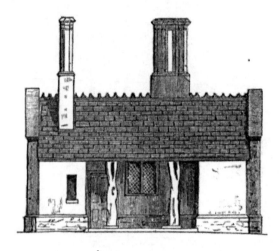

Back front.

ugly one is an exception, and is very seldom seen. In most cases the lodge is similar in character to the mansion to which it permits approach : a Gothic house, hence has a Gothic lodge, and an Elizabethan

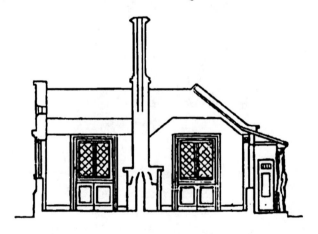

Section.

house a lodge of the same character; frequently it is in the Rustic style that would suit either. Of this the present design and the following are examples.

This design was made for one story only, and it is placed so as to command, or have a view of two roads by which it can be approached; the plan shows a living room, 13 ft. by 13 ft., a scullery, *g*, 12 ft. by 9 ft., a larder, *h*, and two sleeping rooms. It has a porch, formed with trunks of trees, enclosing a seat or bench. The back front is made of a pleasing character, having a covered way to the closet and coal cellar, *l*.

The section shows the height of the rooms, 11×6 from floor to collar beam. The construction was to have been in the common fashion in brick, with red brick facing, and compo dressings round the windows and top of chimney stack, the latter in cut red brick. An erection of this kind could not be completed under a cost of about 370*l*.

Plaster cornice for a drawing-room.

DESIGN *No.* 9.

A PARK LODGE.

Front elevation.

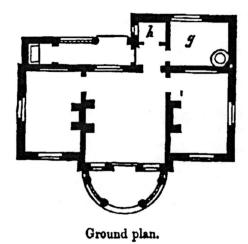

Ground plan.

THIS design was a second study for the same small building illustrated in the previous design. It was intended for a different site, and so placed as to command only one road of approach. It could have been seen for nearly two miles previous to reaching it, and was placed about twenty feet behind the entrance gates; the front had a rustic porch intended to contain rustic seats. The plan shows a

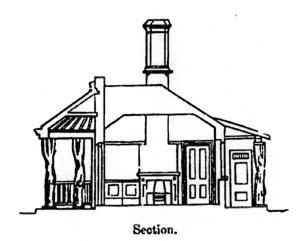

Section.

living room 18 feet by 14, a small scullery, *g*, larder, *h*, and two sleeping rooms each 13 feet by 10 feet. The section is taken through the centre of the building, showing the front and back porch. It could be constructed for about 375*l*.

Either of these lodges could be constructed in concrete, the walls twice the thickness, the chimney stock in brick and cement, and their cost would be reduced.

DESIGN No. 10.

AN ENTRANCE LODGE TO A PARK.

THIS lodge stands within an ancient park in Kent. It occupies a triangular piece of ground and commands three roads of approach. The building is

Perspective view.

strictly in accordance with the style of the old family mansion within the park itself, which is a celebrated structure of the times of Elizabeth and James I. The

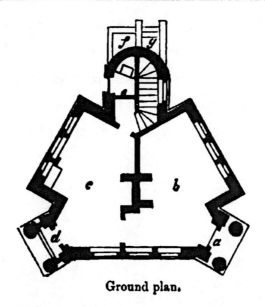

Ground plan.

perspective view represents the lodge as seen from the avenue of trees within the park, the road coming

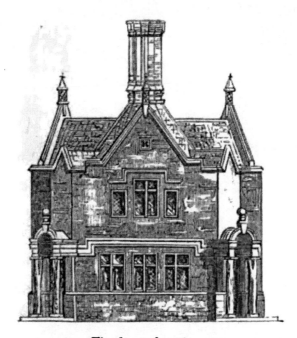

The front elevation.

between.   In the ground plan, p. 105, *a* is the porch, *b* the living room, *c* the scullery, and *d* the larder; *g* are the steps leading to a vault under the stairs, used for coals, and *f* is the stone cover over the dry well.   Considerable care and attention were

Perspective view of back and side fronts, from a photograph.

bestowed in working out the details of this building, which was wholly erected by the workmen of the estate, with bricks and stone also from the estate. The lower part or plinth of the structure is of ashlar ragstone in random courses, the top course header

faced, the joints worked fair, and a sunk splay in the
top tooled fair, the course rising nine inches on the

Plan of upper floor.

face, with an average depth in the bed of eleven inches.
The string over the lower windows is in moulded brick,

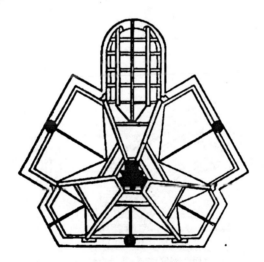

Plan of roof timbers.

faced with compo,—the gables and the chimneys are
constructed and finished with cut red bricks. The

Side elevation.

Details of entrance porch.

finials, of which there are three, are copied from those of the old mansion, and cost each 3*l*.   The front and side elevations are here given, together with the details of the entrance porch.   The columns were formed of trunks of trees, with an entablature and pediment of brick tiles and compo, with iron ties securing the whole.

The brick walls were splashed externally in four colours, black, white, red, and yellow, which gave a very pleasing tone of colour to the whole.   The plan

Finial.

Finial.

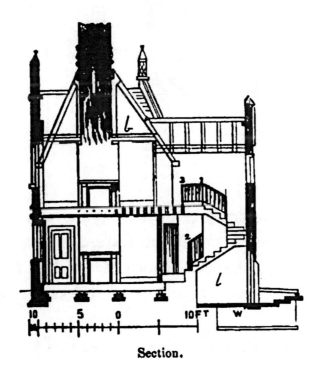

Section.

of the upper floor shows the rooms like the lower, each of the average length of 21 and a width of 10 feet. The staircase leads conveniently to the two upper rooms; *a* is a trap-door to permit furniture and large baggage to be lifted up from below. The sections show the construction of the roof, the timbers

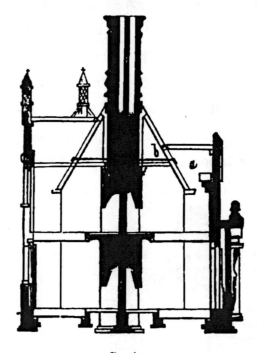

Section.

of which were firmly secured by iron straps, *b b*. The chimney forms a prominent feature in the centre of the building, the construction of which is shown in the annexed cut; *c* are corbel bricks, *b* the iron strap.

The last two illustrations are sections through the

coal-cellar and the dry well. The photographic view shows the small circular gable over the staircase. There are only six of these gables, as a seventh could not be obtained, or it might have been called the

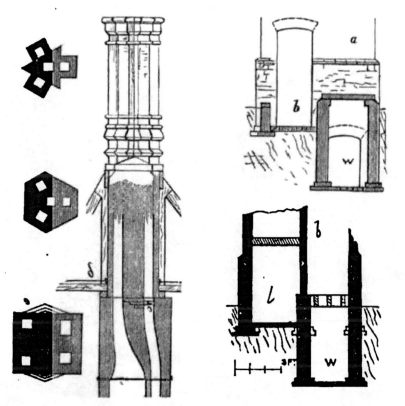

Plan and section of chimney stack.

" house with the seven gables." The structure cost 526*l*., the cottage design No. 2, on the same estate, 311*l*., both in full.

DESIGN *No.* 11.

AN ENTRANCE LODGE AND GATEWAY TO A PARK.

Perspective view.

THE first erection of an entrance lodge and gateway to a country park, is often considered of sufficient importance to meet with very full and careful

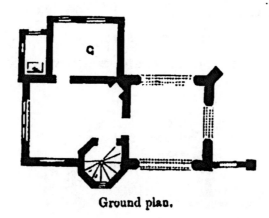

Ground plan.

consideration. If the park is an ancient one, the old castellated style for the entrance lodge will mark its character, and it is generally chosen, although the

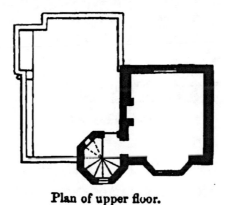

Plan of upper floor.

building or mansion within the park itself may be of more recent style. The family architect, in such cases, will have to make various sketches before one is

I

selected that gives general satisfaction. The castellated Tudor design shown in the perspective view, was the first one made under such circumstances, and several designs were submitted before it was put aside, and one selected similar in style and character to the mansion within the park, and which was soon carried out.

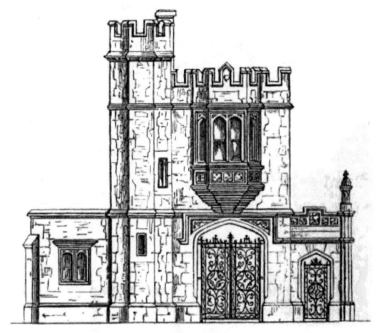

Front elevation of lodge.

The ground plan, p. 113, shows the lodge to have very little accommodation, one small room 15 feet by 11 feet, with a scullery attached; indeed, one of the principal reasons for giving up the design was that the steep character of the ground did not admit a larger erection. The staircase of the lodge led to one upper room over the gateway; this was 13 feet by 13 feet. The elevation of the lodge is shown at p. 114.

The details are plain and bold; a shield of arms with quatrefoils is placed over the side entrance; these and the ornaments on the bay-window are the chief enrichments.

Elevation of half gate.

The lodge was to have been erected with ragstone ashlar for the quoins and red-brick facing for walls,—the bay-window and all the strings and battlements were to be in Caen stone. The iron gates were to be of wrought iron in the olden style. An elevation of one of the gates is given, showing a thin ornamental pattern within a strong iron frame.

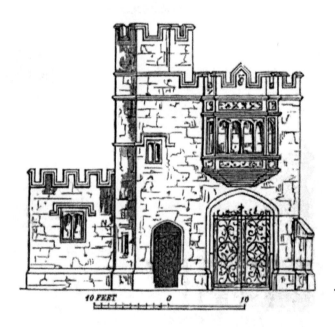

Elevation of second design.

The parts, ¼ full size, are shown; *a* is the top rail, *b* the circular bar, *c* a section and elevation of the hanging rail, and *d* the meeting bar.

The accommodation required by the gate-keeper who was to occupy the lodge was greater than could be well provided on the site the building was to stand on. What he did ask for was given in a second

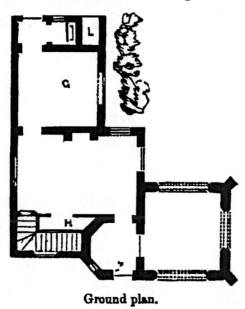

Ground plan.

design, which, as it shows a different treatment of the elevation, is here illustrated. In this the rooms are

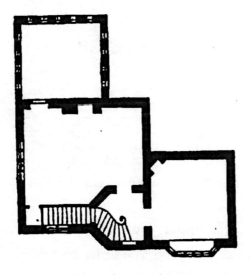

Plan of upper floor.

larger, as may be seen by the ground plan ; *e*, the back room, is intended to be used as a boy's sleeping room ; *h* is the larder under the stairs, and *l* is a place

Details of bay-window, second design.

for coals. The upper plan shows the room over the gateway ; a second room was to be added by taking up the walls of the lodge.

The elevation of this design was considered more quaint and characteristic of the olden style than the first ; its window is copied from one at the old gate-house to the abbey at Montacute in Somersetshire, both as to dimensions and detail. It is rather late in style, and not a very good example, but it is here given with a few sections and details to a larger scale.

The vignette affords a plan of an old English garden, with its labyrinth, fountains, fishponds, and flower beds.

DESIGN No. 12.

A STOVE FOR AN ENTRANCE HALL.

Elevation of stove.

THIS stove is intended to fill a recess in the hall
of a Baronial Mansion, placed on a marble pavement with groups of ancient armour, pikes and

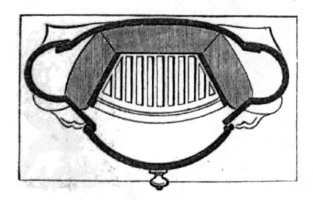

Plan of stove.

helmets, and the other like warlike implements of
ancient times, surrounding it. The plan shows its
interior to be filled with fire-clay. It is only a

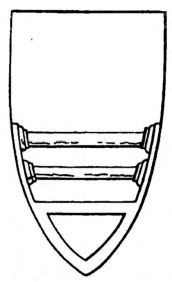

The front of stove, the shield or door open.

Side of stove.   Section of stove.

common iron stove, but with a more artistic outline or figure than is generally seen ; the section shows the construction. A moveable box is placed within the pedestal to receive the ashes; the smoke flue leaves at the back ; the helmet opens to receive a cup of water; the section shows the construction. When the shield is open the fire is seen ; this could be made partly open, so as to allow the fire to be wholly closed in.

The vignette is a portion of a French design for an iron balconet. In France these balconets are regarded as necessary protections at the window openings. In England they are used chiefly for holding flowers.

DESIGN *No.* 13.

QUEEN'S GATE LODGE, HYDE PARK.

THE formation of that new and important suburb of London, known as Queen's Gate, South Kensington, resulted, as is well known, from the exertions of His Royal Highness the Prince Consort. It

First design, Gate Entrance to Hyde Park.

promises soon to become the most fashionable and attractive portion of the Metropolis, as the land is engaged for the purpose of applying it to national objects connected with the Arts and Sciences, by the

Perspective view of Lodge, Queen's Gate.

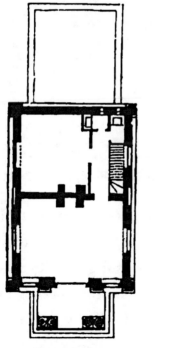

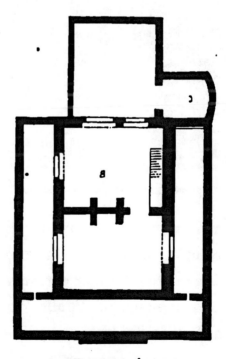

Ground plan.   Basement plan.

Government. Consequently, with the beauty of the situation, this has led to the erectiou of a large number of first-class mansions of the value of from 20,000*l.* each to 3000*l.* (leaseholds). The author of this work, at the time of the purchase by the Government, was surveyor to the principal estate in that locality—that of the late Charles, Earl of Harrington ;

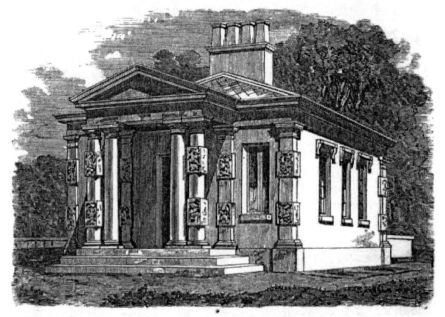

Perspective view of Lodge opposite the Exhibition Road, Hyde Park.

and an opening to Hyde Park, for the chief new road, being granted by Government, he had to submit designs for the new entrance lodge and gates to the Commissioner of Public Works. The first design he had made had previously been submitted to the Prince. It was on a large scale, an archway being placed in the centre, with gates and lodges on each side. But as the new entrance had to be made at the expense of the builders of the Harrington estate, designs of a more modest character were chosen.

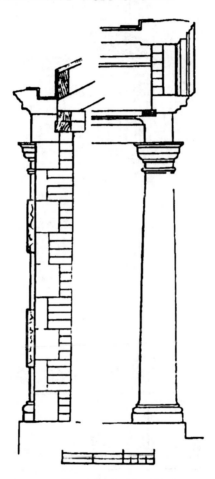

Lord Llanover, then Sir Benjamin Hall, was the Chief Commissioner of Public Works, and took great interest in the designs, repeatedly visiting the spot, and having various studies made; indeed the works were carried out under his supervision and direction.

The opening into Hyde Park was 140 feet in length; this was filled up by the gates and railings, a lodge being placed within the park.

Front elevation.

The view shows the lodge as it was erected by Mr. Aldin, one of the building lessees of the Harrington estate; it cost him about 800*l*.   The iron gates and

Side elevation.

railing were put up by Mr. W. Jackson, the chief building lessee on the same estate, at a cost which amounted to upwards of 2000*l*.

The lodge contains two rooms on the ground floor, the front room being 17 feet by 12 feet, the back room 13 feet by 11 feet. The basement has two rooms of the same size; with a small yard, a place for coals,

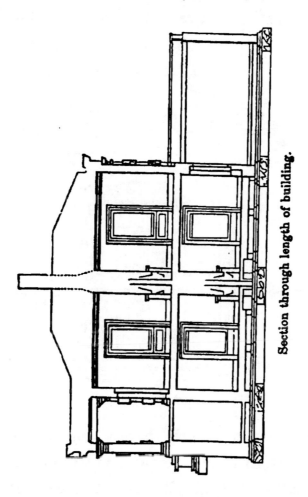

Section through length of building.

and a dry area surrounding the whole. The plans are shown under the perspective view; the front and side elevations on page 128; the small portico has the centre columns without rusticated blocks, so that no

square edges or projecting parts obstruct the entrance
of persons into the lodge.

The section through the length of the building
shows the two upper and the two lower rooms, with
the sunk yard; it does not show clearly the section
of the ground outside the building; the level of this
is 18 inches below the floor of the upper rooms.   The

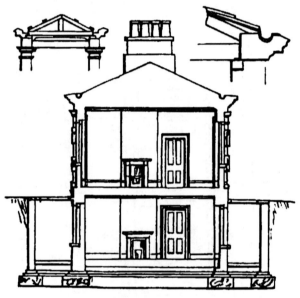

Cross section.

basement is completely buried, but as the small
structure stood upon a mound and was protected by a
dry area, this was of little consequence.   The cross
section next given shows the level of the outside
ground correctly, with the two dry areas.   Over this
cross section are given two small details of the construction of the roof.

The building was of stone and brick, the ashlar front of the walls Bath stone, and the cornice of Portland—this was made so as to form the gutter.

The lodge has lately been taken down, and reconstructed on the opposite side of the entrance gate. So completely was this done that only one small block of stone was required to complete it, and this was only a replacement of one broken. The structure itself has been reproduced by the Government as a lodge opposite to the Exhibition Road. In the cut at page 127, is given a section through the portico and a section through the end wall.

The first design, made by the author, was intended to embody the views of His Royal Highness Prince Albert, in regard to the arrangement of the buildings for the purpose of Science and Art then proposed to be erected on the newly-purchased estate. They comprised one for the collection of pictures, at that time occupying only half the building at Trafalgar Square; this, the new National Gallery, was to be surrounded with other structures, affording ample accommodation for the chief learned and artistic Societies of London. A large central Hall of Arts and Sciences was to be placed in their midst; the whole to form a metropolitan institution for the promotion of scientific and artistic knowledge as connected with industrial pursuits. It is well known that the surplus funds of the Exhibition of 1851, amounting to the sum of 150,000*l.*, were offered by the Royal Exhibition Commissioners at the instance of the Prince, for the purpose of carrying out this grand conception. The report of the House of Commons' Committee on the National Gallery strongly recommended the offer to be accepted, and Parliament at first assenting, voted another sum of like amount for carrying out the entire project. The sum of 300,000*l.* was found, however, insufficient for purchasing the whole of the ground required, and a further grant of from 25,000*l.* to 27,000*l.* was voted by Parliament, and a sum of 15,000*l.* was given by the Royal Commissioners. Mr. Cubitt was engaged to obtain the ground, and the roads through the Harrington estate were planned by him in conjunction with the author, who aided him to the utmost of his power in obtaining the land requisite to complete the site required for the various buildings proposed to occupy it. This site was 2100 feet in length, by an average breadth of 1200 feet, and consisted of about 56 acres; the level of the ground on the north of Kensington being about 36 feet higher than the portion at Brompton. Another block of land, upon which the Department of Science and Art is at present placed, made a space with an average width of 700 feet—in the whole 86 acres.

In sketching the design for the general building, of which a bird's-eye view is here given, the author only took the 56 acres—the view shows only that portion of the building facing the Prince Albert's Road, now called Queen's Gate. It is placed in the centre of the land, so as to have large open grounds surrounding it. These at any time could have been covered up for the purpose of national exhibitions similar to those of 1851 and 1862. By putting the level of the ground floor of the new building about ten feet above that of the Kensington Road, a sub-basement would have been obtained, over 30 feet in height, affording ample space for arranging and storing works of art, as well as for receiving articles to be exhibited, or a great portion of them, from the upper parts of the building, should the latter be wanted for any special purpose, and affording room likewise for all minor business departments. The Hall of Arts and Sciences was to be placed in the centre of the mass of building : a portion of the dome is seen in the view at the upper left-hand corner. This room was to be made 300 feet in length, by 180 in width. Two galleries for paintings, each 1000 feet in length and 80 feet in breadth, were to be placed on each side of the Central Hall. The sculptures from the British Museum were to be deposited in the central smaller halls of approach. The various Societies were to occupy the side-wings,

View of Queen's Gate, Hyde Park, with the National Gallery and other buildings, as suggested by His Royal Highness the late Prince Consort.

each having its meeting and lecture room, and all necessary offices and apartments. The public were to enter at the porticoes seen in the view, and the carriages of the professors at the gateways in front. Two roads were proposed traversing the ground from north to south, and giving easy access for vehicles to every part of the building.

In the small block plan attached to the view, placed on the upper right-hand corner, *b* is the Prince Albert's Road, *a* the Exhibition Road, and *c* and *d* the roads north and south.

The design was placed before the Prince at one of the Architects' meetings at the Earl de Grey's, and it was exhibited at the Royal Academy in the same year. The House of Commons, however, after granting such a large sum of money for the purchase of the land, expressed its disapproval of removing the National

Gallery from the present position, said to be the finest site in Europe, and the Fellows of the Royal Academy were informed that the portion of the building they then occupied would be added to that of the gallery. A view of the gates and lodge as at present executed is here given.

It cannot be supposed that a sum of 340,000*l.* would have been expended by the nation for the purpose of giving the Horticultural Society a perpetual lease of the best portion of the estate purchased. It is already evident that the gardens are not well situated there. The smoke of the district will not permit the growth of delicate plants, and their exhibitions are supplied from the gardens at Chiswick. In much less than fifty years their grounds will probably be the centre of London, and consequently the noble conception of His Royal Highness has still a good chance of being carried into effect. The Society will be smoked out when the city bounds are extended. The present National Gallery building will be wanted either for a Bank of England or a Royal Exchange, and my Lord Mayor may follow the example of the India Directors, and leave the Mansion House, to move to Whitehall. A tunnel under the Exhibition Road takes visitors into the grounds direct from the railway, that now makes them as easy of access from the heart of the City as Charing Cross itself.

A few remarks may be made here on the great rise which takes place in the value of land in any fashionable neighbourhood of London required for the erection of buildings.

The Harrington estate at Kensington Gore, containing in the whole 93a. 3r. 27p., was the joint property of the Earl of Harrington and of the Baron de Villars, through the right of his wife, the Baroness de Graffenried Villars. Previous to 1848 it had been some time in Chancery. In that year Mr. John Gaunt Lye was appointed auditor and agent to the fifth Earl of Harrington for the whole of the property. The rental of the Kensington Gore estate amounted at this time to 2779*l.* 9*s.* per annum. Through Mr. Lye's exertions, he having . received a power of attorney for the purpose, the estate was taken out of Chancery, and a division took place on the 7th May, 1850, at Mr. Lye's office in Lancaster Place. For the purpose of division, one portion—that charged with maintaining the Cromwell Almshouses—was valued at 41,996*l.*, and the other at 40,552*l.* Cards representing each portion were placed in a hat, and the one representing the 41,996*l.* was taken out by the Baron.

In 1851 the Earl's portion was let to Mr. W. Jackson on a building agreement for 99 years, at 100*l.* per acre, or 4600*l.* per annum. In 1852 the Baron de Villars sold his moiety to the Royal Commissioners for the Exhibition of 1851 for the sum of 153,793*l.* The Commissioners only wanted a small portion of the Earl's property. The first offer made by Mr. Cubitt to the surveyor of the estate was 40,800*l.* for 17 acres, or at the rate of 2400*l.* per acre. This was declined, and after a little negotiation the sum of 54,716*l.* was obtained. The matter was settled on the 7th of March, 1853; Mr. Jackson the builder received 7964*l.* as compensation for the loss of so much of his building land.

More land was purchased by the Royal Commissioners to make up the site they required; in the very middle of the latter was a field which had only been used as a place for beating carpets. It belonged to the Smith Charity estate, and fetched a rent of about 40*l.* per annum; this field was obtained by giving in exchange an outlying one on the Villars estate, the building value of which was estimated at 800*l.* per annum.

The Royal Commissioners, after squaring the site they required, and putting aside the portion now occupied by the Department of Science and Art, parcelled out the remaining outlying portion into three blocks, and let them on building leases. The first and most important of these was secured by the author for an employer, at a rental of 1500*l.* per annum, on condition that the fee of each house plot could be purchased within 6 years after the lease was granted; it contained about 2 acres. And these are now the only freeholds that can be obtained. This plot is now covered with buildings of the selling value, as leaseholds, of 250,000*l.*, and it produces an improved ground rental. For the purchase of the whole fee, the sum to be paid was 46,500*l.*, so that for a portion of this land which the author of this work, as surveyor of the property, sold in 1852 for little more than 3200*l.* per acre, the value had risen, in 1860, to no less than 23,250*l.* per acre.

It is only since Hyde Park has become almost the centre of the metropolis, instead of being in one of its rural districts, that attention has been paid to supply it with ornamental lodges and gates. The country was so long occupied with the importance of the war with France, which terminated so gloriously to the honour of our country, that the Royal Parks were left in a very neglected state; and the gates and lodges, particularly the entrance into London by Knightsbridge, were mean in character, and totally unworthy of the purpose.

Londoners of the present day have no notion of the wretched state of Hyde Park as it existed fifty years ago. The side next Park Lane, now a beautiful walk, adorned by the gardener's utmost skill with several varieties of flowers and shrubs, was then a narrow sunken road, which for the most part continued, by the side of the boundary wall, all the way from Oxford Street to Piccadilly. This, when improvement commenced, was filled up, and laid down in grass; and a wide Mall, with two foot-paths, was formed on the higher ground, and enclosed by handsome iron posts and rails. Some extensive gravel pits existed in the middle of the park; these were filled up, one only being permitted to remain. The surface of the park was generally levelled and manured, by which the herbage has been greatly improved. Numerous seats were placed about the park for the convenience of the public; clumps and avenues of trees were planted. The Serpentine was cleansed for the first time; it is just now recleansed. A new drive, nearly a mile in extent, was made through the most distant and beautiful part of the park, to lead to Kensington Gardens; and generally, all the roads were macadamized, and enclosed with posts and rails. To connect the roads north and south of the Serpentine, a handsome bridge was erected, from the designs and under the superintendence of Messrs. Rennie. This has much conduced to the accommodation of pedestrians and horsemen.

About twenty years after these great improvements were effected, Queen Anne's garden, at the extreme termination of Kensington Gardens, was thrown open to the public; the kitchen garden belonging to Kensington Palace was let out on building leases, and a road formed through it connecting the town of Kensington with Bayswater. This road, called the Queen's

Palace Gardens Road, is now covered from end to end with first-class mansions. The improvements continued, and are being still carried on.

The lodges and gates, at the chief entrances into the park, were put up at the expense of the nation. When any building operator required an entrance into the park, for some new outlying district, he bore the expense of the construction, working under the direction of Her Majesty's Chief Commissioner of Works. The Government lodges at Cumberland Place cost 2151*l.* One of these has been lately removed to widen Park Lane.

The two first lodges, with gates opposite Stanhope Street, cost 5062*l.* The single lodge at the end of Grosvenor Street, with the iron gates, cost 2929*l.*, and the fountain 340*l.*

The grandest of all these erections, that at Hyde Park corner, adjoining the Duke of Wellington's mansion, cost 17,069*l.*

The first lodge and entrance gates put up by a private building contractor was the Albert Gate, erected by the late Thomas Cubitt; the lodge is sunk, its flat roof being on a level only eight feet above the ground, and containing two small rooms, with a little yard and scullery. The iron railing forming the carriage gates and entrances to the foot-paths is of the same height as the lodge, and extends about 60 feet;

the stone piers have on them the old stags which formerly decorated the stone piers at the entrance of the Ranger's Lodge in Piccadilly. This gate gave an entrance by Hyde Park to Belgravia, and very much raised the value of that district.

The next lodge and gate were put up by Mr. Kelk, opposite the fine mansions at Prince's Gate. This is known as the Prince of Wales's Gate.

There are two lodges in size and plan exactly similar to the lodge at the Queen's Gate. The gates and railings are very plain; they are 12 feet in height, and extend to a length of 77 feet.

The Queen's Gate lodge and gates are certainly the chief of all the erections put up by building contractors; their cost was 2800*l.*, as previously mentioned. Both in ornamentation and character they vie with the best erections put up by the Government. The length of the iron-work between the stone pedestals is 140 feet; the height of the common rails, 11 feet above ground; the height of the standard and lamp, 18 feet; there are two carriage gates, each of 15 feet opening, and two entrances for foot-passengers, each of 10 feet opening. The stone pedestals at each end are 6 feet in width by 15 feet in height. The iron-work is designed to represent a group of spears; the author wished to surmount the pedestals with groups of military arms similar to those of the trophies of

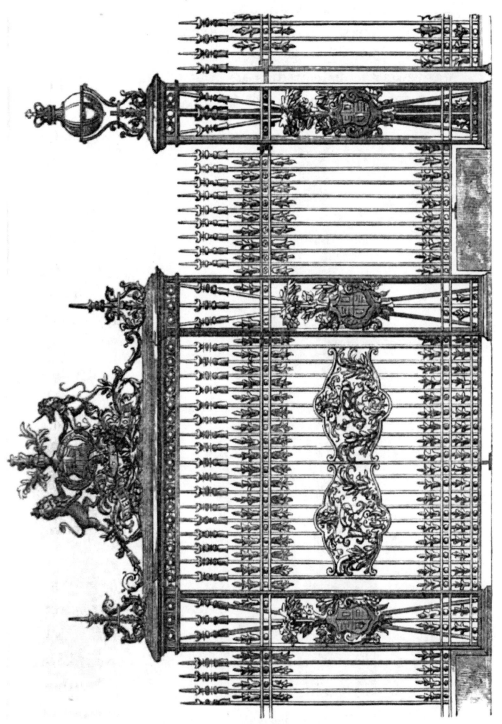

Design No. 13.   Elevation of centre of iron-work, Queen's Gate.

Marius on the balustrading in front of the Senatorial
Palace, Rome.   These could have been constructed in

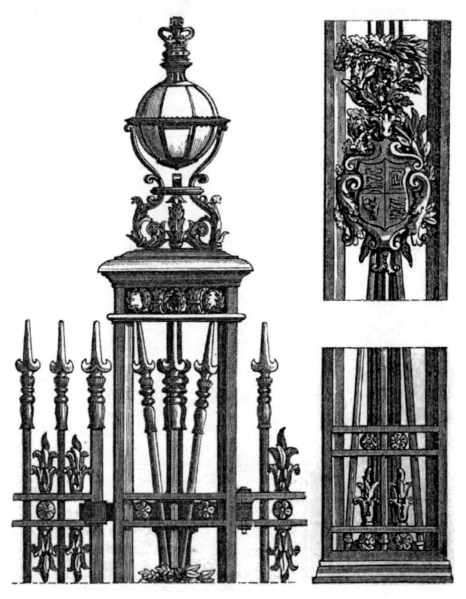

Elevation of one of the Iron Standards.

stone, at little expense.   Sir Benjamin Hall wished for

marble statues, and on Prince Albert's suggestion models were made of two reclining figures, by Mr.

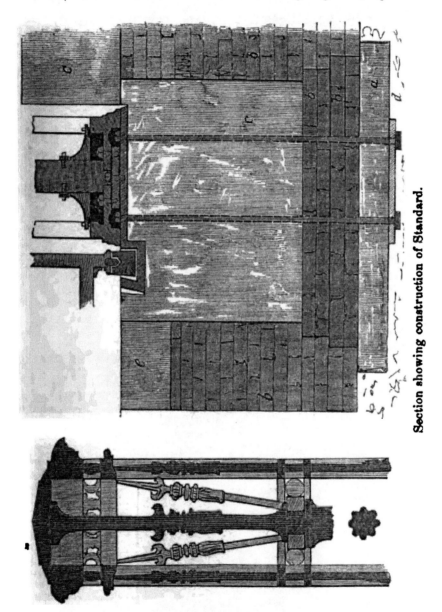

Section showing construction of Standard.

Theed, representing "Morning" and "Evening." These would have caused great additional expense to the

L

builders, who wished, as the entrance was a great
improvement in the value of the Earl of Harrington's
property at Kensington, to place, on the piers, two

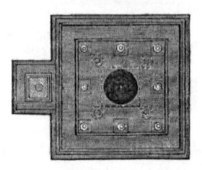

Plans of Standard at various heights, showing construction.

fine antique statues of Hercules then on the gates at Elvaston in Derbyshire, a country seat of the Earl's. But as the statues belonged to the estate, and were entailed property, they could not be removed, and the Earl objected to their being taken down for the purpose of casting. The effect of the whole is much injured by the pedestals remaining unoccupied. The plate on page 143 represents the centre of the ironwork, surmounted by the Royal Arms.

Iron block and ball latch.

The gates and railing are of very superior construction; they are the work of Mr. Turner, of Hinde Street, Manchester Square. They have been pronounced by the Government officials as requiring little attention, and that the gates open and shut better than any other gates in the park. Page 144 gives an elevation

L 2

of one of the iron standards. Each is two feet in width; there are ten of them; four, those belonging to the carriage entrances, being surmounted by lamps. The small size of this volume will not allow a full illustration of the ornamentation to be given, but it admits that important part, the construction, to be clearly shown. Page 145 gives a section of one of the standards, *d* is a layer of concrete, 1 foot 6 inches in height and four feet in width, which goes all through; *a* is the York landing, 6 inches thick and

Wheel block.

5 feet square; *b* is the brickwork, this goes all through; *c c* represent the blocks of Portland stone; and *e* is the granite curb 8 inches by 10 inches in section, within the entrances.

Page 146 gives the plans of the standards at different heights, showing the several plates given in the section; and on page 149 is a section of the wrought-iron coupling-bar with its brass bush.

The gates move on a hardened steel socket of circular form, working within a steel box, as shown in the section.

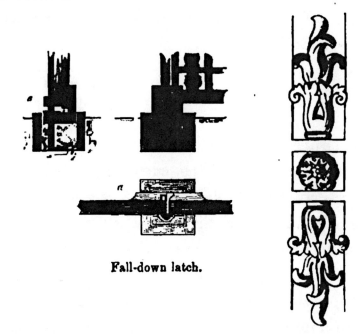

Fall-down latch.

Iron block and ball latches are provided for each of the gates. On pages 148 and 149 are cuts of the wheel block, with the plan, elevation, and section of the stopping-piece or fall-down latch. The stopping-

Coupling-bar.

piece is keyed into the granite curb in the centre of each gateway; *a a*, is the lower rail of gates; and by its side is a small portion of the ornament between the rails.   That the effect of the whole structure was very much injured by the unfinished state of the pedestals was the opinion of Lord Llanover, who sent the following letter to the architect, expressing his dissatisfaction :

Great Stanhope Street,
July 11, 1859.

SIR,

The works at the Queen's Gate, Hyde Park, are very well executed, and the entrance, as completed, produces a good effect; but that effect would be materially improved if the gates and the railings, and the ornamental works were relieved by colour, and some of the parts gilt as I intended they should be. The two pedestals are also without the groups which were to form the superstructure of the square blocks. The work so far as it is executed is very well executed, and I am quite satisfied with it so far; but I shall not consider it completed until the groups are placed on the pedestals, and the best effect will not be produced so long as the iron-work remains wholly black.

I am, Sir,
Yours faithfully,
LLANOVER.

C. J. Richardson, Esq.

ON

THE FOUNDATION AND BASEMENT WALLS
OF BUILDINGS,
DAMP PREVENTION,
AND FIRE-PROOF CONSTRUCTION.

THE foundations of buildings require careful consideration. When a house approaches completion and shows cracks in the upper walls, they arise either from insufficient attention having been given to the solid character of the earth forming the site, or from bad construction at the basement. The building in fact settles down unequally. As a settlement of every building is certain to take place upon its completion, the greatest precaution should be taken to make it as equable as possible. No portion should settle deeper than another, and this can only be secured by care at the foundations.

It often happens that portions of a selected site are of unequal quality. In such cases it is necessary to excavate the worst portions deeper, to reach a good stratum, and to take the brickwork lower, no filling up beyond the usual thickness of concrete being allowed.

There is another very serious evil, in building, to

be guarded against. Owing to the moisture of the earth rising through the foundations and saturating the walls above, the health of the occupants of such houses may be seriously affected by its presence in the walls. About twenty years ago it was the universal practice in good buildings to place wide stone landings—three times the thickness of the wall above—under the foundations, for the purpose of preventing the damp from rising as well as to spread the width of the wall.

A bed of concrete is now used as a substitute for this plan; the engraving below shows the best method

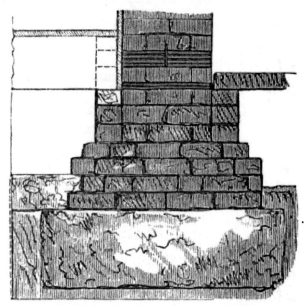

Section of a proper foundation for a wall.

of constructing foundation walls. A trench, three times the width of the wall is dug, at least 2 feet

6 inches in depth. · Into this is thrown a quantity of concrete, which soon dries and becomes solid. In the superior class of buildings a layer of concrete, six inches in thickness, is placed entirely over the ground, inside the foundation. Upon this concrete the walls are built, the lowest footing being twice the width of the wall above. On a few courses above the top footing a course called a " damp course" is put; this is shown at *a*, page 152.

Two courses of slate are laid in cement; but other materials are often used, as a thin sheet of lead, for the whole width of the wall. Zinc might answer, but it has not yet been tried. A thin coat of asphalte, or asphalted cloth, tar, pitch, or a plain coat of cement are also often employed, but the two courses of slate in cement are considered sufficient. The first course of bricks above the ground is often formed entirely of air bricks, originated by Mr. Aldin, the builder, of Kensington. Each brick has eight or ten perforations, $\frac{1}{2}$ inch in diameter, through its whole length ; a small piece of perforated zinc is placed upright between the bricks to prevent insects from entering. This is shown at *b*. The timbers and stone flooring of the basement do not enter the walls, but rest upon dwarf walls, the joists having oak sleepers to rest on. The brick fenders of the foundations are entirely filled with dry rubbish or ironfounder's ashes, and the stone hearths

bedded solid either in mortar or concrete. This is
the construction shown in all the designs of this
volume.   To illustrate still further the attention given
in constructing foundations, the engraving below is
given, showing a section of a foundation executed
several years ago at Westminster, where the ground
was uncertain.   Its scale is only half that of the
previous figure, the upper wall being 3 feet in thick-

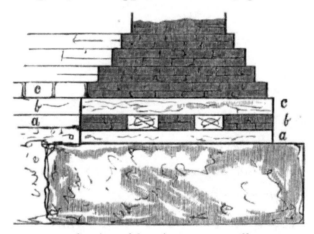

Section of foundation to a wall.

ness instead of 1 foot 6 inches.   Above the bed of
concrete, which is 9 feet in breadth, by 3 feet in
thickness, are York landings, *a*, 4 inches thick and
exceeding 6 feet in width.   Upon these are laid two
lines of wood sleepers, *b*, bedded in brick and cement,
the size of each sleeper being 12 by 6 inches, and in
long lengths.   Above this is a course of planking, *c*,
placed diagonally across the wall; each plank being
12 inches by 6 inches, and about 9 feet in length.

Above this are the footings, each two courses in height : in the return walls the landings, sleepers, and planking are placed a course higher, so that they might be tied together. The brickwork goes down twelve feet, and invert arches are turned at every opening.

In order to keep the walls as solid as possible in the lower part of a building, the ground floor joisting should rest on projecting corbel bricks as here

shown,—the joists going between the cross walls rest upon projecting bricks, the upper one being of peculiar strength ; tall tiles are put between each joist against the wall, for the skirting in cement to be formed upon it. Air bricks in open iron-work, two to each front, are placed so as to admit air within the joisting.

This mode of construction is carried throughout the ground floor.

The stone landing of the passage by the side of the servants' stairs, is supported on the part next the wall by corbel bricks, and on the other side by an iron

Section of stone landing of passage.

bar let into the wall at each end; as shown above. In the upper floor, the joisting should be reversed and go front to back, notched on wall plates let into the wall, thus tying both walls together.

The introduction of rolled iron girders into buildings renders fireproof construction very easy. They are made of all sizes, and can be placed over any

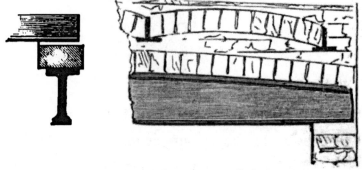

Section of kitchen roofing.

opening, so as to carry the weight above them. Kitchens in many London houses are constructed in the back yards, with an area between them and the house. This confines all the smell of the cooking to the precincts of the kitchen. As it is very important that no roofing should interrupt the light from the back ground-windows of the house, the roof of the kitchen is so constructed that the yard is only moved upwards; it belongs to the ground floor and not to the basement. For this purpose, cast iron girders, standing on brick piers, bear up rolled iron six-inch girders, between which half-brick arches are turned. Above all these is concrete, cement, or asphalte. The courses of tiles and cement are laid at such a slope as will be sufficient to take the water off quickly. It is easy to put skylights, or any kind of opening, in this construction, and to make the whole water-tight.

This figure shows a way of supporting walls over openings, instead of the old method of arching in brick; the iron girders or plates have often no timber between them; they rest upon iron shoes or stone slabs, their depth being proportioned to the opening and the weight above. Strong large hollow bricks or tiles are placed over them, and above all is the brickwork.

Support over opening.

The upper floors of buildings are made fire-proof in a similar manner, and for this purpose there are several excellent patented methods. The iron girders are closed up by brick arches, or filled between with concrete. The only objection to this mode of construction for upper floors is the great weight, and the walls require to be made of extra strength. Several years ago a hollow brick was used to form such arches and roofing, *e.g.*, the dome of the Rotunda, at the Bank of England, is formed with them. The brick is somewhat similar to a flowerpot, but flat and closed at each end. There were several varieties of these cone bricks, as they were called; a few are preserved in the Soane Museum. One sort was $7\frac{1}{2}$ inches in height, $4\frac{1}{8}$ by $2\frac{3}{8}$ inches at the top, and $3\frac{2}{8}$ by 2 inches at the bottom. They were curved inwards with a small opening, 1 by $\frac{4}{8}$ inch in the centre. The edges of the brick were slightly splayed, and the sides scored; these were as strong as the common bricks, and very much lighter. When the East India House was pulled down a large quantity of these bricks was obtained; they were brought to Kensington, and the builders did not know what they were intended for; their purpose being pointed out, they were used up in the construction of fire-proof flooring.

Fire-proofing.—A method of rendering buildings nearly fire-proof was introduced about 1770 by Mr. David Hartley, M.P. for Hull. It consisted in placing thin metal plates between the flooring boards and the joists, so as to prevent any upward currents of air. For domestic buildings the system was one of great value. After several successful trials it obtained considerable notoriety, and being thought capable of an impossibility, that of rendering a Theatre fireproof, it was applied to the Pantheon Theatre in Oxford Street. On that structure being burnt to the ground the plates lost their character, and went out of use. It was clearly a mistake to apply them to such a building. Thin iron plates hung at a short distance below the ceiling were successfully adopted by Mr. Walter Crum, to prevent the spread of fire from one room to another in his calico printing works, near Glasgow.

Damp.—The damp rising from foundations is more easily guarded against than damp coming against a building laterally. Houses in exposed situations and subject to driving winds, are often very wet inside the walls, the rain being driven through them. Sometimes the best construction will not keep out wet. As a rule, a well-built wall wherein proper material has been used, should not be damp.

A rectory, not far from Salisbury, where the author was engaged a few years ago, was in such an exposed situation that on three of its sides no tree or any other object in a direct line could be seen for three miles. Clothes, if placed against the external wall of the dressing-room, were often quite wet. The Rector had tried several preventives himself; one was a mixture, used to water-proof cloth—a wash of soap and alum.

The ingredients were mixed in the following proportions: ¾ lb. of mottled soap to 1 gallon of water. This mixture, when in a boiling state, was laid over the surface of the brickwork steadily and carefully with a large flat brush, so as not to form a froth or lather on the surface, and was permitted to remain twenty-four hours to become dry and hard. Another mixture was then made in these proportions: ½ lb. of alum to 4 gallons of water, which after standing twelve hours, in order that the alum should be completely dissolved, was applied in like manner with a flat brush over the coating of soap. The coating had to be very often renewed. The wall most exposed was made free from wet by being covered with a coating of cement.

Walls exposed to damp should be coated with a thin layer of Portland cement, mixed with a little plaster of Paris, and after this is thoroughly dry, it may be hardened and rendered impervious to water by painting it with boiled linseed oil and red lead, mixed together.

In very exposed situations all external walls should be battened, lath and plastered within, or built with a hollow cavity in the middle, with proper bond and a proportionate increase of thickness,—the hollow could be filled with concrete, or the back of the bricks covered with pitch. There are several other methods for keeping walls free from damp. One is to saturate the walls with some kind of mastic, or a wash composed of two or three parts of resin and one part of drying oil, to the extent of as many washes as the wall will absorb. This must be quite dry at the time, or be dried by means of a small portable furnace. The plan is effectual, but it is a difficult operation to perform. A cement composed of lime, boiled linseed oil, white lead, and sand, has been recommended.

Besides these various compositions, there are several excellent well-known paint and metallic cements, which have stood very severe tests, and are largely made use of; but walls properly constructed should not require their application.

Plaster ornament for a ceiling.

M

DESIGN No. 14.

A SMALL COUNTRY RECTORY.

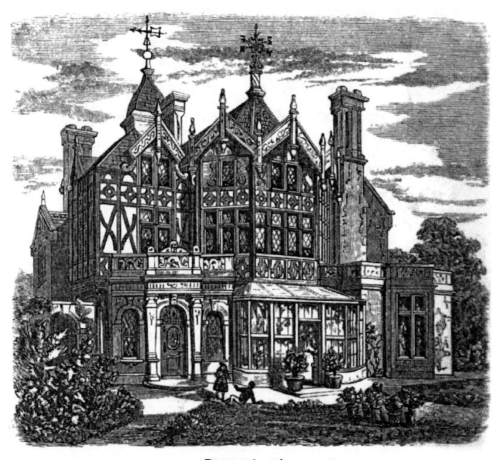

Perspective view.

THIS design was made for a country clergyman
residing near Montacute, in Somersetshire. It
was arranged according to his express directions in
every particular, both as to style, and in regard to the
number and size of the rooms on each floor. Living
in the immediate neighbourhood of some of the finest

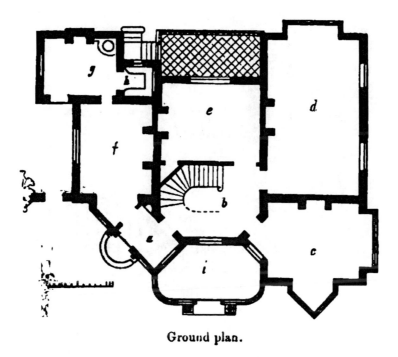

Ground plan.

old English mansions, he was anxious to have a
residence in the old decorated style of wooden architecture, certainly the most picturesque of all the styles
our forefathers have left us. The timber dwelling is
found in almost every county throughout England,
with their projecting windows and highly ornamented
bargeboards; several large houses in Cheshire and

Shropshire remain to satisfy us that such construction, when properly carried out, is very lasting. The timber used requires to be felled at the right time, and to be properly seasoned before being placed up; which must be done on a brick or stone foundation. Dwellings constructed in this way were anciently

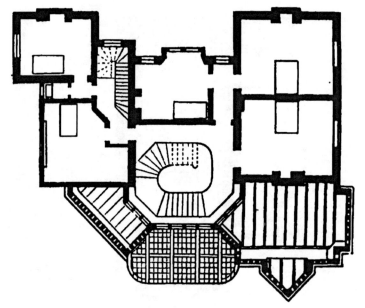

Plan of upper floor.

called post and-pan houses. They have been known to rock and bend before severe storms, and to stand intact while adjoining buildings have been blown down. Large palaces were formerly constructed in England of wood; the chimney flues and fireplaces alone being of brick. The sketch-book of John Thorpe, an Elizabethan architect, a copy of which is in the fine library of the Art Museum of South Kensington, illustrates several of these dwellings.

With the present design it was the intention of the rector to carry out the work himself, the necessary drawings being provided him. The building is small and compact. When much adornment is intended, it is necessary to confine the expense within

Ornament in ceiling of study.

bounds; if a cheap large house with plenty of accommodation be required, then four walls and an overhanging roof alone need be given. The view shows the principal front of the building; on page 163 is the ground plan; *a* is a small hall having a window looking into the conservatory on the right; the door leading to the servants' department is on the left;

c is a small study, 16 ft. by 14 ft., with a decorated ceiling, containing the shield of arms of the owner. The drawing-room, *d*, size 28 ft. by 15 ft., has the

The ceiling of drawing-room.

ornamental ceiling of bold Elizabethan character; this covers the whole ceiling, and the effect of such orna-

Cornice of drawing-room.

mentation is very good.   Often, in the olden times, a portion of the rib moulding was gilt, the ground of the ceiling being of a light blue; ceilings of this kind exist which represent foliage and flowers, giving the effect of a garden bower. The preceding illustration shows the present ceiling. The simple rib moulding is in plaster, with small flowers and pendants. The section of the rib moulding to a large scale is shown in the cut; which also gives the cornice and frieze of the room; *e*, in the ground plan, is the dining-room, 16 ft. by 12 ft., this opens on to a terrace paved with

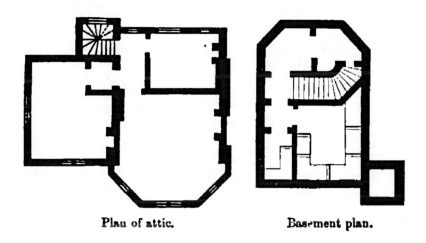

Plan of attic.   Basement plan.

marble in black and white squares—the present ornamental tiles were not in common use at the time the design was made; *f* is the kitchen, *g* the scullery, and *h* the larder. A small enclosed servants' yard, with place for coals, wood, and other conveniences, is in front of the kitchen. The yard has a separate entrance from the front. This is the whole of the accommodation given on the ground floor. The one-pair plan shows the five bedrooms. These are

without dressing-rooms, there being no space for them.
A small turret staircase leads to the attic floor.   This
gives two large bedrooms and a small one for the

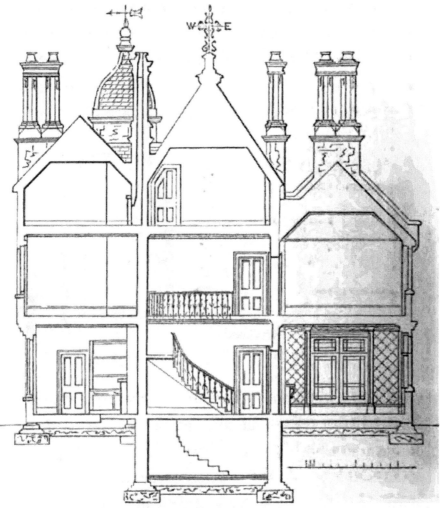

Section through building.

servants.   The large bow-windowed room might serve
as a nursery.   The tower was carried up and contained a bell.   The basement plan contains a large

and small wine cellar, and one also for beer; there
are four cellars, besides an inner cellar under the
stairs.

The principal staircase is very light and cheerful,

Front elevation.

having on one side three large windows, with a ledge
or stand for flowers. It was proposed to panel it
entirely with oak, and have an ornamental ceiling
similar to that in the drawing-room, with a pendant

in the centre. The section is taken through the drawing-room, staircase, and kitchen, and shows the form and height of the rooms above; also the stone stairs to the cellars.

It will be seen that the walls rest upon a concrete

Details of gable ornaments.

foundation; the scale is too small to show the damp course or the ventilating bricks, as previously described (see page 159). The chimneys are shown carried up nine inches square, excepting the kitchen chimney, that being 14 inches by 9. The staircase was to have a plain Elizabethan iron railing, and the whole of the wood-work to be coloured and grained oak; the roof was to be covered with slate, these requiring a less solid base; ornamental ironwork crowned the summit of the principal roof over the staircase. An illustration of the front of the building is given on page 169.

The figures on page 170 illustrate various kinds of

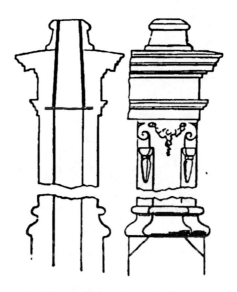

Section and elevation of chimney.

treatment for the carving of the finials and pendants, and the ornaments of the small gables; it being usual in these structures not to have any two parts of ornamental detail exactly alike. It has all to be carved by hand, and requires only slight extra trouble on the part of the architect to make separate patterns for the workmen. A section and elevation of one of the chimneys are shown also; they are fitted with the small cap introduced and used so extensively by the late Mr. Thomas Cubitt, at Belgravia and Pimlico; this will

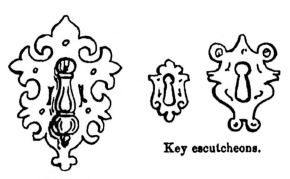

Knocker.   Key escutcheons.

Oak corbel.

be found fully illustrated in the chapter on chimney and flue construction.   At the time this design was made, this plan was not known. The chimney is shown with an iron funnel 2 feet in height, a chimney-pot, in fact, let into the stone work at top, having no projection within for soot to lodge. Two of the stone balustrades are illustrated. Every separate balustrade in such buildings should be of a different pattern.

Stone balustrades.

The knocker on the entrance door, the key escutcheons for the doors, and a corbel in oak from the entrance front, are illustrated on page 172.

An external frieze.

DESIGN No. 15.

A SMALL COUNTRY HOUSE.

The front elevation.

THIS building was intended to be only a comfortable country house for the residence of an eminent provincial solicitor. It was directed to be made of superior character, as the owner, being a person well known in the county, considered that the

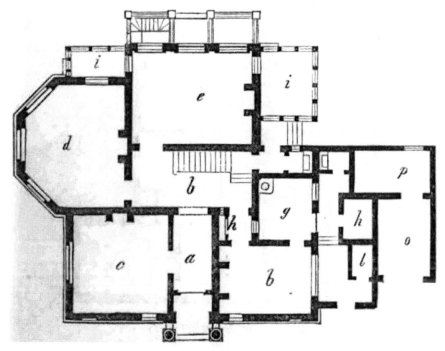

The ground plan.

eyes of the whole neighbourhood would be upon it. The situation was on one of the roads leading out of Maidstone, and as the land in which it was to stand was taken on lease for 99 years, nothing beyond a superior gentlemanly character could be given to it, as it is only in freehold houses that any superior or ex-

pensive architectural adornment should be indulged in.
The Roman or Italian style, as being the most appropriate and the one best understood by builders, was
adopted.

The front of the house had no prospect, the side of
the road opposite to it showing only a high bank with

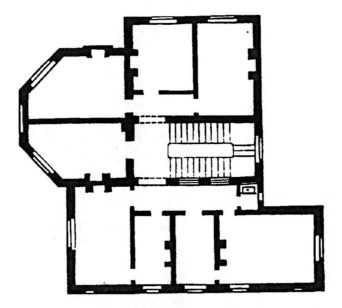

The plan of the upper floor.

boulders of ragstone, peculiar to the county of Kent;
and for this reason none of the principal windows
looked towards it.   The back-front and side, however,
turned towards the hills between Maidstone and Ro-
chester.   Very precise directions were given as to the
arrangement, size, height, and number of the rooms.
The study, c, was to be on the left of the entrance-hall,

and its size 16 feet by 12 feet. It was made 16 feet square. The drawing-room, *d*, having the chief prospect, was to be the principal room. This was made 20 feet by 17 feet. The dining-room, *e*, was 20 feet by 16 feet; both rooms looked into conservatories, *i i*. The back front faced the north—a very favourite aspect for the principal rooms with many of the noble-

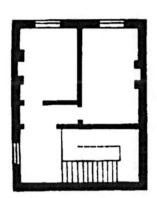

Plan of second floor.

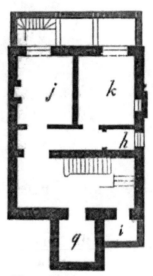

Plan of basement floor.

men and gentlemen of Kent; the reason being that the flowers in the gardens under the windows, turning towards the sun, present a cheerful and agreeable appearance to the occupants of the rooms.

The dining-room had steps leading down to the garden; the kitchen *b*, scullery *g*, and small larder *h*, were on the right of the entrance, the kitchen and the study having small windows by the side of the entrance,

N

so that all visitors coming to the house might be seen. The servants' door was in the small yard by the side

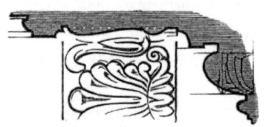

Frieze of drawing-room.

Frieze of dining-room.

Section of cement skirtings.

of kitchen, with a place for coals; *o* is a small chaise-house, and *p* a stable for a pony; *l* is the dust-hole.

The upper floor had to contain five best bedrooms; these can be seen in the plan. Their sizes were 17 feet by 12 feet, and 16 feet by 10 feet. There were three dressing-rooms, the largest 12 feet by 10, the two smaller each 12 feet 6 inches by 6 feet. The second floor contained two rooms for servants, one 16 feet by 10 feet, the other 12 feet by 10 feet. The basement had a footman's pantry,

12 feet by 9 feet 6 inches, and a dairy of the same size. This had steps down to it in the area. There was a wet larder with a window, a wine cellar, and a beer cellar.

The interior was plainly finished, with nothing

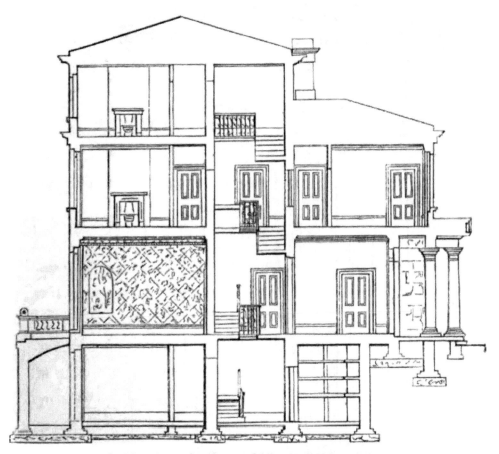

Section through entrance-hall and dining-room.

beyond the best modern enrichments. The whole of the interior had Keen's cement skirtings. The staircase had a skirting flush with the wall, so as not to take away space from the stairs; this is shown at page 178. There were ornamental roses in the centre of the ceilings of the principal rooms. The section of the interior is made through the principal entrance,

Elevation of portico.

across the staircase and dining-room; and in the upper floor, through two of the dressing-rooms.

The only architectural feature in the front of any

importance was the portico (see page 180). A bold and prominent effect was given to it. The estimated expense of the building was 2151*l.*, full price put down as 2250*l.*

The vignette is an elevation of an Elizabethan balustrade, in stone, intended to crown a cornice, and to be placed in an elevated position against the sky line.

DESIGN No. 16.

A COUNTRY VILLA.

THIS villa, which has just been erected in Berkshire, in the neighbourhood of Windsor, is
intended as the country residence for a lady of rank.
The living rooms are large and noble, and the accom-

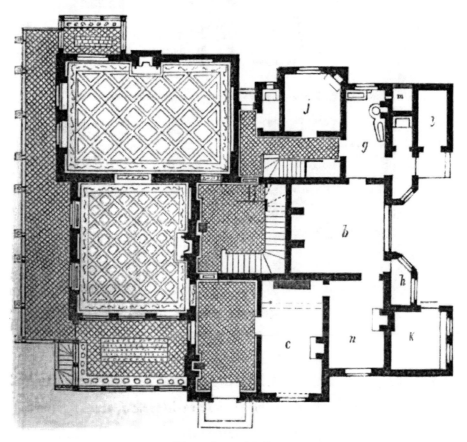

Plan of ground floor.

modation for a small establishment ample.   The plate
(page 182) shows the garden front, and above is the
ground plan. The two principal rooms, the drawing and
dining-rooms, are respectively 25 feet by 18 feet and
21 feet by 18 feet.   They are to the left of the hall ;

this, of moderate size, leads to the principal staircase, which is of very easy ascent, each step rising less than

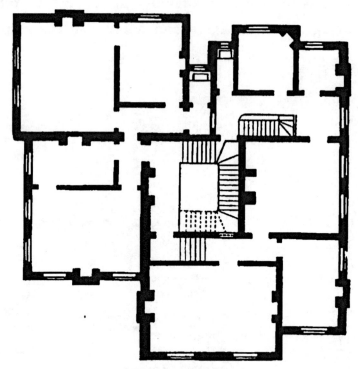

Plan of upper story.

6 inches. The second landing opens to the servants' staircase; *b* (see page 183) is the kitchen, size 15 feet by 14 feet, with the larder *h*, leading directly out of it,—*g* is the scullery, with an oven, and a shoot into the dustpit *m*, *n* is the housekeeper's room, and *j* the butler's pantry; *c* is the lady's room or study. This was enlarged, by taking down the partition, marked on

Plan of wine cellar.

the plan by the dotted lines, to allow of a splendid oak cabinet being placed there. A door in the room opens direct into that of the housekeeper; *k* is the dairy,

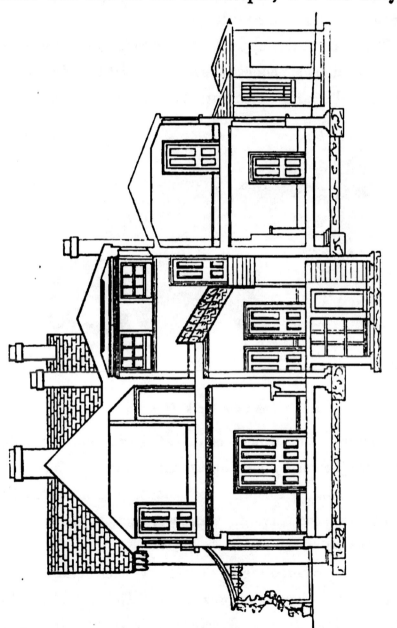

Section through drawing-room, staircase, and kitchen.

and *l* a place for coals. The wine cellar was at first intended to be placed under the principal flight of stairs, descending a few steps: but a large one, *b* (see page 184), was afterwards made.

The plan of the upper story shows it containing two large principal bedchambers—each with a dressing-room, and a large room with two fireplaces serving as

French cut pine woodwork, from the exterior.

a nursery, but which could at any time be made into two rooms by putting up partitions.

The servants' sleeping apartments, the housemaid's closet, and the servants' staircase, occupy the remaining portion of the plan.

The cost of erecting the carcase of the building, including the wine cellar, was 1108*l*. The cost of finishing, putting up the principal staircase in Portland stone, and leaving all work required to be painted with two coats, but exclusive of papering, stoves, iron-work, marble mantelpieces, conservatory, verandah, and exterior deco-rations to roof, was 1550*l.* Mr. Hock-ley, of Kensington, was the builder. When the mansion was finished so far, all ornamentations, &c., formed an agreeable occupa-tion for the lady to complete from favourite examples seen by her on the Continent. The ex-tra parquet flooring in the dining and drawing - rooms is

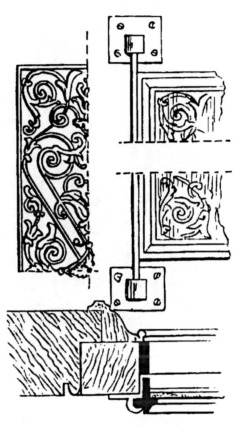

Plan and elevation of iron glazed case-ment to entrance-door.

from Switzerland. This cost 148*l.* All the stone flooring of the hall, staircase, passages, and con-servatory, is covered with tiles from Italy; these are about 8 inches square, but not so well made as the English kind, although more artistic. Each has a small figure put in by hand, which is different on every tile. The tiles are faced with a white china ground and look extremely well. The common tiles cost 16s. per 100. The grotesque figured

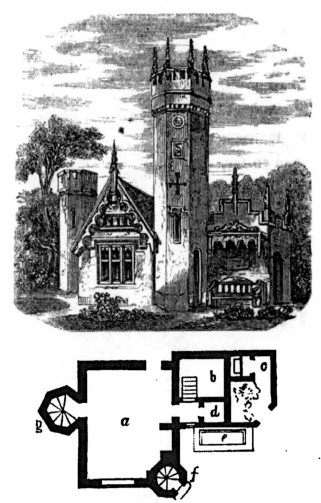

Plan and view of remains of old house.

tiles, of which the illustration on page 189 shows four, cost 2l. per 100. They were supplied by M. Giustiniani, of Naples. The marble chimney-pieces were

to be supplied from Italy. The ironwork of the staircases, and the panel to fill up the opening in staircase, shown dotted in the upper plan, were supplied
from Paris. It is different from any ironwork that
can be procured here, of elegant design, and covered
apparently with a thin coat of zinc. This gives it a
silvery metallic appearance, and it does not require

Four of the Italian figured tiles.

painting; it is really a coating of glass, and is termed
the *lavenant* process. It is said to be a great preser-
vative of the iron, and can be put on in different
colours. Each of the windows of the principal rooms,
and the hall, is fitted within with Price's steel revolv-
ing shutters. These cost 75*l*. The upper windows
on the outside have iron balconets, likewise from
France, and the roof, surrounding the principal parts,

is finished with the French cut pine patterns. They
were supplied by M. Jules Millet, of 12, Boulevard du
Temple. The entrance-door has the two upper panels

French iron staircase railing.

filled with French castings, executed in a fashion
different from the English mode; but one quite
worthy to be followed. The iron panel is placed on

the outside, with a light iron glazed casement fitted behind it. This in warm weather can be opened, so as to admit fresh air into the hall. The plan and elevation of the casement shown from the inside, on page 187; by the side of it is one quarter of the external iron casting.

It may be remarked that these French patterns, both in iron and wood, are not finished off as clean as they would be in England. The castings appear just as they came out of the sand, and the wood pattern exactly as the machines or saw left them; but they are extremely elegant, and the metallic appearance of the ironwork is very pleasing.

The former house is pulled down, except a portion, permitted to remain, which is formed into a decorative building for the garden; the plan (page 188) shows *a* the old kitchen, *b* the wine cellar made into an ice-house, *d* a lock-up closet, *f* a prospect tower, *c* a closet in a small enclosed garden, and *e*, a garden seat.

On page 190 is a pattern sent from Paris for the staircase railing.

DESIGN No. 17.

A DOUBLE SUBURBAN VILLA.

Perspective view.

THIS building was intended for erection on a leasehold estate at a little distance out of London. It would have been of rather plainer character, but the view (page 192) shows the design first made. The frontage, or width of ground for each house, was

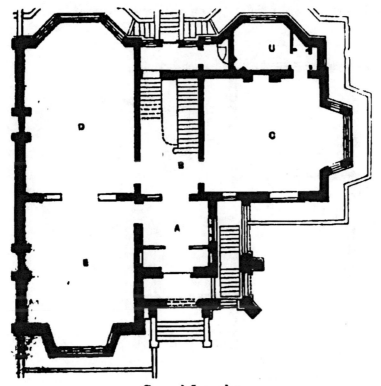

Ground floor plan.

60 feet, the depth 150 feet. The character of the building was of the domestic style of the reign of Henry VII., and the accommodation it afforded is given in the several plans. The ground plan shows two large rooms *D* and *E*, the drawing and diniug rooms, which can easily be opened into each other by sliding back the

inner doors into the partition ; *C* is the library, with
a book-room leading out of it.   *B* is the staircase, of
a size rather larger than that generally allowed in
London houses.   Very often, sufficient attention is
not paid to this highly important part of our dwellings
by builders, nor full space allowed for it.   A good

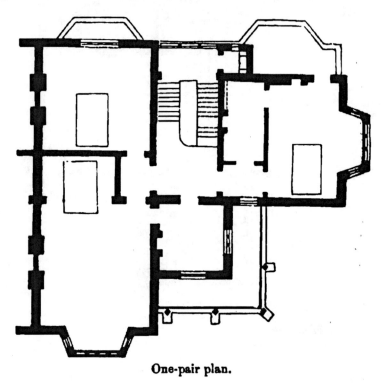

One-pair plan.

staircase should have, at every six or seven steps, a
landing of at least 2 feet 6 inches in depth.   Where
winding stairs are used they should have a good sweep ;
the tread, in the centre, should be 1 foot in width, the
riser never more than 6 inches in height—less even
would be better.   It is also of considerable importance

in a staircase that the height of the steps in the various flights should be the same. Some of the most costly and important of the builders' houses in London, erected on highly rented land, have the staircases so confined that these, an architect's well-known rules, are

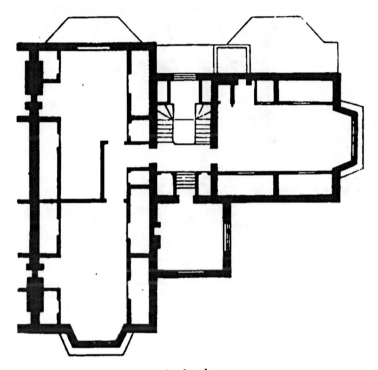

Attic plan.

wholly put aside. Staircases with risers of 6 inches in height from the ground to the one-pair floor, increased to near 7 inches to the two-pair, the latter flight containing .probably 30 steps in a straight line without a landing, render a house almost uninhabitable.

A servants' staircase is a most desirable addition to

a large house.   The present building was not considered of sufficient importance to have one.   It was
proposed to be placed between the tower and the
dining-room, but it was rightly considered that the
two staircases should be put together so that the

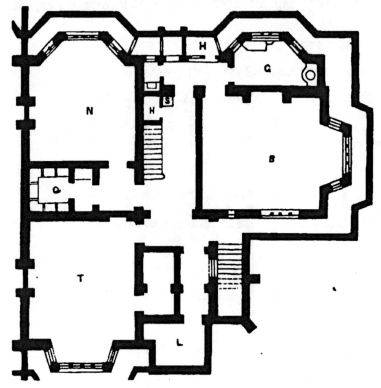

Basement plan.

landings of each, on every half space, should be on
the same level, separated only by a door, and giving
the servant immediate access to every floor of the
house.   A position between the library and staircase
would have been most proper, but there was not
sufficient width ; it would have interfered with the

kitchen, and would have made too intricate a plan, which, for houses to be erected on leasehold land, is

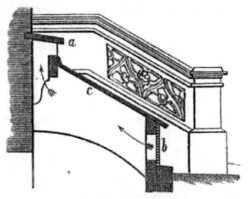

Section of roof to larder.

objected to by builders unless directed by the party purchasing.

With a servants' staircase follow a large housemaid's closet, sink, &c., which must always be provided where

Section of steps to garden.

possible.   The plan of the one-pair shows three large
bedrooms and one dressing-room, with the tower room,
which was intended either for a morning room, a

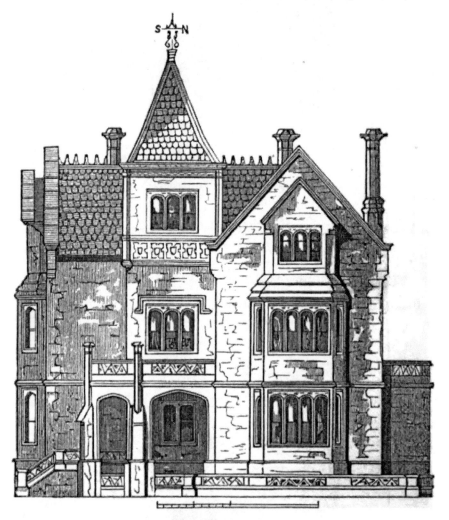

The side elevation.

school room, or a boudoir.   There is a large conservatory on the principal landing of staircase, and a closet
leading out of it.   A good-sized aquarium with a

regular supply of water could be easily arranged in the centre of the conservatory. The attic plan contains three large rooms for servants, and the tower room

was to be used as a smoking room, or as a play room for the children.

The basement contains a private breakfast or dining

room, *T*, with a large store closet, having an opening one foot in height filled with perforated zinc opposite

Half elevation of small library.

the window of the passage; *N* is the housekeeper's or servants' hall; *B* the kitchen 23 feet by 18 feet, with *G* the scullery behind, *H, H,* the larders, *S* position for a lift, and *L* a place for coals. The basement stairs should have been on the side adjoining kitchen.

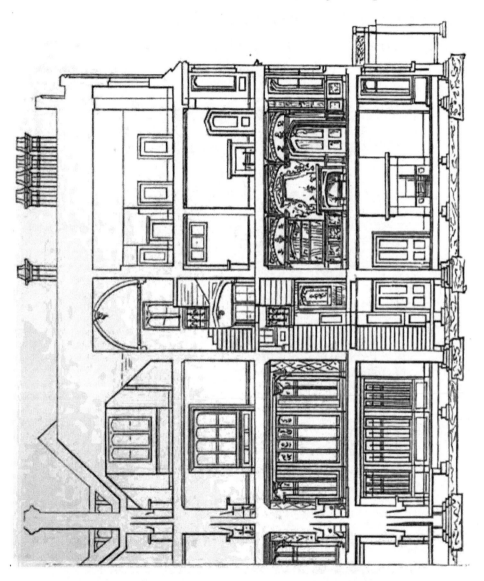

It is a difficult thing in this class of house to confine the smell of the cooking to the kitchen. An endeavour was made here to effect it. The kitchen

had no direct entrance to the body of the house, the
servants going through the passage, by the side of the
area, from which it was well ventilated, to get to the
common staircase. This had a window at the top, not
shown in the plan. The small section on page 197 shows

Elevation of hall screen.

the mode of ventilating the larder ; *a* is a slab of slate
let into the wall, *b* a pane of perforated zinc, *c* iron bars
glazed with thick glass, so that whatever the weather,
there would be full ventilation, the fresh air always
entering and the confined air leaving the room. This

is the usual mode, in large houses, of covering the external passage leading from the kitchen to the house.

Details of hall screen.   (See page 206.)

The general view shows the front and side of the two houses. The elevation of the side front is given on page 198.

The three small illustrations on page 199 are various details of the exterior. One is a part section of the roof of turret, showing the timbers and the vane at top, an elevation of one half the upper gable window, and

Plan and elevation of entrance garden-gate.

half of one of the small front windows; these portions of the exterior, together with the arcade at the entrance and balustrade over it, were to be executed in stone.

The Gothic window by the side of the arcade is an example from Berstead Church, in Kent. The gentleman for whom the design was made caught a sight of it in the "Architect's Sketch Book," and requested it

might be introduced as a small window in his library.
An elevation of one half of it is given on page 200.

The general section (page 201) is of one of the
houses taken through the drawing room, the staircase,
and the library. The staircase is well lighted, having
a conservatory and closet on the first half-space landing. The ceiling of the staircase is finished with
groining and pendant flowers; the stairs have a

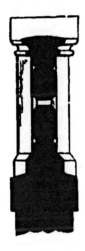

Balustrading on garden wall.

plain Gothic iron-railing, painted and lightly gilt;
the section shows the party-wall between the two
houses.

The entrance is divided into an inner and outer
hall, divided by a Gothic screen in carved oak, the
various openings of which, together with the upper
panels of the folding doors, are filled with embossed
glass. This keeps the house warm, and prevents cold
draughts from entering; a second glazed screen

separates the inner hall from the staircase; the effect of the screens when there is plenty of light behind is extremely pleasing. It was for such a screen that the door-handle illustrated at an earlier page, as a vignette, was made.

Of the first of these screens, that in the hall, only the larger lower and upper panels were to have white

Balustrading in front of house.

embossed glass; the smaller openings were to be filled with richly coloured embossed glass; a small elevation of the hall screen, and portions of its details to a larger scale, are given on pp. 202, 203.

The chimney pieces were proposed to be of cast iron, and to be painted and slightly gilt.

The expense of construction of the pair of villas would be nearly about 7800*l.*

Front.

Cut-wood canopy to a door at West Brompton, a short distance beyond the Metropolitan District Railway. It has been constructed about twenty years, and stands well.

One of the side trusses or corbels.

DESIGN FOR VILLAGE SCHOOLS, AND READING ROOM.

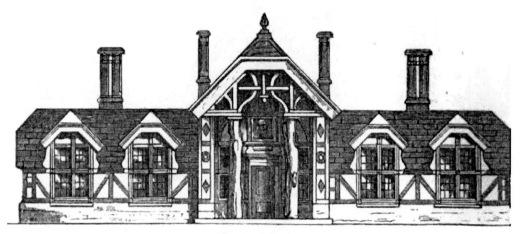

Front elevation.

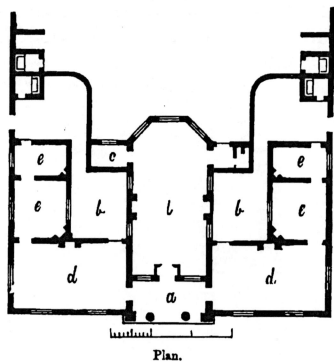

Plan.

THIS building is about to be erected in the county of Norfolk. It will contain a boys' and girls' school, with two rooms each, forming a parlour and bedroom, for the master and mistress; *a* is the entrance porch, *d* and *d* are the two school rooms, and *e* and *e* the living rooms. The centre of the building forms the reading, lecture, and meeting-room for the village. The small room *c*, leading out of it, is a book room for the secretary or attendant; *b*, *b*, are open yards; each master and mistress have private entrances, and yards to themselves. The construction is of the cheapest kind; on a brick foundation, quarter framing is placed, filled in with brick, and plastered inside and out. The columns in the centre are trunks of trees, standing on stone slabs, and each has a flat stone capping. This building complete should not cost more than 850*l*. It is much to be desired that every village should have a room set apart, distinct from any public-house or tavern, where newspapers and books can be provided, lectures given, and various entertainments supplied the villagers.

DESIGN No. 19.

A ROMAN CATHOLIC CHAPEL AND SCHOOLS.

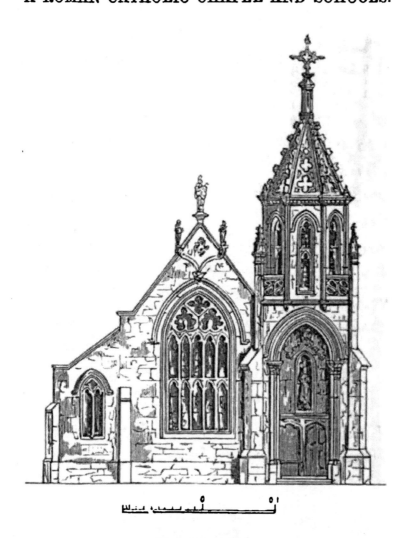

Elevation of front.

THIS design was made for a building intended to occupy a site leading from the High street in a

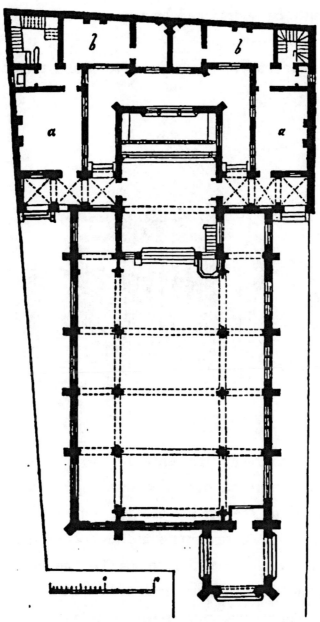

Plan of chapel and schools.

P 2

very fashionable district, immediately out of London.
The ground was rather confined in area, and from its
position, being behind the houses in the street, it
could only be approached by a narrow avenue between
two of the houses.

The plan was an endeavour to make the most of

Transverse section of chapel.

the space afforded; the entrance to the church, a
small tower with an open decorated spire, was placed
at the end of the avenue of approach; *a a*, are the
schools, which have immediate access to the space
before the altar; *b b*, the rooms for the teachers or
priests, had staircases on each side leading to rooms
above. These buildings were kept low, so that as

much light as possible should enter from the window above the altar. An elevation of the front of the chapel is given in our first illustration. The section looks towards the chancel, showing the chancel arch and pulpit in front, the altar, and the decorated

Porch in the High street.

window over it; the latter contains a large cross formed of white embossed glass, on a richly coloured glass ground. Above is the elevation of the porch, proposed to have been placed at the entrance of the avenue of approach.

DESIGN FOR A BATH HOUSE, AND SUMMER ROOM.

Perspective view.

THIS design was made for a building intended to occupy a prominent position in a park in Kent; it would have commanded an extensive view over the Weald and surrounding country. The lower ragstone foundation already existed, being portions of an ancient building which had formerly stood there, and this held a fine spring of pure cold water, which runs down into a lake at a lower level in the park. Occupying a position in which it could be well seen, it was desirable

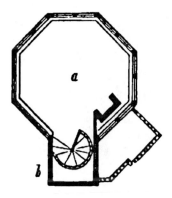
One-pair plan.

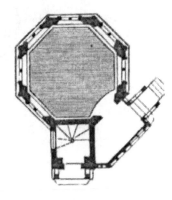
Ground-floor plan.

that the building should form a picturesque object, and to effect this the Old English style of wooden architecture was chosen.

The view shows the back and side of the building, with the entrances, these being here less exposed to the weather than if they had been in front facing the open country. The ground-floor plan shows the cold bath with a small dressing-room; the bath was octangular in form, and fifteen feet in diameter. A small iron circular staircase led to the upper room ; this was eighteen feet in diameter, with a domed ceiling, the sides of the room having iron

Side elevation.

casemented windows, and over them a bold ornamented plaster frieze ; the fire-place was adorned with oak carving. The fine prospect from the windows of the Weald, and the lake and park scenery in front, would have made this an extremely pleasant room.

The lower story of the building above the ancient

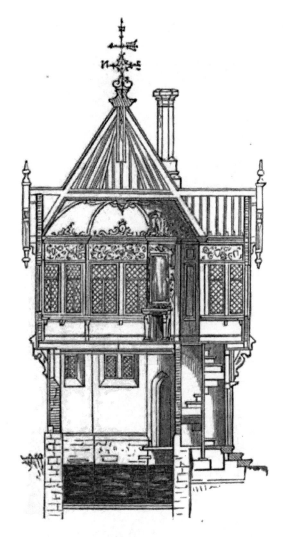

Section.

ragstone foundation was of brick, nine inches in thickness, with quarters on the outside, brick-nogged;

carved oak inch plank was then to be screwed to this quartering, and the inner spaces filled with cement; this it was proposed to dust with small bits of coloured

Entrance.

glass. The building was intended to be strongly constructed, as it was to stand on an elevated site in the most exposed situation in the park. The entrance, of which an elevation is given above, had two carved oak columns, having iron rings fixed to them. A small shield of arms was above the entrance; the whole of the oak was to be stained and varnished. A portion of the exterior is given on a larger scale.

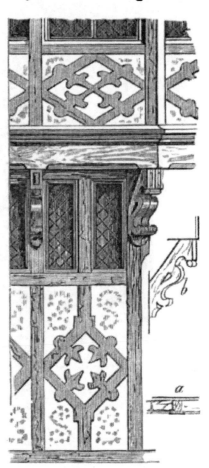

The upper story was in quartering, brick-nogged, faced externally with carved oak planks and plaster, and plastered inside as below. The small plan, *a*, in the illustration, shows this; *b* is an elevation of one of the carved oak trusses, and these were carried right round the structure.

An elevation of one of the small gables is shown in the next cut, with its richly carved barge-board, and turned pendants and finials.

Portion of exterior.

The plan of the iron casements is given, p. 220; *a* is the frame fixed to the wood quartering, *b* the loose frame fixed to receive the loose frame, *c d* is the glass, and *e* the hinge and staple; a representation of the small turn-buckle is shown, and lastly the plan of the flooring over the bath; the joists, each 9 inches by 4 inches, and 9 inches by 2½ inches, were strapped down

Elevation of one of the small gables.

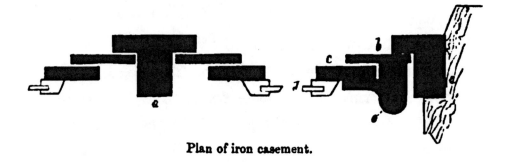

Plan of iron casement.

eight or nine inches into the wall, where necessary.

Turn-buckle.

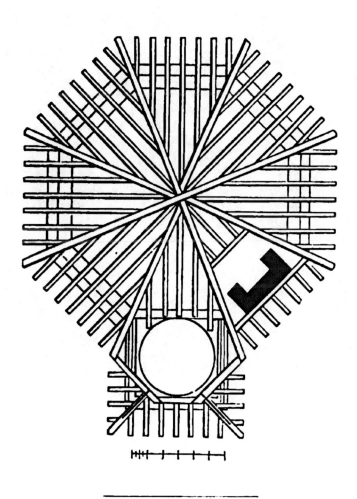

DESIGN No. 21.

DESIGN FOR A SMALL COUNTRY VILLA.

Perspective view.

THIS mansion was erected in Devonshire, for a gentleman having a numerous family. It consisted of three floors:—a basement story, ground

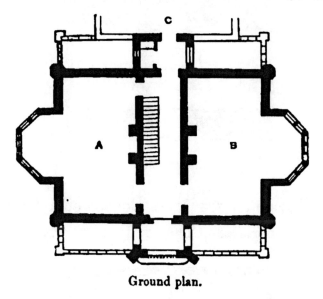

Ground plan.

floor, first floor, and attic. The picturesque style of the time of Henry VII. was adopted, and the construc-

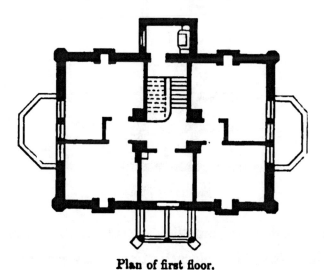

Plan of first floor.

tion was of brick with stone ashlar facings for the walls. The decorated portions were of stone ; but red

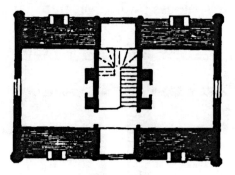

The attic floor.

brick and stone, or red brick alone, would have been equally appropriate.   The red brick with compo-

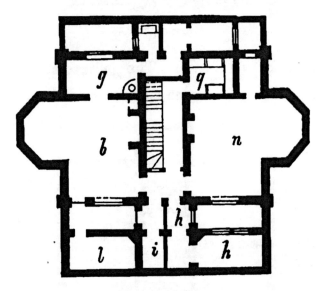

Basement plan.

dressing and enrichments would have been the cheapest.   Considerable attention was given to obtain a picturesque character for the building, and the chimneys were so placed as to obtain one. The height to the top of gable was 38 feet 6 inches. The ground floor, given on page 223, contained two

View of entrance porch.

rooms, *A* and *B*, each 28 feet by 16 feet, without the bay. The porch was enclosed from the hall.

The upper floor had five rooms, intended merely as sleeping apartments. All had fireplaces, except the centre front one, and that is shown supplied with a flue pedestal, a contrivance by which an upper room

Q

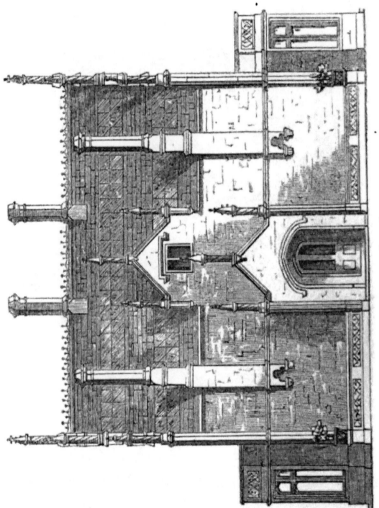

The front elevation.

can be warmed by one of the fireplaces in a lower
room, which prevents waste of heat.   The attic floor
had two good-sized rooms without fireplaces, for the
servants.

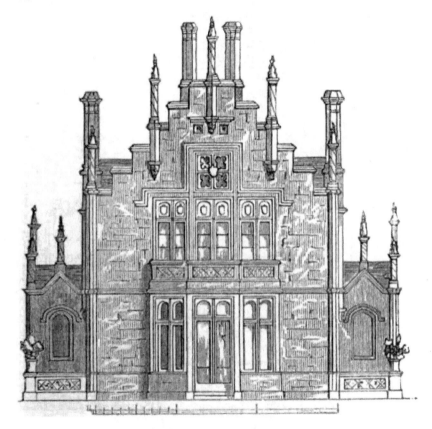

The side elevation.

The basement floor had good accommodation.   One
large room, that marked *n*, was for the housekeeper,
with space for a.bed.   It could be used as a private
breakfast or dining-room; *b* is the kitchen, 20 feet by
15 feet 6 inches, with a large space in the bay.   The

Q 2

scullery *g* adjoined the kitchen ; *h* is the larder, *q* the wine cellar, *i* the beer, and *l* the coal cellars.

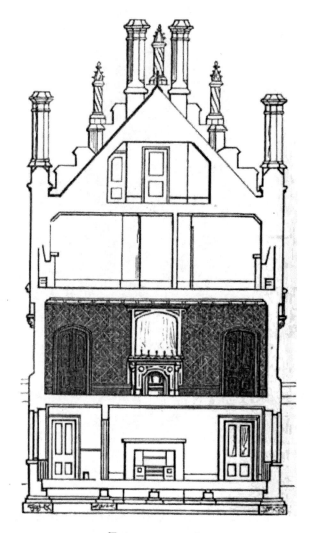

Transverse section.

Another design for the porch is given on page 225 ; this is of a more decorative character than that seen in the view.   It had on it the shield of arms of the proprietor. It was to be constructed entirely of stone, the portion above the archway being richly carved. The front and side elevations of the exterior of the building, of which representations are given, show the extreme simplicity of the design.

The transverse section (page 228) shows the interior; this is taken through the kitchen and

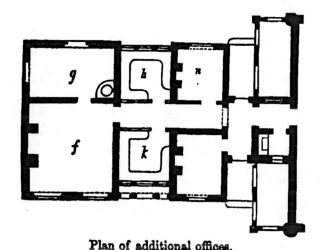

Plan of additional offices.

scullery in the basement, looking towards the fire-place and through the living rooms and attic above.

This design has, with various alterations, been adopted in several places for different parties, stripped entirely of its ornamental character, and merely having four walls and an overhanging roof, in plain cottage style. It forms the cheapest model that can be given for a villa. One was erected a few years back that cost considerably less than eight hundred

pounds.   It had the basement floor but no attic, the
upper rooms being heightened by having an open
collar-beam roof.   One addition made to it when it
had no basement was in extensive external offices, as

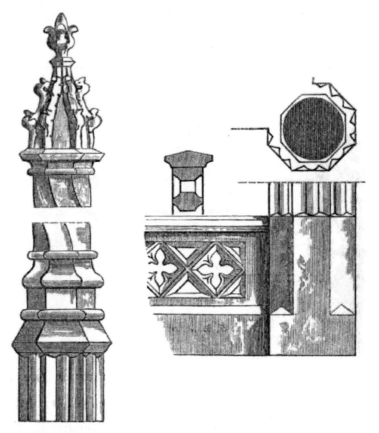

Elevation and section of external balustrade and angle buttress.

seen in plan on page 229: *f*, the kitchen, is 18 feet
square, with its scullery *g*, 18 feet by 10 feet; *h* is the
larder, 9 feet 9 inches square, and *k* the dairy, of the
same size, with a northern aspect.   The two small
rooms by the side, one marked *n*, were intended for a

study or school-room, and a footman's or butler's pantry, with a separate entrance and an outlet from the house into the garden; the servants' closet, and boot and knife cleaning place, were at a little distance away, together with the place for coals and wood. Some details of the exterior on a larger scale are given above.

The vignette shows the best proportion that can be given to stairs intended for a public building; the rise of each step being 6 inches, the tread 13 inches. In private dwellings the tread is made smaller by half an inch.   When the rise can be made $5\frac{3}{4}$ inches only, much greater ease can be obtained in the ascent.

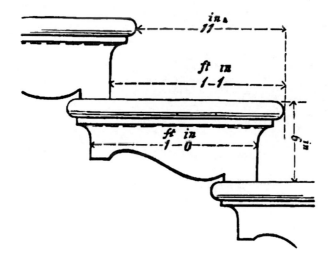

DESIGN No. 22.

A VILLA IN THE OLD ENGLISH WOODEN STYLE.

Perspective view, garden side.

THIS structure was intended to bear the resemblance, as near as possible, of a first-class old English half-timbered house, the post-and-pan dwelling of our forefathers, which seems to have been an especial favourite throughout the country. It was easily constructed at a time when timber, chiefly chestnut, was far more plentiful than at the present day. Such were the most picturesque of all our domestic buildings; the timber cottage, with its projecting windows, and highly ornamented barge-boards, is found in every village. The large houses in Cheshire and Shropshire, which still remain, prove that such constructions are as lasting as brick and stone, provided the timber is felled at the proper time, and thoroughly seasoned before it is made use of. Houses of this kind have been seen to rock and bend in severe storms, while adjoining buildings, comparatively strong erections, have been blown down; this was known to have been the case with Park Hall, near Oswestry in Shropshire. Such buildings were called by different names, as will be shortly described in detail, according to the materials of which they were composed.

The design afforded on page 234 was taken from an elevation given in " John Thorpe's Sketch Book," one of the richest illustrations of wooden architecture. It was to have been erected in a Kentish village, with

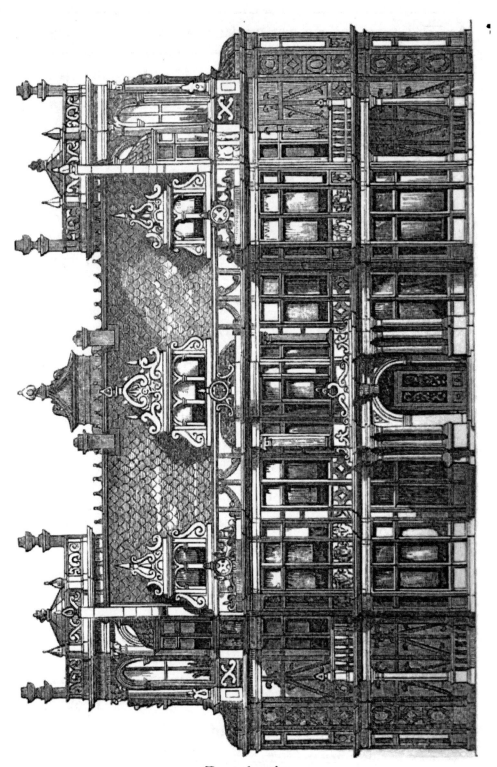

Front elevation.

its front towards the road, on high ground, the road looking down to a wide extent of open country. The garden side of the house commanded a fine prospect. Advantage was taken of the steep descent of the ground to build the kitchen and scullery, with a day room for the children, apart from the main building.

The plan of the basement is given on p. 236 ; *a* is the kitchen, 18 feet square, the scullery *b*, was at the side, and the larder *c*, at its side ; *d* is the place for coals, a passage *e*, leads to the day room, *f*, for the children ; *g* is either the cook's room, or a sleeping room for a man servant ; *h* is the passage up to the house, *i* is the dry larder, *j* is the butler's pantry, with a strong room for holding plate ; this was intended to be a sleeping room. *k* is the wine cellar, *l* the back staircase which went from the lower floor to the attic, *m* is the principal staircase, and *n* a place for stores. The roof of this lower building was to be formed with flat girders, and brick and tile in cement, making a terrace-walk above; the chimneys were taken up from the lower building to the higher one, as shown in the side elevation by the dotted lines. The kitchen, and the whole of the basement, was to be paved with the best Seyssel asphalte. It is laid on a solid foundation, on a thickness of ground lime. The objection to the black and British asphalte for the interior of rooms, is that a fine dust rises from it, which, in sweeping, affects the eyes of the occupants of the apartments.

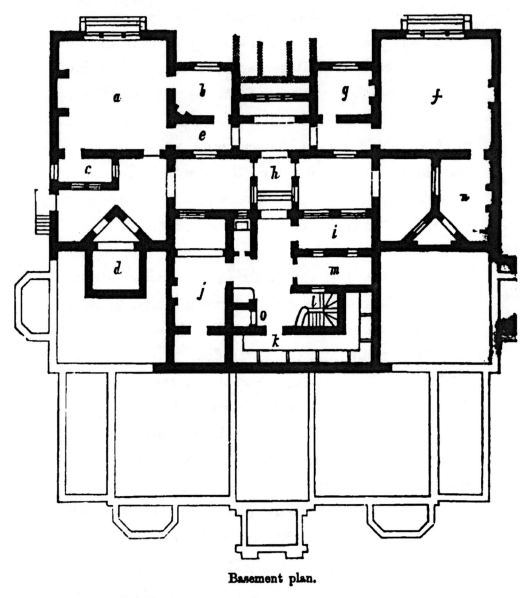

Basement plan.

The plan of the building was not intended to be in the old style, but to be arranged, as far as possible, according to modern notions, without any great hall, or stone screen within it.   A noble stone porch was

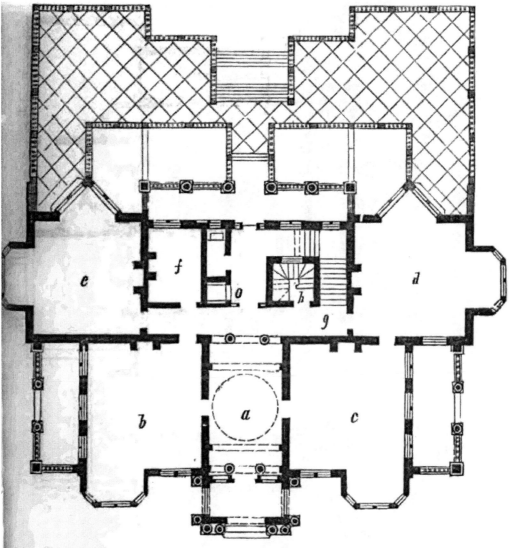

The ground plan.

placed in front, resembling slightly an ancient arch-way.   The hall is 20 feet in length by 12 feet in

breadth.   The breakfast and eating rooms, *b* and *c*,
20 feet square, are on each side; both have bay

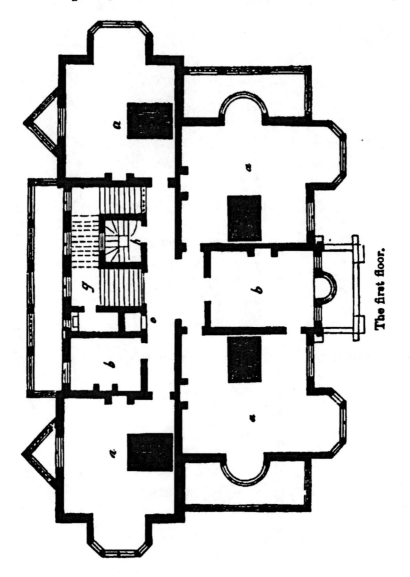

The first floor.

windows, with an exterior colonnade and terrace.   The
drawing-room, *d*, and the library *e*, are each 18 feet
square; both have bay windows, and the angular

window peculiar to the Elizabethan architecture. These windows open on to the terrace. *f* is the

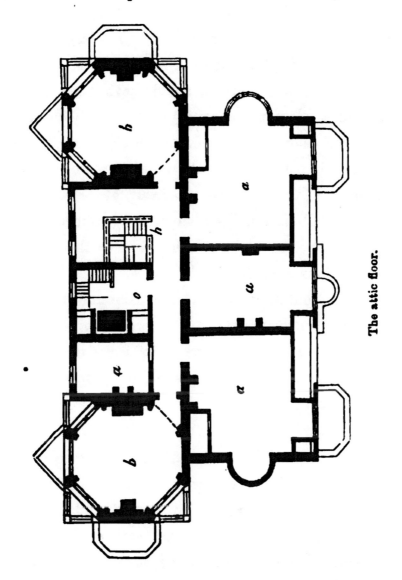

The attic floor.

gentleman's dressing-room, *g* is the principal staircase containing the servants' staircase, *h*, within it; *o* is the lift. At the back of the building is a colonnade commanding a view of the country, and beneath is the terrace, with its balustrading and steps to the garden.

The one-pair floor contains only four large bed-rooms a, a, and two dressing-rooms b, b. One dressing-room, that in front, could have been con-verted into ·a pleasant morning room; each of the two principal bedrooms in the front could easily have been formed into two; a small dressing-room taken out of each. Terraces were in front of these two rooms, the small circular bow-window opening on to them; the principal staircase only led to this floor. The servants' staircase led to the attics.

This floor contained three large servants' rooms, with two small octagon rooms. It was proposed to form the front rooms into one, with a circular roof, covered with scroll-work and flowers, in the form of a garden-bower, similar to the gallery ceiling at Burton Agnes in Yorkshire. In this ceiling there are about a dozen varieties of flowers and bunches of leaves, which were placed in a scroll-stem in various positions so as to vary the pattern. The flowers and leaves could have been painted in their natural colours. These rooms, however, could not be spared, so it was proposed to turn the two octagon rooms into what may be termed garden-bower rooms, and to attempt growing dwarf fruit-trees in them, as practised in Germany.

The roofs of these rooms were to be constructed in iron and glass, and covered internally with wire trellis-work, the warming to be effected with flue pedestals, two in each room, one taking the kitchen flue and the other house flues, the corresponding pedestal in the other room to have the remaining flues in that side of the building. The illustration on page 242 shows a plan and section of one of these rooms.

The tower in the centre of the back front contained a cistern for the supply of the house; the closets beneath could have Moule's earth system applied to them, the earth to be brought up by the lift o, dried in the bower rooms, and deposited in an enclosure in the tower room from which it could descend to the closets.

It may be here remarked that the closets throughout the whole of these designs are in such a position that the dry-earth system could be easily applied to each. In cottages that have the flues in an external wall, and where this system is introduced, the earth deposit should be placed against the flue, and the closet adjoining.

The lift o, shown in the plans, connects every floor with the basement; it permits coals and other heavy articles to be lifted up, receives the speaking tubes leading to the basement and children's day-room, and any bell wires that may be required.

R

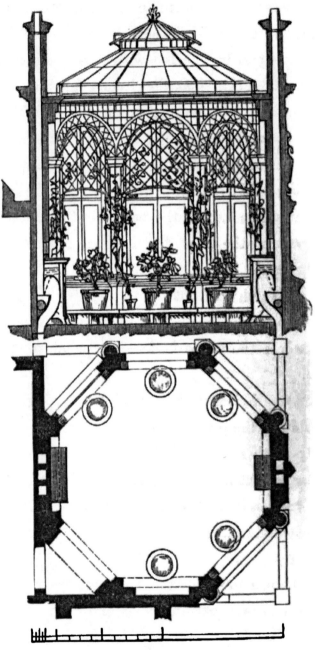

Plan and section of garden bower-rooms.

Side front.

R 2

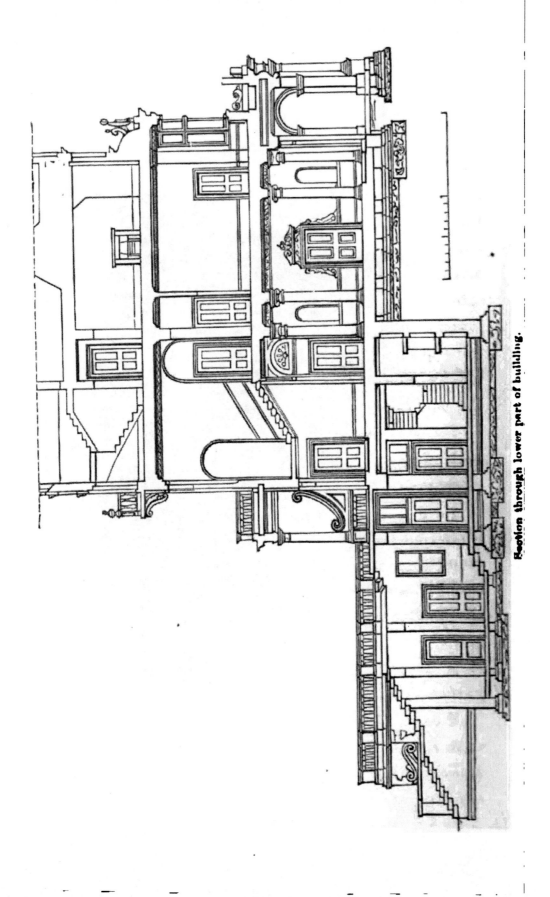

Section through lower part of building.

The first elevation given shows the front of the building, having a length of 87 feet. Although the structure was to be an imitation wooden house, the timber was merely intended to be an appendage to the brickwork. The exterior walls were to have been two bricks and a half thick on the ground-floor, two bricks above. The wooden posts and pans were let into the external half brick, and well built in, the ornamental woodwork in inch oak screwed to the wood-quartering, the space between them filled with plaster, with an ornamental pattern-stamp on it, and the columns and entablature were of oak.

The next elevation given is that of the side front, with its gable, in the centre of which is a small circular window, opening on to a terrace over the colonnade; the scroll at the side is a construction to permit the flues from the lower portion of the base-ment to ascend the tower walls; flue sweeping doors could be placed there. A section of the lower part of the building is given, taken through the centre of the house, showing the principal staircase and the external steps to garden. The perspective view shows the garden front.

Wooden houses were once the chief kind of con-struction in England. The great fire of London would not have been so serious in its results if such constructions had not been almost universal.

In many parts of England these houses have other designations. There is a mode of building peculiar to each, and adapted to the kind of material that the districts offer. In Cambridgeshire, for instance, many of the houses are formed entirely of " Clunch," a kind of indurated chalk marl, of which there are extensive quarries at Roach, near Burwell. Others are of gault, a local term for the blue clay which lies below the gravel of Cambridgeshire, and forms the immediate substratum in the low ground about it. This is beaten up with chopped straw, then formed into blocks of large size, and dried by the sun. A writer in the " Cambridge Portfolio," in his remarks on what he terms the inferior style of domestic architecture, says : " Many of these houses have the lower floor formed of stone or clunch, in which a framework of wood is raised, consisting of studs and wall-plates with strong posts at intervals and some cross-pieces as a tie. The joists of the upper floor are laid in the wall-plates, and project about a foot or eighteen inches beyond the wall beneath. The smaller timbers have tenons which are fitted into mortices in the larger, and secured by wooden pins. The interstices are filled either with durable boarding, double lath and plaster, clunch or bricks, laid level or obliquely. The better houses of this description have gables, with ornamented barge-boards with hip-kobs and corbels or brackets, more or less carved, under the ends of the principal timbers of the upper floors."

The barge-board is sometimes called berge-board, verge-board, parge-board. It was a board fixed to the ends of the gables of timber houses, to hide those of the projecting timbers of the roof, and throw off the wet. They were generally richly carved and very ornamental. Occasionally some of these of the date of the 14th century are met with; those of the 15th and 16th, many of the Elizabethan character, are very common. We have few of the better class of these half-timbered houses, in which the decorative labour of our ancestors was most conspicuous, remaining in our towns and cities; but in Edinburgh, York, Chester, and Newcastle there are still a sufficient number of specimens to prove the truth of these remarks. In the towns of Normandy and the Netherlands numerous buildings, and indeed whole streets, may be seen which still exhibit the perfect counterpart of our old Cheapside, as it appeared before the great fire. Troyes, the capital of Champagne, still retains its ancient buildings, and the chestnut-timber houses of Caen, which were raised, or restored, during the period in the 15th century when it was in the hands of the English, show us what our cities once were, and, of course, the extent of our improvements. London formerly possessed the richest examples. At the corner of Chancery Lane, in Fleet Street, there once stood a five-storied house in timber, each story projecting; the whole of the timber and the gables being richly carved. In this house once lived the celebrated Isaac Walton.

The other most common application of this kind of house is " half-timbered." In some counties the woodwork is not in patterns. It appears that when a greater degree of elegance was required the uprights and beams were carved, or the houses were pargetted, that is, coated thickly with plaster, in which embossed or indented ornaments were used. This kind is very common in nearly all the English counties. The origin of the word *parget* appears to be doubtful. We find *parget*, substantive, and *pargetting, pergetting,* and *pergining*, verb, in old writings, of various kinds of plaster work, used inside and outside of houses, particularly about the time of Elizabeth; the word *parget* was used as far back as 1450.

The half-timbered houses generally had the woodwork (studs and posts) painted black or tarred, with the intermediate spaces of brickwork whitewashed. Many of these houses have been plastered over in modern days. In London several of them have been refronted, and we lose sight of the woodwork, and imagine we see fresh-built houses.

In some parts of the country we see numbers of

cottages built of mud mixed with chopped "haum." This is commonly barley stubble. The word appears of foreign derivation ; in high and low German, Dutch, Danish, Swedish, halm ; Ang.-Sax., healm; Icelandic, halmr, stubble.

The haum is used to give the mud strength. These houses, previously described in connexion with concrete erections, were built about a yard in height at a time; each part was allowed to dry before further addition was made. The openings for windows and doors were cut when the wall became firmer; the walls were then smoothed off a little, and whitewashed. These houses are said to be very strong, and to last for many years. In the Midland Counties they seldom exceed one story in height, but in Devon, Somersetshire, and Hampshire, this composition is a common material for gentlemen's houses two and three stories in height. It is there called *cob*, the derivation of which word remains in obscurity, unless it is a short term for *cobble*, or a coarse clumsy performance. A cob-wall was one composed of straw and clay beaten up together.

In Kent, the half-timbered houses are called wood-noggin houses, because the pieces of timber were called wood-nogs. Nog is properly a wooden brick, which is inserted into walls to hold the joiners' work ;

nogging is the term for the brick-filling partitions between the quartering.

Sometimes, but very rarely, there is no projection of the upper story over the lower one. These openings in the windows are common, and all have richly carved barge-boards.

In some of the Kentish villages there are several noggin-houses plastered over, with a ground in which flowers and patterns are worked in another colour. Some have a red ground and white flowers, others a black ground and white flowers. The wooden frame is always built on a substructure of brick or stone, called the " under-pinning." Numbers of the houses in Kent are covered at the sides with weather tiles; here the brickwork is carried up to the first floor, in which the wooden framework is placed, and laths nailed across, in which the tiles are hung; the shape of the tile varies. Some are diamond-shape, and others finish with circular ends.

In Warwickshire, Oxfordshire, and Gloucestershire, we meet with half-timbered houses, which are there called brick pane houses, but very few of them are worked in patterns.

In Northamptonshire the half-timbered houses are commonly called studded or framed houses, because the framework is put up before the spaces are filled up. The studs are upright between the posts, which are larger than the studs. There are also " wattle," and " dab-houses," and sheds, which are constructed of studs, sills, and wall-plates. Between or into the studs are laid, horizontally, plaited or wattled strong hazel twigs, or other underwood, and on both of these a thick coat of plaster or mud is laid or dabbed. A wattle is a hurdle made of four or five upright stakes, and hazel branches, woven closely and horizontally into the stakes—Anglo-Saxon, *watel*, a hurdle or covering of twigs ; in some counties they are called " flakes," merely from their being thin and flat. In Sussex and Devonshire, and in the South of England, wattled hurdles are called " Raddles." In a little Dictionary for children of the date of 1608, we find " a hartheled wall or ratheled with hasile rods or wands." The word *hartheled* is the same as hardilled, and the Dictionary spells hurdill *hardill*, Ang.-Sax., *hyrdel*, Low Germ., *hoidt*, Dutch, *horde*, Germ., *hurde*. *Ratheled* is from the same derivation as *raddled*. What in one county is " wattle and dab," is in another " raddle and dab." *Dab* is here used as a substantive, but it is properly a verb—to dab on, to sprinkle, or bespatter. In French, *dawber*, or *dober*, to smear, hence " to daub." These mud cottages are very common even in the richest counties of England. In South Northamptonshire are red sandstone houses frequently possessing stone mullions in the windows, and dripstones.

Further northwards, as in Shropshire, Cheshire, and Lancashire, we find a better description of the half-timbered houses in many of the manor houses built there. Lord Liverpool's seat at Pitchford, near Shrewsbury, illustrated by Habershon, is a fine and a very large example, although the pattern is not so elegant as many of them. Joseph Nash and other artists have made the best of these familiar to us by their publications. Cheshire is the county most abounding in them. In the southern part of the county of Lancashire they are called " post-and-pan houses." Post is an upright piece of timber, used in various ways, such as gate-post, door-post, a jamb-lining. The word "post" is found in many languages, commonly meaning an upright. In Ang.-Sax., *post*, a post, Frisic, *post*, a beam, German, *pfost*, French, *poste*, Latin, *postis*, a post.

" Pan," in Lancashire, certainly means a beam, and is the common name for it (beam not being used), although we do not find the word *pan*, a beam, noticed in most of the glossaries as it deserves. In the Craven Glossary, " *post* and *pan*," a building of wood and plaster alternately. *Pan*, totally to fit : " Weal and woman cannot pan, but woe and woman can," is the complete old English proverb, in which the word pan is used. In the glossary of Tim Bobbin, " Pan " means to join or agree. In Hunter's Hallamshire

Glossary " pan," properly in building, is the wall-plate—the piece of timber that lies on the tops of the posts, and on which the balks rest, and the sparfoot also. *To pan*, to apply to closely. In Brockett's North Country work, *pan* means to match, agree. The idea of a pan for a beam would seem to be a shortened word for span, but it comes, it is said, from the old word *pan*, denoting to close or join together, to match, fit, apply, agree. From this, or the origin of which, came pane, or panel of wood, or wainscot, pane of glass. Ang.-Sax., *pan*, a piece, hem, plait; pan hose, patched hose, because pieces are fitted into them.

In Warwickshire and Oxfordshire they call a post-and-pan house a brick-*pane* house, because the wood-work divides the building into rectangular spaces, filled with *panes* of brickwork.

In Forby's Suffolk Vocabulary *pane* is a division of work in husbandry, also strips of cloth. The slits in Elizabethan dresses are called *panes*. Du Cange, in his *Glossarium Mediæ et Infimæ Latinitatis*, has *panna*, a carpenter's word, signifying a square piece of wood of 6 or 7 fingers on a side, which being placed on the rafters of the roof, and retained by wooden supports, carries the asseres. The " Glossary of Architecture" construes a pan as a lathe; but of this there seems some doubt.

There is a remarkable example of the word *Panna* in the Close Rolls of the 9th of Henry 3rd, membrane 5, page 65, though the word in the printed copy is erroneously spelt *pauna*.

De posti-
bus et pan-
nis datis.

Mandatum est Hugoni de Neville quod habere faciat Baldivinium de Veer duos postes et duos *pannas* in bosco nostro in Deresle, de dono nostro ad se habergandum apud Thrapston. Teste rege apud Westmonasterium XV die Octobris, anno nono.—That is : The King orders Hugh de Neville to give Baldwin de Veer two *posts* and two *pans* out of the Royal forest of Deresley to build a house at Thrapstone.—" Habergandum" is from *habergo*, to build a house, which seems to be derived from the old German *habe*, goods and possessions, and *bergen*; in Ang.-Sax., *boergan*, to defend, keep, and protect. *Habe*, goods, is from the German *haben*, Ang.-Sax., *habban*, to have and possess. In Du Cange we find " Habergagium vel habergamentum, domicilium domus," that is, a place to keep goods in. This account is given us by the writer in the " Cambridge Portfolio," who adds, " That it is probable the house alluded to in Thrapstone was merely a shed." He gives a great many derivations from the word *pan* in French. He says that *pan* or *post* is a *post* and *pan* wall, perhaps with boarding in the panes instead of brick or stone. A post-and-pan house therefore signifies one formed of uprights and cross-pieces, and this appears to be the most rational name for them. The patterns of the woodwork are sometimes extremely elegant; at Park Hall in Shropshire, one represents balustrading intermingled with quatre-foiling, while the plaster ceilings inside the building are of excessively rich character. In many of the old post-and-pan houses, the windows are between every post, running the whole length of the house in each story, rendering a remark of Lord Bacon's true, that in such houses you did not know where to become to get out of the sun or the cold. They are now sometimes called "bird-cage houses," from the effect at a distance. Some of these old mansions had the hall extending to the roof, and this was carried down to a very late period. At Kirby in Northamptonshire, a seat of the Lord Chancellor Hatton, built by the architect, John Thorpe, Inigo Jones altered the timbers of the hall roof and gave them an Italianized character. He was, previous to his visit to Italy, one of the chief and most celebrated masters of the then fashionable Elizabethan style, which was carried down to a later period than is generally supposed.

The superior class of wooden houses were for the gentry, the wattle and dab houses for the hind. This cottage, then, must have been little better than a miserable shed. Cottages still exist in the north of

England, amid the northern counties, that are bad at the very best. The tenants have to bring everything with them, partitions, window-frames, fixtures of all kinds, grates, and a substitute for a ceiling. Certainly the improved concrete cottage, if it could be erected at a small expense, would be a great advantage to them. Its partitions, and even its roof, the latter covered with slate, might be securely formed of strong hurdles, and a cistern for water easily placed just below it. The walls, if covered with a good Portland cement face, will last for many years, and, if the roof be so formed as to protect them, for warmth, comfort, and cleanliness such cottages are unsurpassed.

It is to be regretted that the combination of workmen forming the various Trades' Unions, has so raised the price of labour that it has reacted against themselves, and the workmen's houses, roomy, and formed of sound, lasting materials, can no longer be constructed at a cost that would allow a fair percentage on outlay.

Lord Bacon paid particular attention to building, and he had several fine mansions. He received his Sovereign at one, *Gorhambury*, who on her remarking its great size, said, " It was not that the house was too big, but that her Grace had made him too big to inhabit it." His essay on building gives such a complete picture of what the nobleman's house was in those days, that it is here quoted.

" First, therefore, I say you cannot have a perfect palace, except you have two several sides : a side for the banquet, as is spoken of in the book of Esther, and a side for the household ; the one for feasts and triumphs, and the other for dwelling.

" I understand both these sides to be not only returns, but parts of the front; and to be uniform without, though severally partitioned within ; and to be on both sides of a great and stately tower in the midst of the front, that, as it were, joineth them together on either hand.   I would have, on the side of the banquet in front, one only goodly room, above stairs, of some forty foot high : and under it a room for a dressing or preparing place, at times of triumphs. On the other side, which is the household side, I wish it divided, at the first, into a hall and chapel (with a partition between), both of good state and bigness ; and those not to go all the length, but to have at the farther end a winter and summer parlour, both fair ; and under these rooms a fair and large cellar sunk under ground, and likewise some privy kitchens, with butteries and pantries, and the like.   As for the tower, I would have it two stories, of eighteen foot high apiece above the two wings ; and goodly leads upon the top, railed with statues interposed ; and the same tower to be divided into rooms, as shall be thought fit.   The stairs likewise to the upper rooms, let them be upon

a fair open newel, and finely railed in with images of
wood cast into a brass colour; and a very fair landing-
place at the top.   But this to be, if you do not point
any of the lower rooms for a dining-place of servants;
for otherwise, you shall have the servants' dinner after
your own; for the steam of it will come up as in a
tunnel; and so much for the front; only I understand the height of the first stairs to be sixteen foot,
which is the height of the lower room.

" Beyond the front is there to be a fair court, but
three sides of it of a far lower building than the front;
and in all the four corners of that court fair staircases,
cast into turrets on the outside, and not within the
row of buildings themselves; but those towers are not
to be of the height of the front, but rather propor-
tionable to the lower buildings.   Let the court not be
paved, for that striketh up a great heat in summer
and much cold in winter; but only some side alleys
with a cross, and the quarters to graze, being kept
shorn, but not too near shorn.   The row of return on
the banquet side, let it be all stately galleries: in
which galleries let there be three or five fine cupolas in
the length of it, placed at equal distance; and fine
coloured windows of several works: on the household
side, chambers of presence and ordinary entertainments, with some bedchambers; and let all three
sides be a double house, without thorough lights in the

sides, that you may have rooms from the sun, both for forenoon and afternoon :—cast it also that you may have rooms both for summer and winter; shade for summer, and warm for winter.   You shall have sometimes fair houses so full of glass that one cannot tell where to become to be out of the sun or cold.   For embowed windows, I hold them of good use (in cities indeed, upright do better, in respect of the uniformity towards the street); for they be pretty retiring places for conference, and besides they keep both the wind and sun off; for that which would strike almost through the room doth scarce pass the window; but let them be but few, four in the court, on the sides only.

" Beyond this court, let there be an inward court of the same square and height, which is to be environed with the garden on all sides; and in the inside, cloistered on all sides upon decent and beautiful arches as high as the first story; on the under story, towards the garden, let it be turned to a grotto, or place of shade, or estivation; and only have opening and windows toward the garden, and be level upon the floor, no whit sunk under ground, to avoid all dampishness: let there be a fountain or some fair work of statues in the midst of this court, and to be paved as the other court was.   These buildings to be for privy lodgings on both sides, and the end for privy galleries; whereof you must foresee that one of them be for an infirmary, if the prince or any special person should be sick, with chambers, bedchamber, ante-camera, and recamera, joining to it; this upon the second story.

"Upon the ground story, a fair gallery, open, upon pillars, and upon the third story likewise, an open gallery upon pillars, to take the prospect and freshness of the garden.

"At both corners of the farther side, by way of return, let there be two delicate or rich cabinets, daintily paved, richly hanged, glazed with crystalline glass, and a rich cupola in the midst; and all other elegancy that may be thought upon. In the upper gallery too, I wish that there may be, if the place will yield it, some fountains running in divers places from the wall, with some fine avoidances. And thus much for the model of the palace; save that you must have, before you come to the front, three courts, a green court plain, with a wall about it; a second court of the same, but more garnished with little turrets, or rather embellishments upon the wall; and a third court, to make a square with the front, but not to be built nor yet enclosed with a naked wall, but enclosed with terraces leaded aloft, and fairly garnished on the three sides; and cloistered on the inside with pillars, and not with arches below. As for offices, let them stand at distance, with some low galleries to pass from them to the palace itself."

The vignette is an elevation, with enlarged details, of a design for a weathercock or wind vane.   In buildings where there are many on the roof, they are sometimes seen pointing different ways, and it is of importance they should be properly constructed.   The construction necessary to prevent these differences is shown in the two sections on each side the elevation ; *a* is a gun-metal rod, in which is fixed the small steel rod *b* ; this moves in a piece of agate fixed in a small block of copper *c* ; the agate is marked black in the left-hand section.

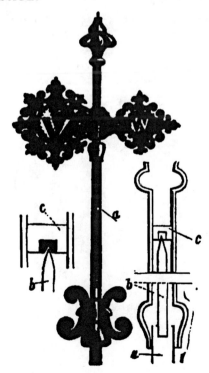

DESIGN No. 23.

A GARDEN SUMMER-HOUSE.

Perspective view and plan.

THIS small circular erection was designed from the express directions, as to style, size, form, and plan, of the gentleman for whom it was made, and who had it constructed. It was of wood, standing on a brick foundation, with a quaint room in the centre, completely lined with match-boarding, stained

Elevation.

oak and varnished, the ceiling having hanging pendants. The lead lights of the sashes were glazed with various specimens of old coloured glass.

The view and plan are illustrated at page 262; the plan shows the general arrangements; the porch had seats on each side, and the back portion of the

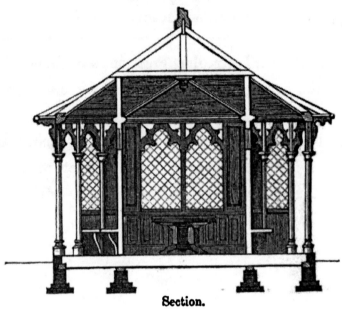

Section.

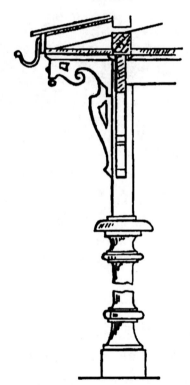

Detail showing construction.

summer-house was enclosed for a single seat. The
elevation given on page 263 shows, as well as the
view, flower-pots on supports in the roof. These were

Gate to a flower-garden.

omitted in execution. The section shows the building
as constructed; it is taken through the porch. The
interior room and the enclosed seat behind the illus-

tration gives the detail of a portion of the construction.

Elevation.   Section.

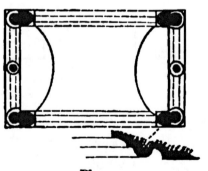

Plan.

The building had no fireplace, being merely intended for summer use; it was placed on an elevated site, and commanded a fine view.

No small structure can be made too expensive in construction if it is to be placed in a beautiful flower-garden. However pretty its ornaments may be, they are sure to pale by the side of the natural objects surrounding it. The small gateway shown in view on page 265 was constructed entirely in oak with a slab-slated roof. It stood at some distance from the dwelling, to which it formed a conspicuous object, and it was the entrance to an enclosed flower-garden. An elevation, section, and plan of it are given on page 266.

The vignette represents an open ironwork console or holder for a meat-jack for the kitchen fireplace: it is of French design.

DESIGN *No.* 24.

A SMALL COUNTRY RETREAT, OR FRENCH MAISONETTE.

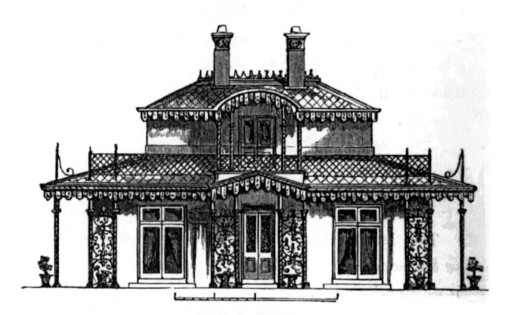

The front elevation.

THIS is a study for a small villa in the modern French style, one which has lately been introduced into several buildings of domestic character in England, the woodwork being sent from France. The

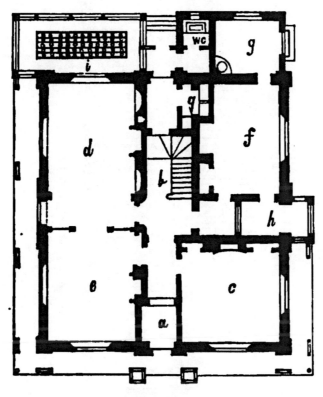

Ground plan.

chief feature of the style is the machine-cut ornamental wood; it is of common deal, about an inch or a little more in thickness. When placed up, and coloured a light fawn colour or plain yellow, it is extremely pleasing, and has the merit of being very cheap.

The design has an ornamental iron verandah

completely round two sides of the building, with small
upright standards taken through its roof, which are

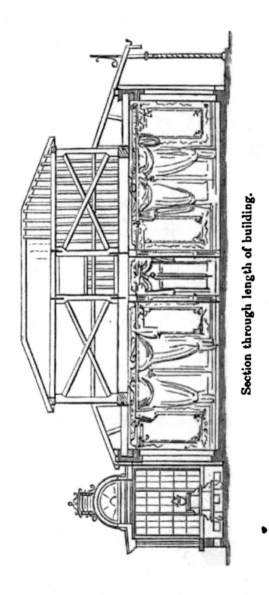

Section through length of building.

connected together with zinc wire-work; the intention
being to permit flowering plants to grow over it, so

that the front should be crowned with flowers. The villa is only intended for summer use, being confined in its accommodation. The ground plan, given on page 269, shows *d* and *e*, the drawing and dining

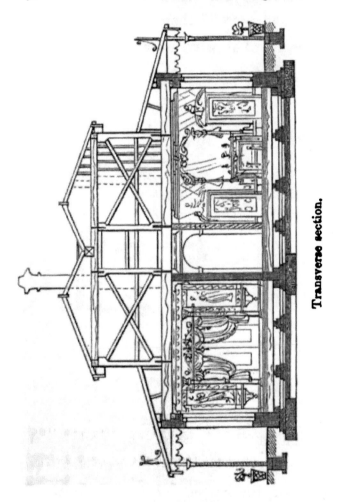

Transverse section.

rooms, divided one from the other by curtains hanging on a glazed screen; the length of the two rooms is 42 feet, their breadth 15 feet. They are decorated gaily in French style; the room *c* can be used as a study, but it is intended for a sleeping room; the kitchen *f* has a large larder *h*, but it would be desirable if the kitchen was formed a short distance away from the building, and connected with it by a passage; the rooms *f* and *g* could then be made into a bed and dressing-room. The wine cellar is at *g*, and a conservatory *i*, is placed at the end of the building.

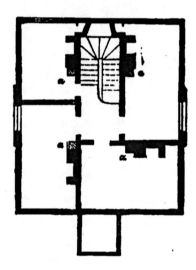

Plan of one-pair.

The elevation of the front of the building and the two sections show the general construction of the upper part of the house. This was in timber, the flues alone being of brick.

The plan of the upper floor shows four rooms; each of the flues is supplied with its pedestal, so that should the house be occupied in winter, these upper apartments could be kept well aired by the fires in the lower apartments, without any attention from the servants. The framing of the upper portion is correctly shown in the section copied from the working drawing.

Portion of verandah.

An elevation of a small portion of the verandah, showing its iron work, is given; and an illustration to a large scale shows its ornamental zinc guttering, and the carved wood French ornament, a section showing

T

how they are fastened on ; and the zinc gutter placed in front is likewise given.

Elevation of zinc gutter, and cut woodwork.

Section of the same.

The following is a design in purely French taste for the circular top over the entrance porch on the upper floor.

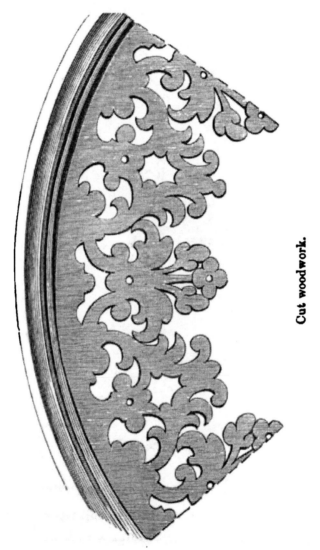

Cut woodwork.

The roofs of buildings in this style should be covered with zinc. The French are as much before

us in their use of this metal as they are with their
cut woodwork.

Roofs covered with zinc could be made flatter, and
have a covering or floor of boards, each board ½ an
inch apart. An illustration is given of such a construction; it has a light iron railing with a scroll

Design for roofing.

against the brick parapet; and supports a stand for
flowers. With the absence of offensive smoke, and
with the use of the flue pedestal to supply warmth,
the upper parts of our houses could easily be formed
into conservatories.

The interior of the building was intended to be as

profusely decorated with the cut woodwork as the exterior. The staircase balusters were of a rich pattern, the whole being stained after some ornamental wood, and varnished.

Staircase balusters.

The expense of constructing such a building would be 2450*l.*

In this style of cut-wood decoration the French certainly excel us. Some English examples, very common in our railway stations, are shown below. The most ornamental is a pattern used by the author some few years ago; a rose is introduced to cover the fastening of the cut pattern to the fascia behind.

We have in England a carving-machine, known as Irving's patent, that was a few years since much worked at a manufactory in Pimlico by Mr. Pratt of Bond Street. At one time it bid fair to exert a most important influence upon the production of this kind of cut-wood decoration. It could make such carvings with the greatest ease and rapidity, whether in stone or wood. The machine was a simple drill in a moveable arm, worked either by steam or a hand-wheel, on a moveable table; the combined motion rendered it capable of carving any form, however intricate, from the largest Gothic window-head, to the smallest screen. At Pimlico it was under the architectural superintendence of R. W. Billings. It is still used, together with Jordan's patent for carving, at Lambeth.

The vignette gives a pattern for cut-wood balustrading.

DESIGN No. 25.

AN ELIZABETHAN VILLA.

Perspective view.

THIS design was made a few years ago for a
gentleman who was a great admirer of our old
English architecture, and who desired to have a

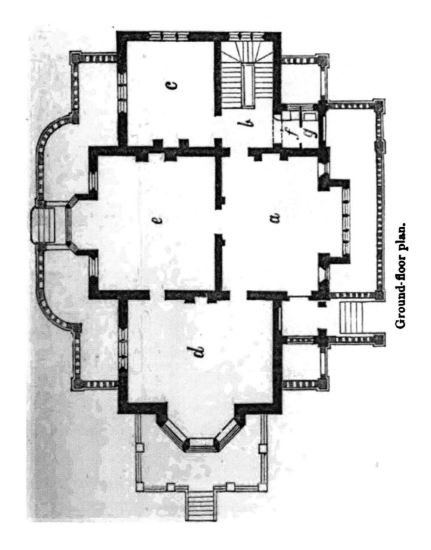

Ground-floor plan.

dwelling with its chief characteristics, both internally as
well as externally, but with all modern arrangements.
He intended to purchase a piece of land in the neigh-

bourhood of London for the purpose of erecting the structure upon it.   Producing the design was a labour of love to us both, and many a pleasant evening we

Balustrading of staircase.

spent together in studying the details as to what we should like to have in each room, without troubling ourselves about what the expense would be ; unhappily he did not live to carry out his intention, and the drawings were laid aside.

Section of hall.

The exterior is a study from the celebrated building, Rushton Hall in Northamptonshire, erected in the

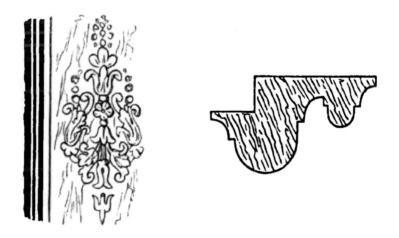

reign of Elizabeth, by Sir Thomas Tresham. On the estate in the forest, about a mile from the house, is that curious and unique building, the Triangular Lodge,* which served as a secret place of meeting for the conspirators of the Gunpowder Plot.

The ground plan shows only a small and single staircase *b*; considerable discussion took place upon this; the great staircase was first planned in the hall *a*, but a billiard-table was imperative, and the hall alone

Elevation of hall fireplace.

could receive it. The smaller staircase was made ornamental, with carved oak balustrades having a

---

* First illustrated by the author in his work, "Architectural Remains of the Reigns of Elizabeth and James I."

small brass ornament between, for the children to lay hold of in getting upstairs.

The hall was to be wainscoted all round; the illustration on page 283 shows one side, with the entrance into the dining-room; a section of the moulding of the panels is given on page 283 of full size. A gilt decoration was to have been put in each panel, as shown. An ornamental plaster frieze, containing shields of arms which

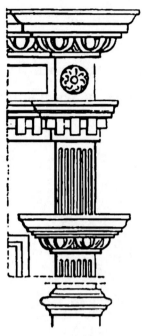

Details of hall fireplace.

Hall stove.

were to be emblazoned, came over the panelling.
An elevation of the fireplace, to have been made in
Caen stone, with its details on a large scale, is given
in cuts on pp. 284, 285.

Portion of hall ceiling.

The fireplace is shown with fire-dogs to burn wood,
with its iron fire-back; but this was objected to, and

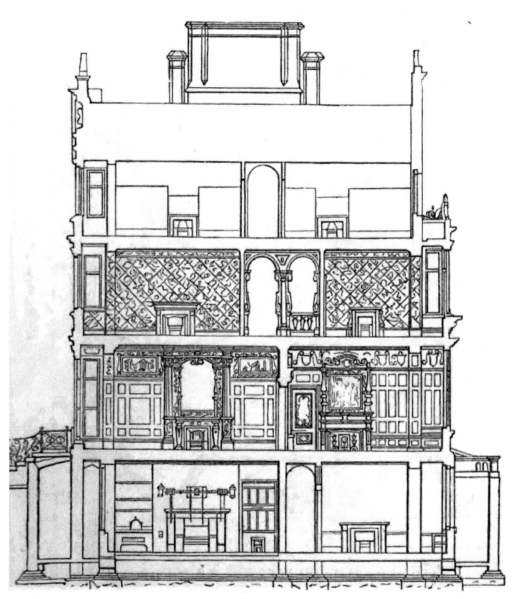

Section.

the stove was selected: my friend having great interest in coal, preferred it to wood.

Dining-room ceiling.

The illustration on page 286 is a portion of the hall ceiling, copied from a celebrated example of the time of Henry VIII. To illustrate every room or give only one-third of the drawings made for this design

would far exceed the limits the present volume allows.
Each of the three rooms on the ground floor had

Pendant.

decorated chimney-pieces, and carved architraves and
panels to the doors. The section shows the height of
the rooms. The dining-room *e* (see ground-plan) was

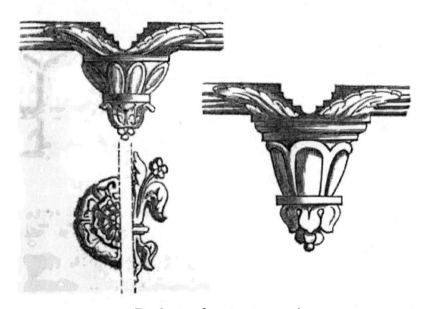

Pendant and centre ornaments.

U

22 ft. by 20 ft. ; the library *c*, 17 ft. by 15 ft., and the drawing-room *d*, 24 ft. by 17 ft., with a large bay window opening on to a terrace—their height 12 ft. 9 in. ; *f* is the lift and *g* the closet. Each of these rooms was to have ornamental flat plaster ceilings with

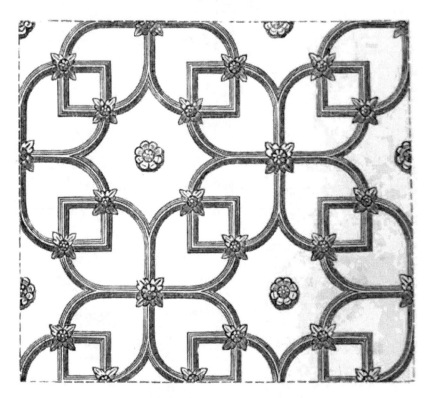

Drawing-room ceiling.

pendant ornaments. These are shown in illustrations on page 289.

The staircase led to a gallery in the middle of the building on the first floor, dimly lighted at each end by the staircase and passage windows. The first floor (page 292) contained a morning room, *a*, in the centre, 15 ft. by 12 ft., with a bow window ; and three bedrooms *b, b, b*, with two dressing-rooms *c, c*, one with a bath and a closet.

Library ceiling.

The attic plan (page 292) contained three large rooms for the servants, *b, b, b*; a housemaid's closet *e*, and in the recessed space by the side a large slate cistern for water. The basement (page 293) contained considerable accommodation: *d* was intended for a private room for the family, *a* the kitchen, *c* larder,

b the scullery, *i* beer-cellar, *g* butler's sleeping-room,
e butler's pantry, *h* wine-cellar, *l* place for cleaning

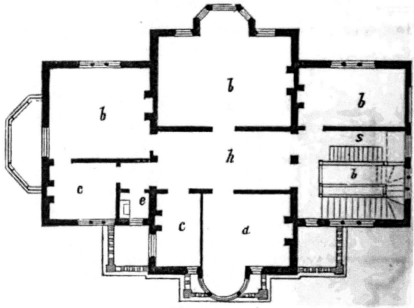

Plan (page 291).

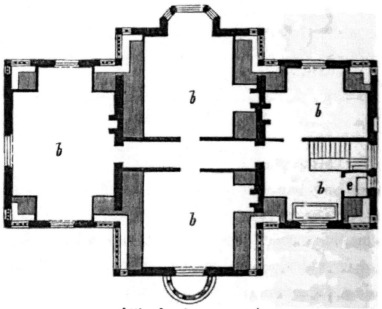

Attic plan (see page 291).

knives. The housekeeper's room *f*, and servants' hall are in the front, and *j* is the lift for dishes to ground floor, *k* the coal-cellar. An open area was made on two sides of the building.

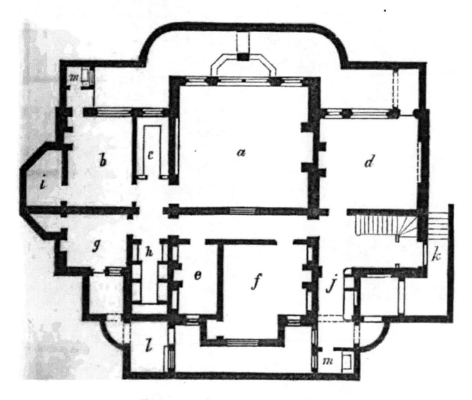

Basement plan (see page 291).

It was intended to construct the basement fire-proof, and to have the flooring chiefly of asphalte, laid on brick and concrete, solid with the earth ; having a width of stone at the fireplaces. Small openings into the areas were to be made for water to run off, so that the floors could be at any time flooded from a

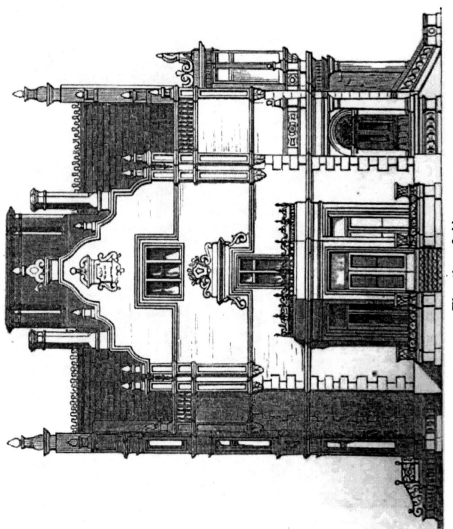

Elevation of aisle.

hose. The skirtings for eighteen inches above the floor were to be in asphalte, so that no beetles or other vermin should find their way in. It was a

Ironwork on terrace.

subject of discussion whether all the other floors and skirting should not be of a similar description. The three elevations of the building are given : they were

Ironwork on bay-window.

to have been in red brick with compo dressings, and the balustrades in artificial stone. One peculiar portion of the exterior decoration was the ironwork in

lieu of stone balustrading.   The bay window and the
terrace were surmounted with this ironwork ; that on
the terrace was to be formed so as to sustain heavy

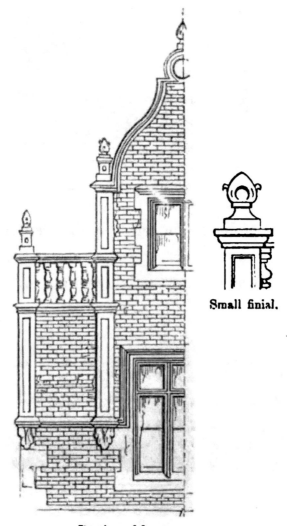

Small finial.

Portion of front.

earthenware pots of flowering shrubs :—an elevation
of the two examples is given on page 297.

The mouldings on the exterior of the building were small and simple; this is shown in illustrations on page 298. Various designs were made for the

Balustrades for first floor.

balustrading; three of these, with the ornament containing a shield of arms in the centre of the side gables, are likewise given.

The expense of constructing this design with all the ornamentation shown, would have been great. A

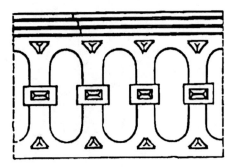

Lower balustrade.

considerable portion of it, when it came to be estimated and the specification and working drawings were made

Ornament in side gable.

for the builder, would have been left out, and the whole made more simple.   The design would not have materially suffered for such deductions; all the general forms or the simple outline of the exterior would have been preserved. The chief deduction would have been made in the ornaments of the interior, or these might have been only partly done. Such a design, with a moderate amount of decoration only, would cost about 4700*l.*

The vignette shows French and English cut-wood patterns for blind ornaments.

DESIGN *No. 26.*

A SUMMER OR GARDEN VILLA.

Perspective view.

ONE of our most eminent writers on gardens, Repton, remarked that " gardening and architecture, like all the fine arts, have much in common; and the department of architecture which belongs more exclusively to gardens has especially a great affinity to gardening in its broadest principles." In fact, there is much more relation between the two than is usually admitted—a matter already alluded to in the Introductory Essay. Architectural forms and decorations, temples and rustic bowers, seats, &c., are not, as many have observed, unfit for our climate. In western counties they certainly can be indulged in to a large extent; and the fine evergreens and the beautiful grass of this country will, in association with ornamental terraces and sculpture, impart sufficient warmth of tone to render them agreeable. The garden of *Mon-plaisir* at Elvaston, in Derbyshire, and the Alhambra Gardens there; those at Castle Coombe, Trentham, Alton Towers, and Bowood, sufficiently prove how attractive gardens can be architecturally made. In former years gardens were almost universal through every part of England, as is proved by the bird's-eye view, engraved by Kipp, from drawings by Knyff in the book, " Britannia Illustrata," and those of the gardens given in Loggan's " Oxonia Restituta," and the similar work on Cambridge. But gardens, like all other mundane matters, have their periods of change or retrogression; the natural style having almost obliterated the architectural garden of William and Mary. This might have been too precise, as copied

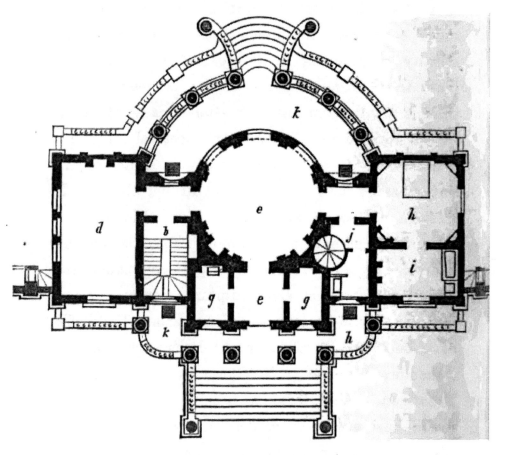

Ground-plan of villa.

from the Dutch model: they were satirized by Pope, thus—

"Grove nods at grove, each alley has a brother,
    And half the platform just reflects the other."

They were called King William's style of fortifications, surrounded with yew edges, cut in variety of forms; those which have been suffered to outlive their original shape are really beautiful. Queen Anne's Garden, now part of Kensington Gardens, is an example. But these gardens were very inferior to those of Italy and France, or even those in England of the Elizabethan age. It is to Italy, the garden of Europe, that we must look for the finest specimens of garden architecture. The Villa Pamphilia or de Belrespiro, situated half a mile out of Rome beyond the Gate of San Pancrazio, is celebrated for its gardens; from them could be observed the whole city of Rome, and surrounding suburbs. The gardens are nearly five miles in circumference, and occupy the site of those of the Emperor Galba. Their arrangement is varied and agreeable; being picturesque without disorder, symmetrical without monotony; and we here observe the art with which the arrangement of a regular garden is made to agree with the rural nature of which it forms a part, and the noble structure it surrounds. It is doubtless the work of the architect of the villa L'Algardi, about the year 1646. They have been ascribed to the French artist, Le Notre, but there is very little of the French style about them; they are wholly Italian, following the lines of the villa, and in the same style or spirit. These are, or were admirable; while the fountains,

x

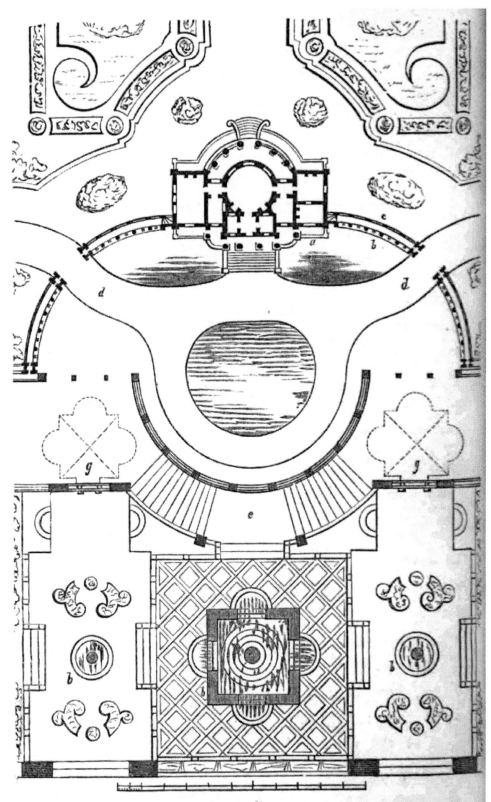

Ground plan of garden and villa.

the cascades, grottos, basins, statues, and the antique
fragments which adorn them are arranged with the

Small group in centre of side left-hand basin.

skill and intelligence of genius. Illustrations are
preserved to us only in a fine Italian work, by Jacobi
de Rubeis, published at Rome, about the middle of

Small group in centre of right-hand basin.

the seventeenth century.   The villa was destroyed by
the French when they crushed the liberty of the Roman
people at their onslaught on Rome against Garibaldi.

In designs of this description the house and garden
should unite, and be lost in each other.   Those parts
of the garden most contiguous to the house should
follow its outline, its walks and terraces, and be so

Fountain ornaments.

placed that the windows and doors of the mansion
could command a perfect view of them.   The province
of garden architecture is, primarily, to supply fitting
appendages and accompaniments to the house, so that
the latter may not appear alone and unsupported.   If
judiciously adopted it will be effective in helping to
produce a good outline, carry down the lines of the

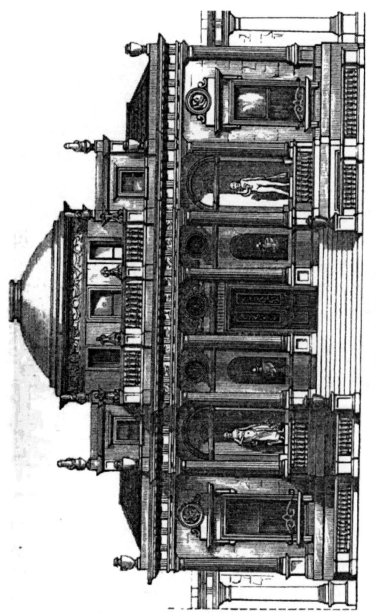

Elevation of front.

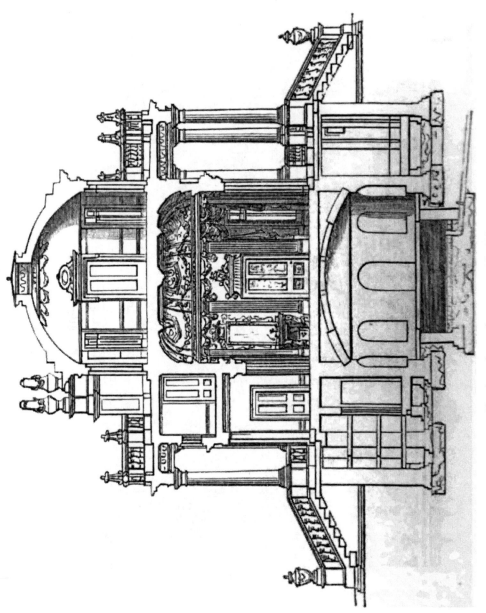

Section through centre of building.

house, and connect it with other buildings, which may be conservatories, ferneries, aquaria, rustic seats, temples, and arbours; and it will provide a

Portion of saloon.

proper basement to the house. Such arrangements afford shelter or privacy to a flower garden, extend the façade or frontage of the house, shut out back yards, stabling or offices, enrich, vary, and enliven the garden, supply conveniences, receptacles for birds, plants, sculpture, or works of art, specimens of natural history, and support for climbing plants. These points indicate refinement, wealth, and love of art, and otherwise blend the various constituents of a garden with the house, and harmonize the two by communicating an artistic tone to the garden. So says Repton, and most of the principal writers on gardening.

Cap in saloon.

Some of the ancient gardens of Asia and Italy were considered among the wonders of the world. They were termed paradises, and were filled with such plants, both beautiful and useful, that the soil could produce; they were enriched with many kinds of works of art, banqueting-houses, aviaries, wells, and streams of running water, indispensable in those warm climates.

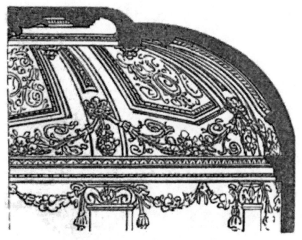

Section of part of saloon ceiling.

An architectural garden, as illustrated in the design at page 302, should have a picturesque outline, a

Plan of the same.

marked boldness and prominence of parts, rather than a mere ornamental detail ; a picturesque effect by changes of level in the ground, by diversity of height

Portion of centre panel.

of the different terraces, and by an arrangement in plan that would produce depth of shade. Every object admitted should fit into its proper place. This

Panel of ceiling.

villa was designed to cover a fine spring of cold water, and thus insure a deep cold plunging bath. It was to be merely a place for temporary occupation and retirement, to renovate the health of the owner. The gardens and fountains externally were only ornamental accessories; the plan at page 306 illustrates these. The villa was approached by two roads *d d*; there was a circle of open lawn between the house and the terraced gardens in front. The latter were approached

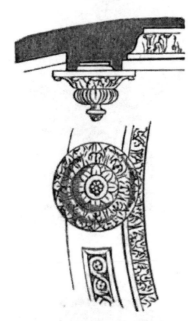

Section and plan of one of centre pendants.

by descending flights of steps. A basin of water and a large fountain, rising from a group of sculpture in the centre, are there shown. By the side are two smaller basins with smaller groups of sculpture, representing sea-horses, cupids, and dolphins. This terrace is paved with ornamental encaustic tiles. At the head of the two side gardens *b b*, are grottos *g g*, with seats on a raised terrace on each side of their entrances. The steps descend to a lower level, and have sea-horses and cupids on their pedestals, with five falls of water from griffins' heads, filling a basin below. A wide

Bedroom ceiling.

walk, and a running stream by its side, were thus gained.

The author at the time he made the design was effecting some additions to a country house, which admitted such a garden to be formed in front of it:

he published his design for it at the time (1850) in the *Builder*.

Drawing-room ceiling.

This villa may be considered a casine, or a retired dwelling on a rather larger scale, similar to the picturesque house at Wothorp, in Northamptonshire, which was erected by one of the Earls of Burleigh, as a place to retire to, while his "great house at Burghley was sweeping." Wothorp was a large building: it was fully illustrated in one of the

Sections of moulding of ceiling.

author's works, from original drawings lent him by the late Marquis of Exeter. The casine, only one size larger than a cottage, was the fashion of the preceding age. Whenever the proprietor of an estate wished to turn hermit, he retired to the casine, a

small temple erected in a portion of his grounds, where
the finest views could be obtained, and the most perfect repose secured. In earlier times such buildings

Drawing-room chimneypiece.

afforded secret meeting-places wherein to hatch
political plots; such a one was the triangular lodge
in a secluded part of the wood at Rushton in North-

amptonshire, the seat of Sir Thomas Tresham, where
the gunpowder conspirators assembled. The casine
of more modern times was not so small, but it con-

tained all the requirements of good living. One
example, is the casine of Marino, near Dublin, built
by Sir William Chambers for the Earl of Charlemont.

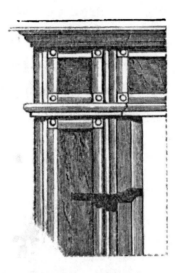

It was square in plan, surrounded by twelve columns,
two projecting flat porticoes in front and back, and
pedimented porticoes at the sides. The entrance was

approached by a noble flight of steps, the pedestals of which were decorated with carvings, and supported crouching lions. Statues and vases adorned the roof. A print of it, from a drawing of Wheatly, was published in 1783. The building contained a small hall or vestibule, a saloon or living-room, 20 feet in length by 15 feet in width. Leading out of this were

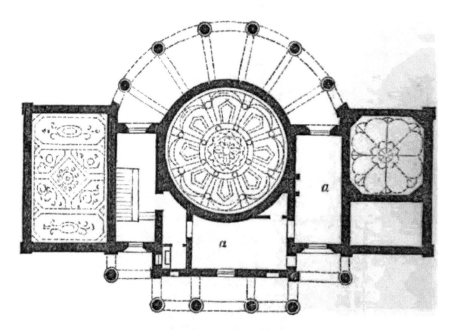

Plan of mezzanine floor.

two small rooms; one a study, the other a bedroom and closet. The basement contained a large and well-fitted kitchen, a scullery and larder, a butler's pantry, and servants' hall, and cellars for ale and wine. Retired buildings of this kind, of larger character and of more importance, were often erected in private

grounds of noblemen and gentry.   One, very similar
to the present design, was constructed by the late
Robert Adam, for a salt-water bath, at Mistley, the
seat of the Right Hon. Richard Rigby.   Mr. Adam
and Sir William Chambers erected a large number of
such ornamental structures.   One of the most elegant

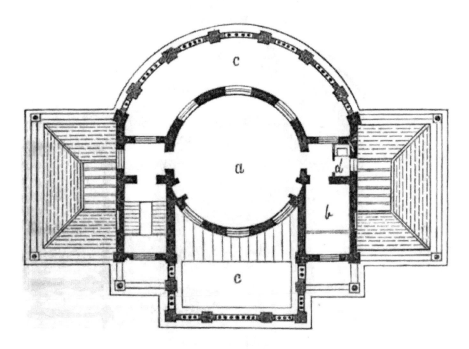

Plan of upper story.

examples, by Mr. Robert Adam, was the rout-house
or pavilion erected for a *fête champêtre* in the gardens
of the Earl of Derby, at the Oaks, in Surrey, in 1774.
The building was internally of the most ornamental
character; there was an octangular vestibule, a hall
30 feet in diameter; this opened into a grand ball-

room, 72 feet by 35 feet within the columns, and
86 feet by 56 feet within the walls.   The supper-room,
surrounding the ball-room, measured 200 feet from
one end to the other, and 20 feet in width.   It was
exposed in its full splendour on the curtains being
drawn; and at the end of the ball-room there were

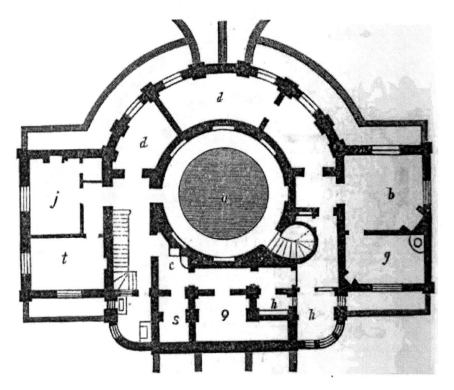

Basement plan.

two tea-rooms, each 20 feet square, on each side of
the entrance saloon.   The author gives these details
in order that he may not be considered too venture-
some in submitting to public notice, in these
economical times, such an ornamental design as the

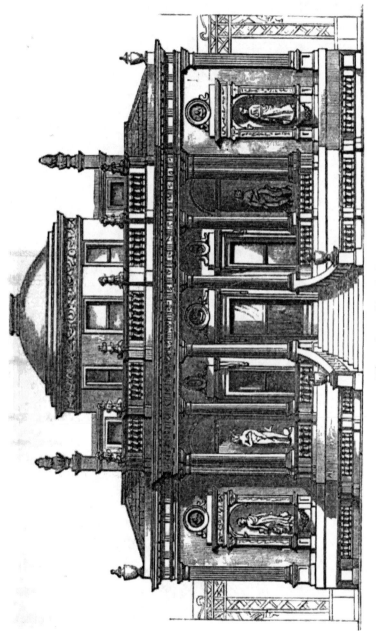

Elevation of back front.

present.   Similar structures of a more expensive character were once very common; but the small

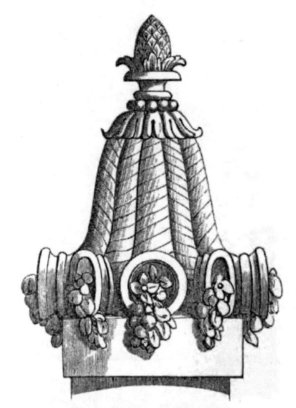

Elevation of top of pedestal.

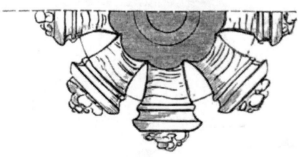

Plan.

retired casine has now gone out of fashion. The ladies consider such secluded buildings as only fit for

laundries, and not preferring themselves lives of perfect retirement and quiet, have brought in the small

Ornament terminating pedestal on attic.

villa where a whole family can dwell, and no selfish
thoughts or gloomy contemplations find place.

In referring to the plan of the villa at page 304, of
which the plate page 302 shows the elevation, *e* is the

Section.

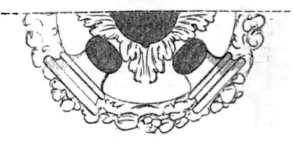

Plan.

small hall 8 feet square, *g* the gun room or waiting
room is on the right, the serving room with a lift from
the basement on the left. The saloon is a highly

decorated apartment, 20 feet in diameter. This is ·
seen in the section through the centre of the building
given at page 310; *h* is the sleeping room, 13 feet
square, with an ornamental ceiling. The saloon serves
as a dining-room and place for meals. The drawing-
room *d*, or music room, 22 feet by 14 feet, is on

Termination of attic pedestal.

the left, *b* is the principal staircase leading to the
upper rooms; this serves also for servants. The
small iron staircase *j*, is for passage to the cold bath
below, *i* is a room for a warm bath. The cold bath,
as shown in the section, is ventilated through a

domed ceiling, but the scale is too small to show this perfectly.

A portion of the saloon is shown at page 311, with a few of its details in the six cuts following it.

Chimney-pot elevation and section.

The bedroom ceiling (page 316) supposes the covering of a tent, upheld by spears and ropes. The colour of the drapery is of a light fawn, the ground a deep ultramarine blue. In the centre of the ceiling

is a small Cupid on a red or gilt ground, a light blue
circle surrounding it. The spears, roses, ropes, and
tassels are gilt and coloured.

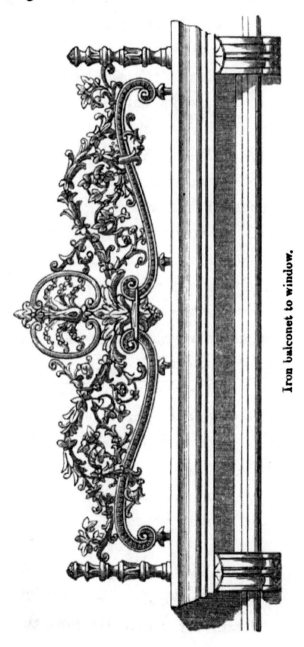

Iron balconet to window.

The drawing-room ceiling is decorated plaster work in white and gold. Its plan is shown at page 317, and three of its details on page 318. Among other decorations of these rooms may be considered the chimney-pieces. The cuts (page 319) give an elevation of the drawing-room chimney-piece, the plan of its shelf above, and a portion of its details to a larger scale beneath. This chimney-piece in the finest statuary marble would cost 80*l.* to execute. Several have been done for the author at that price. They look very well in execution. Two fire-places of less pretensions are shown in the illustrations at pp. 320 and 321; the first was in rouge royal, costing 25*l.*; the last are of marble with slate panels covered with imitation of Brocatelli marbles, these costing 19*l.* 10*s.* each. The illustration of the whole of the details of internal decoration of such a structure would fill a much larger volume than the present; but it is the sole object of the author to give such illustrations of the several designs, that a portion of each part of the building only shall be shown; *k,* in the ground plan (page 304), is an open portico with steps to the garden or park in front of it.

The next plan (page 322) is that of the mezzanine. This shows two of the female servants' sleeping rooms, *a, a,* with a closet; the decorated ceilings of the saloon, drawing-room, and bed room, are also shown; the bath room should have some slight decoration, but this has been omitted. The female servants' sleeping rooms are each 17 feet in length by 8 in width.

The plan of the upper story (page 323) gives a smoking room *a*, with an open terrace *c c*, front and back, a closet *d*, and a cistern room *b*.

Section of window sill and iron balconet.

The basement plan (page 324) shows the cold bath in the centre, with its staircase; the kitchen *b*, the scullery *g*, *h h* the larders, *c* is the lift, and *d d* are men's sleeping rooms; the servants' hall *t*, and house-keeper's room *j*, are on the left, *q* is the wine cellar, and *s* the beer cellar.

The elevation of the back front is at page 325; it has a circular portico and steps down to the garden. An attempt has been made to introduce an original termination for the pedestals on the attics, instead of using the almost universal Soanic bulbous ornament so repeatedly seen in nearly every public building in

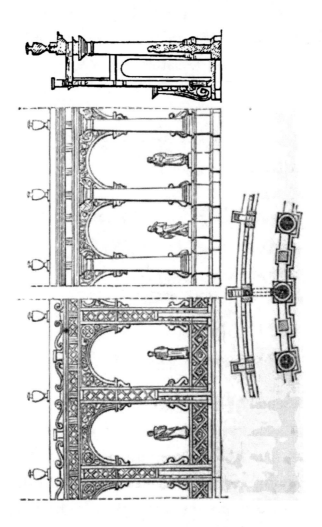

London and the country, and of which the author's late master, Sir John Soane, was so fond. These attempts are given in the figures pp. 326-328; and an attempt is made to give an ornamental chimney-pot on page 330. It will be seen in the figure that the ornamental cement pot or vase contains an iron, or it might be a zinc, lining; this would be kept warm, and a security for the smoke passing out.

The exterior of the building is ornamented with statues and vases, and the windows have iron balconets.

The last remaining illustration to be given is the arcade on each side of the villa, dividing the front and back gardens. The chief portion of this in stone, with statues between the columns and vases over them; at the back of the columns is another front of ornamental trellis work in wood, with scroll stands for flowers—this is supported or upheld by the stone screen; an elevation of each, with a section, is given at page 334.

The vignette gives French and English patterns for cover to external sunblinds.

DESIGN No. 27.

A DECORATED WINDOW.

THIS design was sketched with the intention of making Italian forms rival the tracery of the Decorated Gothic window, and to obtain a rich and variegated mass of painted and coloured glass, without any stiff mannerism or formality. The window was 11 ft. in height with a width of 7 ft.; it served as a screen in one of the principal staircases in a house at Queen's Gate, Kensington; immediately behind it is the servants' staircase, having a large window and skylight. The lower portion of this window is divided into three lights by two pilasters acting as mullions. The circle above the transome is filled with a richly painted subject, representing a basket of flowers and scrollwork on a ruby ground. The basket is formed of emerald glass, the ground of the surrounding portions is richly embossed glass, the chief portions white, the small portions ruby, yellow and blue, the latter with white ornaments upon it. The three lights between the pilasters are filled with embossed glass, and the whole is surrounded by borders of scrollwork richly embossed, stained and painted; the ruby ground is shown in the drawing by vertical lines, the yellow by oblique lines, and the blue by horizontal lines. The expense, including the zinc-work for fixing the glass to the upper portion or fanlight, was 22*l.* 6*s.*; the lower portion cost 8*l.* 10*s.* It was the work of Messrs. Baillie and Co. of Wardour Street.

z

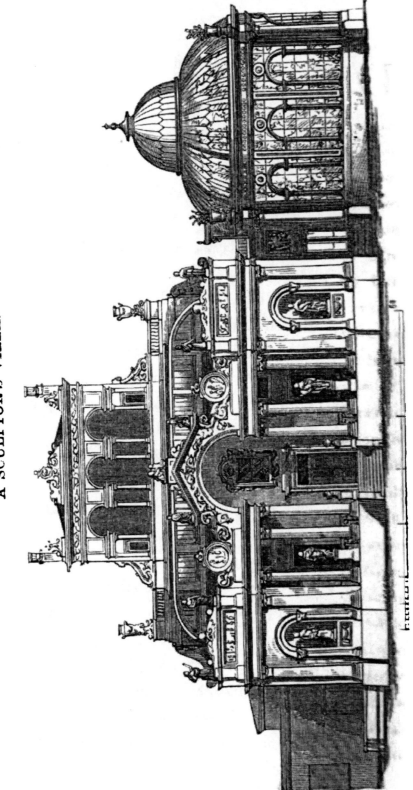

A SCULPTOR'S VILLA.

DURING the year 1850 the author, in conjunction with the late Mr. John Britton, F.S.A., was engaged in making some topographical sketches in one of the western counties of England. He became for a short time the guest of one of its principal residents—a gentleman who had succeeded to the possession of more than a million of money, the result of a relative's gains as a merchant in the City. He had filled the small house he was then inhabiting with a very fine collection of antique bronzes: also with ancient and modern statuary. The house was occupied in every corner with these valuable and beautiful works of art. He was then having another house of larger dimensions erected to receive them. Considerable discussion took place at his table between himself and his visitors, among whom were two or three distinguished men of taste, as to the best method of introducing sculpture into a dwelling of moderate capacity. It was the general opinion that to properly exhibit classic sculpture, a villa the size of those of the ancients, such as are described by Pliny in the account of his villas at Laurentinum and Tusculum, would be required, and that no other would suffice. On his return home, the author, as a matter of amusement, without any thought that his ideas would ever be carried out, made the present design; it was a subject that pleased him, as he had only a few years pre-

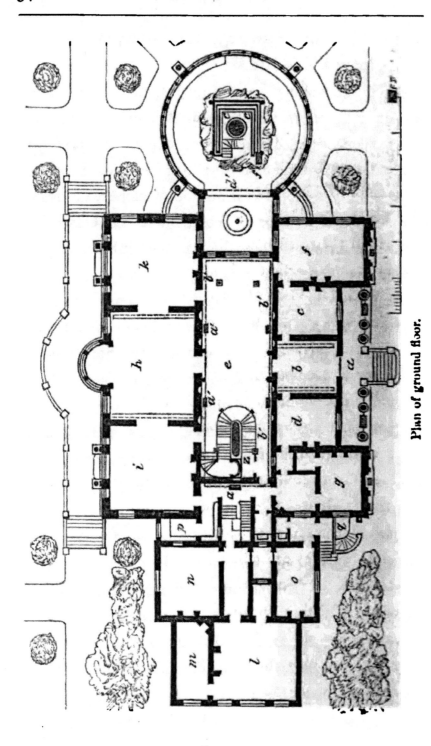

Plan of ground floor.

viously superintended the construction of a small sculpture gallery for the late Sir Francis Chantrey at Pimlico.

The ground plan of this design shows a gallery of sculpture in the centre of the building, a small

Section of staircase.

"Museo Chiaramonti." The principal group at the end, representing the capture of the Queen of the Amazons, is so placed that the staircase winding round it forms its base; the group can be seen from the staircase, and from the galleries at the side, in every point of view. This being a large building, the scale upon which the plans, elevation, and sections are drawn is smaller than the scale previously used in this volume. The gallery, including that portion which forms the ante-room to the conservatory, is 80 ft. in length by 20 ft. in width, which is a poor

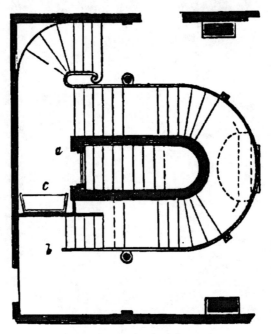

Plan of principal staircase.

imitation of the gallery at the Vatican—the Museo Chiaramonti. This is 280 ft. in length, with a breadth of 20 ft.

But the possession of only a million of money gives a moderate income compared with that of the sovereign popes at the time the Vatican was erected. The

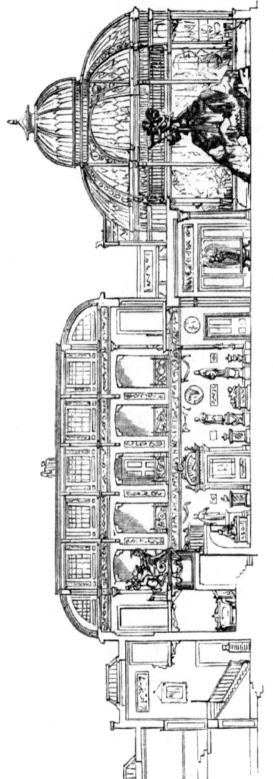

Section through gallery and conservatory.

sculpture is arranged on each side of the gallery, the
bas-reliefs inserted in the walls, the bronzes on small
pedestals, a reclining group is placed in a niche in
front of the staircase. A marble group is placed in
the fountain in the ante-room to the conservatory,
and another in the conservatory itself. A gallery of
this description permits the admission of a large
quantity of sculpture, allowing it to be seen with advantage. The entrance of the building, partly taken
from the front of one of the Italian palaces,* permits
a large quantity of sculpture to be placed in advantageous positions. The plan, page 340, shows an
entrance loggia *a*, the hall *b*, 17 ft. by 16 ft., with
the waiting-room *c*, to the right, the breakfast parlour
d, and the butler's pantry *g*, to the left; *f* is the
library, 28 ft. by 16 ft., entered either from the
gallery or the waiting-room. It has a large window
looking into the ante-room to the conservatory, and
permits a good view of the group of sculpture and the
fountain in the centre; *e* is the gallery, with the
principal staircase, *i* is the dining-room opening into
the picture gallery and drawing-room *h*, *k*.

The section, page 343, shows the general arrangement, and an idea can be formed of its grand

---

* The garden entrance to the ancient palace of the Grand
Duke of Tuscany, alla Trinita de' Monti. The architecture of
Annibale Lippi.

scenic effect in summer, when the doors were opened.
The walk round the conservatory and through the
whole of the gallery would have a length of 170 ft.,
and round the galleries 150 ft. more, giving ample
space to place a very large collection of sculpture.
Underneath the gallery were supposed to be large
cellars for wine. These had a private entrance through
the pedestal of the Amazonian group, as shown in
the plan and section to a larger scale at page 342;
the collection below was supposed to be as valuable as
the one above, and calculated to yield as much enjoyment, and one certainly that would be more highly
appreciated by a greater number of persons. The
villa, however, is on a small scale compared with some
of the noble residences in the county, and the accommodation throughout very scanty. The servants'
offices are shown annexed to the plan; *l* is the kitchen,
24 ft. by 22 ft., *m* the scullery, *n* the housekeeper's
room, *o* a small servants' hall, *p* is a serving room,
and *q* the external entrance to the cellarage.

By the side of the principal staircase is a descent
into the cellars and basement, for the servants, *b*, plan
page 342. The conservatory has a diameter of 40 ft.
and a height of 44 ft.; it is of light construction, in
decorated ironwork.

The one-pair plan shows the sleeping department,
the principal bed-rooms, *b b*, each with a dressing-

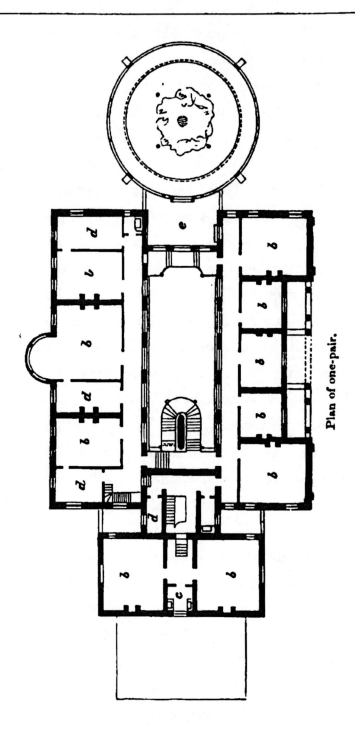

Plan of one-pair.

room, *d d*. These are entered direct from the gallery;
in the front of the building are five smaller sleeping

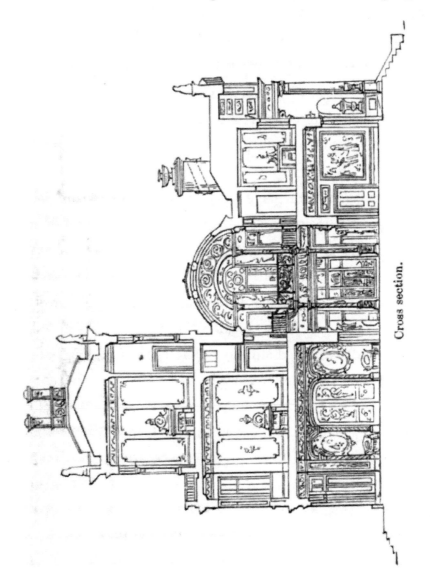

Cross section.

rooms. At the conservatory end the gallery opens on
to the roof of the ante-room beneath, and from this

there is an entrance to a circular gallery inside the conservatory. On the servants' side are seen two large sleeping rooms, and a housemaid's closet; as this portion of the building is kept lower than the other, it could have two or three rooms constructed over the kitchen, or it could be carried up another story. The plan of the principal bedchambers is taken up another floor; the small staircase for this purpose is seen at the end of the gallery.

The cross section (page 347) shows the height of the building, and its general construction. The whole of the principal living rooms in the three floors are of the same height, 16 ft. 6 in. each; 37 steps were required in the principal staircase to ascend to the first floor on one side, and 31 on the other; the roof of the saloon was to be constructed similar to the roof of the Riding-house shown in plate, page 389. Large roofs can be constructed on this principle at a very cheap rate, and it is a very strong and efficient one; the roof of the Pantheon in Oxford-street, constructed by Mr. Sydney Smirke, is of a similar kind; the roofs of the annexes to the Exhibition building of 1862 by Captain Fowkes were on the same principle, but as these were only intended to stand for a year, were very slight. The cross section shows the ventilating flue, proposed and illustrated in a following chapter; the small stack in the low building shows the incline necessary to meet the back eddy of wind from the high building. It would have been better, could it have been effected, to have placed the stack in a position parallel to the high building, and not at right angles to it. The stack on the latter shows two ventilating flues, each with an upward shaft; the whole of the smoke from the fireplaces would be delivered from these two shafts.

It only remains to illustrate the system of warming proposed to have been introduced. This was by a combination of two entirely different systems of warm-water circulation through iron pipes.

The various apparatus of warming buildings by the circulation of hot water, may be roughly stated to be of two kinds, each acting on the opposite principle to the other. The first, or more modern one, is the *closed system*. This has always been preferred by the author, it being more conveniently introduced into a building, less expensive, and giving less trouble than any other, and more certain in its action. In it the water circulates with great rapidity, completely under pressure, the pipes being closed, and the whole of the air expelled from them. The older system is that in which the tubes are not closed, but are connected with a cistern, into which the water is allowed to flow and re-flow; the two may very properly be called the high and low temperature systems, and by these terms they are here designated. With the first, the tubes can be made to reach a higher degree of heat if necessary, by placing a larger proportion of them than is usual in the furnace; but with the second, a temperature of 180 degrees can alone be reached. With the latter, its greater or less efficiency depends upon the position of its open cistern, which regulates the amount of pressure in the tubes, according as its situation is high or low. It was introduced into this country about 1818; the open cistern was placed in the upper part of the house, the boiler being below in the kitchen, thus allowing a considerable pressure in the tubes, and securing a quick circulation of the water. The high temperature system was introduced by A. M. Perkins, Esq., about the year 1832; in its simplest form it consisted of a continuous or endless tube of wrought iron of one inch external diameter, filled with water, and closed in all parts; a portion of the tubing was formed into a coil and placed in a furnace of wrought iron, the fire being enclosed in fire-brick. When it was first introduced a larger amount of tubing was placed in the furnace than is now usually done; with the proper amount, one-tenth or one-eleventh only of the full quantity is necessary, and then it must be obvious that no overheating of the tubes can take place. In practice it is more usual to find objections made to the apparatus not giving sufficient heat, than to its giving too much. The quantity of feet in pipes necessary to raise rooms of a certain size to a given temperature, must be proportioned to their cubical contents, and this depends equally on the situation and aspect of the building, the number of doors, and windows, or skylights; no rule can consequently be given which would be applicable to all places with any degree of certainty.

The pipes being only five-eighths of an inch internal diameter, a very small quantity of water is required to fill the apparatus. A tube called the expansion tube is placed above the highest level of the circulating pipes, and is generally of larger diameter. The object of this tube is to allow for the expansion of the water as it becomes heated; a tube is also placed at the highest level, in order to fill the apparatus, so as to leave the expansion tube empty.

The tubes are provided with screw plugs, so as to be conveniently opened when it is required to fill the pipes with water, and closed again after being filled. This can be done with facility by a servant. The circulation of the water is produced by the application of heat to the coil in the furnace; and as the small size of the pipes admits of presenting the largest possible amount of surface to the action of the fire, it is clear that a greater economy of fuel is effected by it than by the ordinary system of boilers. As the water becomes heated it rises immediately to the highest level of the circulating pipes, and thus forms a column of heated water, specifically lighter than the colder water, which descends to the lower part of the coil. Thus a circulation is effected throughout the whole course of the pipes,* which eventually become heated, and the whole may be regulated exactly to that degree of temperature which is most conducive to a beneficial effect.

To regulate the degree of heat to be given to the tubes, without requiring the necessity of an attendant, advantage has been taken of the expansive property of the iron pipe when heated. There are three multiplying levers fixed in a box, and so placed that the short arm of one of the levers rests upon a regulating screw attached to the flow pipe. On the other end of the series of levers a rod so rests that, upon the slightest movement of the levers, the damper in the flue, which is attached to the rod, is opened or closed, as the case may be. The box of levers is suspended from the hot pipe, so as to leave about two feet in length between the point of suspension and the point of contact with the short arm of the lever.

---

* This subject is fully treated and illustrated with plates in the Author's treatise on "The Warming and Ventilation of Buildings," published in 1837 and 1856.

The operation of this arrangement is obvious, for the instant the pipe becomes heated, it expands and presses the short arm of the lever ; and as the fulcrum within the box cannot move, by reason of the rod which suspends it being cold, it follows that the lever must be depressed, by which action a sufficient motion is given to the damper, to close it at any given temperature at which it may be originally fixed.

The great advantage in the use of this apparatus is the saving of time in obtaining the requisite degree of heat. It often happens that the time occupied in heating the water of an ordinary hot-water apparatus completely defeats the object of getting warmth in any reasonable time, particularly in greenhouses, where it is frequently desirable to get up the heat quickly, to prevent the effect of frost. It has been said that this property of generating the heat rapidly has the disadvantage of not being able to retain it : this, however, is not the case, for, on the contrary, an equal temperature may be maintained for any length of time that may be desired. It is only necessary to make the fireplace sufficiently large to contain fuel enough to last the time the heat is required to be continued, and the damper will regulate the combustion of the fuel and the heat of the pipes, so that there will be no variation for twelve hours together.

There being no boiler to the apparatus, it is free from the ordinary danger of explosion; if a pipe by possibility should burst, no harm ensues, for the water escapes from so small an aperture, that it becomes absolutely cool by its expansion and mixture with atmospheric air.

So little fear of fire exists with the apparatus, that the directors of the principal fire offices readily accept, at the lowest rate of premium, all proposals for the insurance of buildings in which the system is adopted, not requiring even the customary inspection.

The author made drawings of one of these apparatus put up in an ornamental greenhouse in Kew Gardens in 1844; and fourteen years after, the director of the garden, Sir W. J. Hooker, publicly allowed it to be stated in print that no hot-water apparatus in any of their houses had given so much satisfaction; that the heat was given out after lighting the fires more rapidly than in any other of their houses, and steadily maintained at any degree of temperature required. The two systems of the high and low temperature can readily be combined, and the temperature of both large and small tubes nearly equalized. This may be done by using one furnace. A diagram given by Dr. Arnott in a lecture delivered by him at the Royal Institution in March, 1836, with his explanation, will show the principle upon which the combination is effected. Suppose A, fig. 1, is a cistern full of cold water, and B a cistern full of hot water : if the two cocks *c c* are unturned, it is a fact that the water at *d* will be one degree of warmth only above the water at

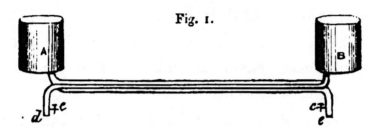

Fig. 1.

A, and the water at *e* will be of one degree less temperature than the water in B. If, therefore, on this principle, some of the pipes of the high-temperature system are passed through the large tubing of the low temperature one, the desired effect is obtained : the large pipes or tablets of one apparatus remain at their full heat, while an additional quantity of inch pipe of sufficiently warm temperature is obtained, that can be carried into rooms and placed in situations into which the warming surfaces of the low-temperature system could not be made to approach.

As regards the low temperature apparatus, if the large pipes belonging to it are laid in sufficient quantity, they doubtless have the effect of producing a moderate degree of heat.

The best way of introducing them into a dwelling-house is to sink them in channels in the floor, with perforated ironwork over them: they are more usually introduced into hothouses, factories, and workshops, where their appearance is not objectionable. A feeling exists in favour of their use in conservatories; in order to show how they can be retained for that purpose, the combined systems are introduced in the plan of the villa here described.

The ground plan shows the entrance hall, the gallery or sculpture saloon in the centre, the principal staircase, the picture room and the servants' staircase, all warmed by the inch pipes; the larger pipes are introduced into the conservatory. In the picture room— that between the drawing-room and the dining-room— and in the hall, the pipes are sunk in trenches in the floor. They are close to the walls, and lined with brick with an inside covering of zinc. These trenches have over them perforated ornamental ironwork; a' a' are pedestals containing coils of pipe; b' b' are pipes behind the skirting, likewise perforated. Where these pipes pass the doorways they are sunk in the floor. In the conservatory d' d' are the large pipes; f is an open cistern, through which the circulation of water in the pipes flows; at g are placed the expansion and filling tubes.

Fig. 2 is an isometrical view of the pipes, furnace, and cisterns complete to a small scale; e is the furnace placed in the basement; f is a cistern of cold water through which the flow and return pipes from the furnace pass : the water becoming heated in the cistern flows out, and returns in the direction shown by the arrows.   The flow pipe, leaving this cistern, passes up to the expansion tube g, whence the tubes run through the building in the manner shown, returning to the furnace.   The pipes d, are two other flow and return pipes, furnished with a stop-cock, by means of which the circulation can be confined either to the house or to the conservatory.   The furnace

Fig. 2.

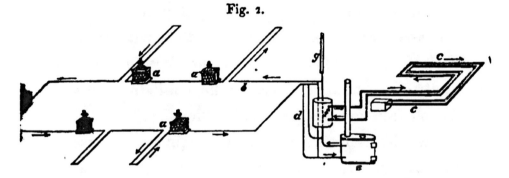

should in reality contain two coils of pipe, having two flows and two returns, the whole of which should go through the cistern f, but the small scale of the plate allows one circulation only to be shown.

Dr. Arnott's principle of nearly equalizing temperatures was applied by him for room ventilation.   Its mode of application is explained in the following extract from his report on " Warming and Ventilating Infirmaries, Workhouses, Factories, and Domestic Apartments," given in the appendix to the Second

Annual Report of the Poor Law Commissioners :—" In rooms where the mechanical mode of ventilation already described (by means of fanners) and now common in factories, has been adopted, an addition might be made to the apparatus for extracting the impure air, which would drive fresh air in, and which, by causing the two currents to pass each other in contact for a certain distance in very thin metallic tubes, would cause the fresh air entering to absorb nearly the whole heat from the impure air going out, and would thus render it at once both pure and warm, and would consequently save, after the room was once warmed, any further expense of fuel for the day, and would avoid, how rapid soever the ventilation, all the danger from draught and unequal heating."

The above idea is extremely ingenious, but as to its practical efficiency, some doubt might be expressed. The temperature of a warm room, even if it was 65°, would be much too low to produce the action described.

A very ingenious application of the small-tube system of warming has been introduced into his dwelling by Mr. Babbage. He placed the furnace in the basement, and divided the whole length of piping by means of a mutiple cock into four circulations, any one of which he could turn off or on at pleasure; one circulation warmed the bath, which, when the cistern that supplied it was once up to 160 degrees (and this it took an hour to obtain), remained sufficiently warm for a bath during 24 hours. The whole quantity of pipe in the building was 891 feet, and the quantity in the furnace 135. The thermometer in the smoke-flue was seldom higher than 212 degrees, when that in the flow-pipe was 240 degrees. Any two or three, or all four of the circulations could be worked together, by simply turning an index provided for the purpose.

The tool-room was always kept at a temperature of from 50° to 54°. In winter the hat-room received a portion of piping, so that coats and gloves, even in the dampest weather, were always kept dry. One circulation was sent through the dining-room a short time before it was used; it was after a certain time turned off and sent through the bedrooms and dressing-rooms. The various rooms in the winter were kept at different temperatures, the dressing-rooms were a few degrees warmer than were the bedrooms : an inducement for early rising. The linen was aired, and warm water provided in the dressing-rooms and for the use of the servants. The apparatus saved labour in cleaning and lighting of fires, and it was economical, the consumption of fuel during the six winter months being about a bushel of coke in 24 hours. The supply of air, and the consequent combustion and quantity of fuel, was regulated by the fire itself. This was never suffered to go out after it had been once lighted, except when necessary to remove the clinkers, and this occurred about once a fortnight. In the morning, about seven o'clock, the fire was well shaken by means of a lever attached to the bars of the grate. Coal or coke was supplied, and the air valve opened. The stop-cock was then turned on to supply the coils for the library and stairs. At about eight o'clock in the evening the stop-cock was turned to heat the coil of the bath, and at eleven o'clock, fuel having been supplied, the air valve was completely closed, and the damper also if necessary. By these means the fire burned very slowly during the whole of the night, and the bath cistern received the warmth thus generated.

These conveniences and luxuries might be more generally applied than they are at present in the dwellings of this country.

DESIGN No. 29.

GARDEN SEAT.

THIS small ornamental structure was designed for a garden in Wiltshire, on an estate near Chippenham. The garden, which is very extensive, rises

Perspective view.

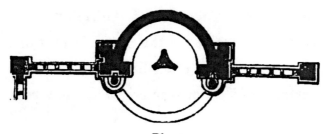

Plan.

in steep terraces up the combe or hill by the side of the mansion, which lies down in the valley. The structure was to be on the highest part of the garden,

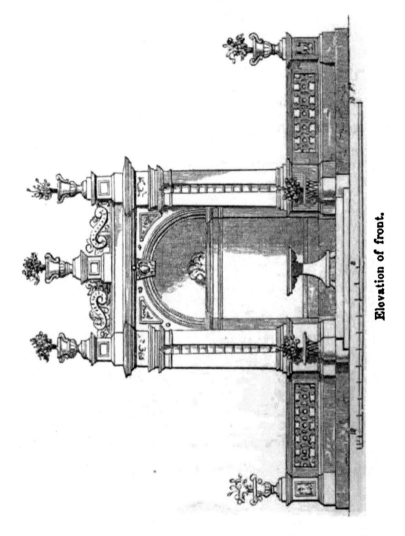

Elevation of front.

commanding an extensive view of the valley, the village, and adjacent country. As the house is in the neighbourhood of several fine old Elizabethan mansions, the design partook of that character. The view represents

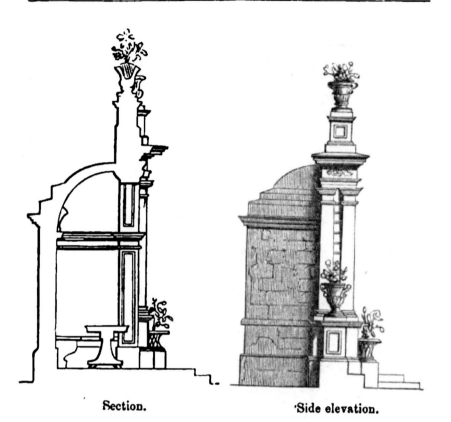

Section.   'Side elevation.

Balustrade.

the structure in its complete state, with the terrace overlooking the valley.   The turret on the tower of the village church is seen in the distance.   The latter

Portion of exterior front.

Portion of the entrance front.

Balustrade (2nd example).

is an agreeable object in the view, being an extremely fine specimen of Decorated English Gothic, and in good preservation.

The plan is beneath the view, and the elevation of the building is likewise given. The whole of it was to have been constructed in stone; the vases were intended to receive flower-pots, so that a constant change of flowers could be placed in them by the pots being changed as often as was desired. A section through the centre and a side elevation are given; the balustrade is from an ancient example, it is five inches in thickness. The mouldings of the exterior are of plain Roman character, without any admixture of Gothic forms. The best examples of our Elizabethan architecture are pure Italian, but possessing a bolder and more picturesque outline, suited to our northern climate, than that shown by the elegant Italian model.

The second balustrade, p. 365, was an after-suggestion, it being considered more appropriate to the design than the first one. Another elevation was made for the same structure; this is shown as Design No. 30; it was to occupy the same site, and to have been constructed wholly in stone.

———

Opposite is a drawing of an ancient chimney-piece at Enfield, bearing the inscription—

Sola salus servire Deo,
Sunt cætera fravdes.

Ancient chimney-piece in the Palace School, Enfield.
(Formerly in the occupation of Queen Elizabeth.)

DESIGN No. 30.

A GARDEN SEAT.

THE turret of the village church is seen through the centre opening; this was proposed to be filled with plain and coloured glass; the detail of the ornament above the cornice is copied from that on

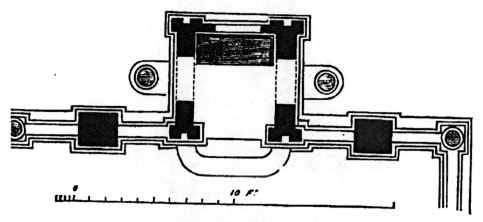

Plan (2nd design).

the gables of Charlton House, Wiltshire, from which the author had just returned, having visited it for the purpose of making drawings and fully illustrating it in one of his publications.

DESIGN *No.* 31.

AN ICE HOUSE.

Perspective view.

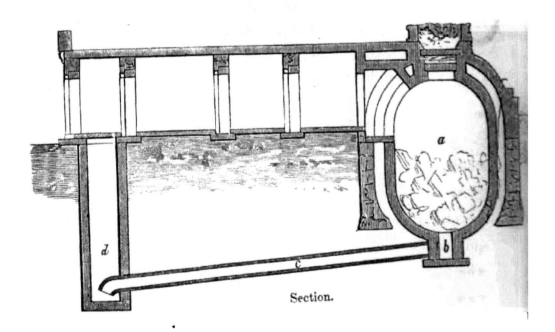

Section.

THIS design represents an old-fashioned ice-house, such as were constructed in the country several years ago, and still are so, where large quantities of ice are required to be stored. This small structure, embosomed amidst trees, impervious to the sun, was formed with the stone of the district, and arched and domed over with bricks. The well *a*, sunk in the earth, is 10 feet in diameter, *b* is a cesspool to receive the water that drops from the ice, and *c* is the drain

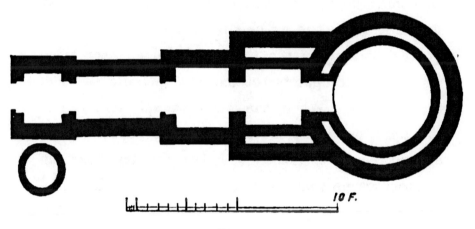

10 F.

Plan.

to convey it to the well *d*; the ice is thrown in from the top, the earth *e*, and the two stone slabs and the straw between them, being removed.

As an additional precaution against warmth, the structure was buried in a mound of earth. This, as it quite destroyed any picturesque effect it would otherwise have had amidst the trees, is not shown in the view.

These ice-wells have not often so long a passage of approach ; one only from 6 to 10 feet in length is sufficient, but double doors and a free current of air across the entrance passage are desirable. It has not often a domed roof to cover that of the well, a common wooden roof covered with thatch placed a few feet above the roof of the well being sufficient ; neither is it often considered necessary to have a well to receive the water dropping from the ice. The ice-well walls may be splayed down to the ground, with proper footings, and an uncovered piece of ground left at the bottom. Over this is placed an open wood frame, which supports the ice, and permits all water to drain off. When the walls are splayed down in this form, buttresses must be added to support them, and the weight of the ice. Every country house in America is provided with an excellent ice-house of the simplest and most practical kind. It consists of a deep excavation in the earth, roofed over with a pointed thatch. These ice-houses are always well filled in the winter, and rarely if ever quite emptied during the summer. An accurate section of such an ice-well, with full directions for its construction, has been lately published.*

---

* "Cheap Ice Well." (Atchley & Co.)

DESIGN No. 32.

A SUBURBAN VILLA.

ONE of the chief peculiarities in small suburban villas that have been erected near London within the last thirty years, is that of making the

Elevation of principal front.

chief room on the basement the ordinary apartment for the family. The confined areas formerly adopted in front and back of the building are omitted, and the earth is sloped up in form of a bank, being adorned with flowers and shrubs so as to look pleasing from within the apartments.   There is usually a side room in the basement, with descending steps to the entrance, which serves as an office to the occupier of the house.   If his business be chiefly in the locality,

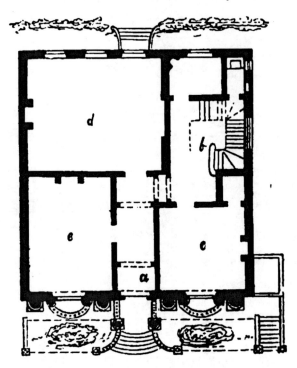

Ground plan.

this is very convenient ; the chief room in the basement is used as a dining and supper room, and indeed, for all common purposes by the family.   It renders it unnecessary to have more than one, or at most, two servants' rooms.   The drawing-room, the library, and the superior dining-room are on the floor above.

This suburban dwelling very much resembles the same class of structure in America, where economy of space is carried out more completely than with us, and the residents are less dependent on servants. Iu the American house, the pantry is nearly always placed between the kitchen and the dining-room, and its chief approach is from the latter, even when the dining-room is on the ground floor. The American

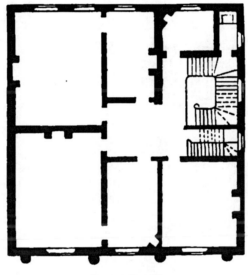

One-pair plan.

house has the office, or place of business of the occupier, on the lower floor, with its separate entrance. The Americans exhibit a compactness of arrangement and an attention to detail that prove they are in no way behind us in a knowledge of what is requisite for household comfort. One peculiarity in the American building is the verandah, which is considered to be in-

dispensable.   It is large and roomy, and often placed
on three sides of the building; the climate, warmer
and dryer than our own, renders such an addition a

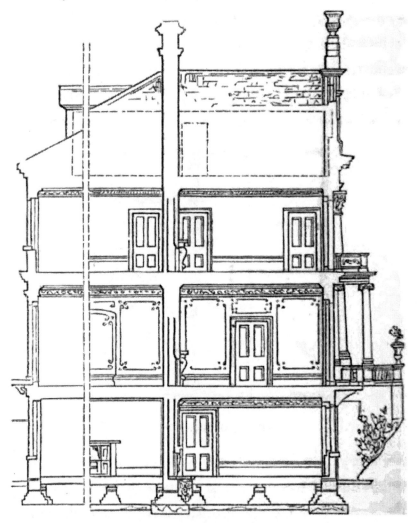

Section through front and back.

great luxury.   Our atmosphere in the winter months
has often been pronounced of leaden gravity, and it
does not permit of any erection that stops the circula-

tion of the air, which would render it stagnant. Another peculiarity in the houses of our American cousins, is that they are often cased in wood. If the house be only two or three stories in height, an 8-in. brick wall is considered sufficient ; this is " furred off outside, and covered with clap boards," in the ordinary

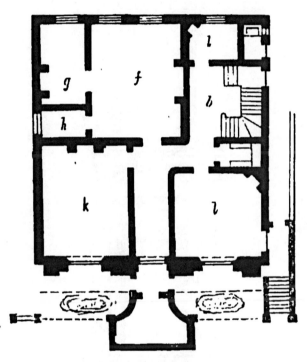

Basement plan.

way followed in a wooden building. Its advantage is, that it is sure to secure a perfectly dry wall. This mode of construction in England would necessitate the painting of the whole of the exterior once at least in every three or four years. One more suitable with us for a wall in a damp situation would be the plan the author pursued in the house on Salisbury Plain, putting quartering against the wall, and covering it with diamond slating. The surface could be varied with coloured encaustic tiles so as to present a pleasing

Front windows.

appearance, proper ventilation being given behind the slating.

The small suburban villa represented in the plate

is supposed to stand on a plot of ground with a frontage of 50 ft.; the construction is in brick and stucco, the small columns of the portico are of Bath stone. The plan shows a small hall *a*, the library *c*, 15 ft. by 14 ft., and on the right with a strong closet. The dining-room *e*, is 18 ft. by 15 ft., and on the left; the drawing-room *d*, is 23 ft. by 18 ft. There is a large commodious staircase *b*, and leading from it a small dressing-room *i*, and closet. This dressing-room might easily be made to contain a bath; the water for the bath in any one of the floors should always be heated by means of a close boiler attached to an ordinary kitchen-range. It is the most simple, economical, and efficient arrangement for that purpose, as no more fire than that used for cooking is required. The cold water is supplied from a cistern at the top of the house, and a continual circulation of the water between that and the boiler goes on, the hot water ascending, the cold descending. Pipes may be branched off from the ascending pipe, which leaves the top of the boiler, and taken to any part of the house, ensuring a supply of hot water to dressing-rooms, nurseries, &c. Instead of a boiler, a coil of iron or copper pipe is often used, rendering the circulation quicker and more effective. The one-pair plan of the suburban villa contains three large bedrooms, two dressing-rooms, and one invalid's room entered from the staircase; to this room the closet could be attached.   The staircase leads up to two large attics for the servants.

The section, p. 376, shows a portion of the front and back of the building, with the construction of the roof, the back wall not being carried so high as the front.   This is done to give the building an imposing appearance from the road, a mode of construction very often carried out in suburban houses.   The basement plan affords good accommodation ; *f* is the kitchen, 18 ft. by 15 ft., *g* the scullery, *h* the larder, *k* the living room, *l* the business office, with its separate entrance.   The closet for the servants is external ; the footman's pantry and the wine cellar lead out of the staircase *b*, the coal cellar is under the portico.   The house thus contains seventeen rooms ; the cost of its erection would be 3260*l.* completely finished.   A detail of the windows is given on a large scale at page 378.

The following is an elevation of the vane, the constructive detail of which is given in a former vignette. The character is Elizabethan, and designed from an example at Oxnead Hall, Norfolk.

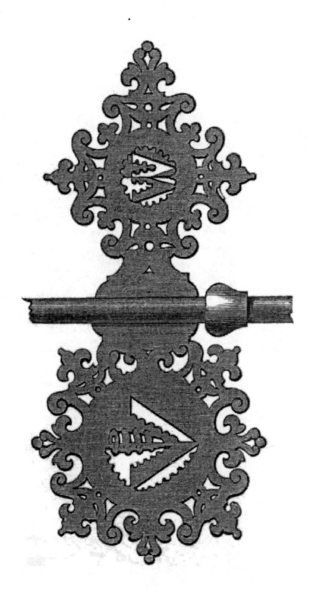

DESIGN *No.* 33.

A SUBURBAN VILLA.

Elevation of Principal front.

THIS design is also one for a suburban villa, or a small country house, on a rather larger scale than the preceding. This villa, dressed with a plain Italian elevation, and of smaller dimensions as to plan, has been erected on several sites near London. The front of the present design was partly taken from a plate in " Nash's Mansions," at the request of a

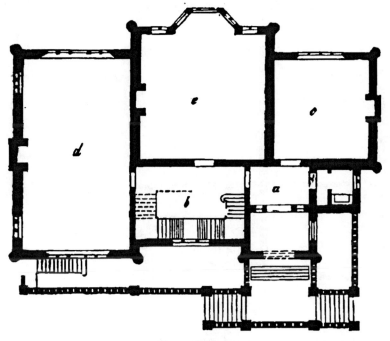

Ground plan.

gentleman who very much admired it, and who was anxious to have a semi-detached villa of the same character. The villa was therefore designed so that another could be placed by the side of it. The two gables form the centre, the chimney stack is between them on the roof; the front was to have a sunk area, topped by a Gothic balustrade, and as there were no principal rooms on the basement floor in the front of the house, this was easily given; the rooms at the back looked into the garden, and these had the ground in front of them sloped up.

The ground plan shows an entrance hall *a*, 14 ft. by 10 ft., with a commodious staircase *b*, 18 ft. by 12 ft., to the left. There was a closet to the right;

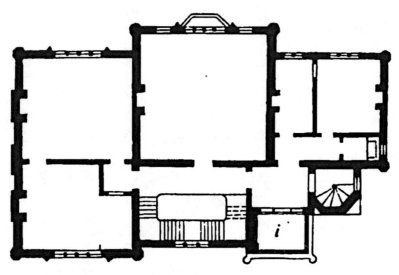

The one pair plan.

a lift from the basement could easily be obtained here. The study *c*, was about 16 ft. square, and was entered from the hall; the dining-room *e*, had a bay window, and was in the centre of the building; it measured 20 ft. square. The drawing-room *d*, was very large, being 31 ft. in length by 16 ft. in breadth, with a large window at each end; this was often considered objectionable, as the occupants of the room can always be seen from the opposite houses, but as this was intended for a semi-detached villa, windows could not be obtained at the side.

The one-pair plan contains one large and three small bedrooms, with a closet. Over the porch was placed a conservatory, and by its side the tower staircase led up to the attic. This contained four good-

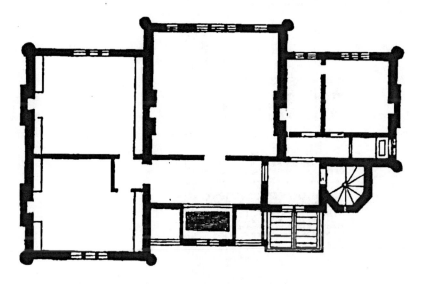

Attic plan.

sized bedrooms, each with a fireplace; there was a housemaid's closet, and a place for the slate cistern to supply the lower part of the house with water; a small cistern on a higher level was placed on the roof of the tower. Another room could easily have been obtained on this floor, by continuing the passage at the housemaid's closet through the centre room, and this was proposed, but it was objected to, as it could not be rendered light and airy.   A second staircase,

Section through portion of building.

from the attic to the basement, could have been formed in the tower, the two closets being placed in a similar position to the one on the first floor. The staircase in the tower led on to the roof. The section shows the height of the various rooms, there being no variation throughout the floors. It was intended to carry out

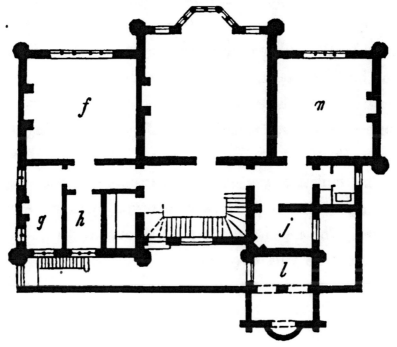

The basement plan.

the style of the exterior in the interior—a medley between the Gothic and Elizabethan; the proprietor having a very large collection of old-fashioned carvings of various styles and dates, picked up at sales, or purchased in Wardour-street (at that time more celebrated for such antiquities than at present). The walls were to be covered with gilt leather and rich tapestries, and with this the architect did not intend to meddle, leaving it all to the taste and skill of the owner, although he has finished several interiors with such materials.

The basement plan shows the kitchen *f,* the scullery *g,* and larder *h* ; *q* is the wine cellar, and *j* the butler's pantry. Then there were two large rooms looking towards the garden, and these were unappropriated. The butler's small pantry had a window looking into the side area; the servants' door was on the staircase; the coal cellar was placed under the steps leading to the porch.

The building was to be constructed in brick and cement, with the porch and external balustrade in stone. The expense would have amounted to 4600*l.,* or the double villa to 9000*l.*

DESIGN *No.* 34.

RIDING-HOUSE AND STABLING.

THIS collection of designs could hardly be complete without a group of stable buildings. To make such a group picturesque is extremely difficult,

Perspective view of riding-house.

and it is very seldom attempted. Such buildings mostly form a portion of the offices which are placed out of view, concealed by plantations or shrubbery, and generally at some distance from the mansion to which they appertain.

The present design, carried out in 1846 and 1848, was for some additional stabling to a baronial park, and it formed a conspicuous object. It stands on the

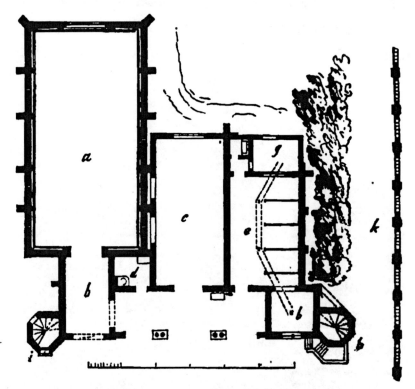

Plan of riding-house and stabling.

eastern side of a quadrangle, the larger stabling being on the west, the offices of the mansion on the north (see above), and on the south there was a terrace-walk overlooking the park. The block of buildings as represented in the plan, comprised a riding-house *a*,

62 ft. in length by 32 ft. in width, a four-stall stable
e, 30 ft. in length, a loose box *b*, 13 ft. square, and
the boiler room, *d*. The dung pit *g*, into which the
liquid manure from the stable was sent, was on a very
low level, and had a cart road at its side. The coach-
house between the riding-house and stable was 40 ft.
in length by 20 ft. in breadth; it had a covered area
in front 44 ft. in length, with a width of 13 ft., and
a well and pump. The prospect tower *h*, as well as
the tower *i*, had iron staircases, which led to the
stud-groom's sleeping room, two harness rooms, and
the gallery of the riding-house.

The latter was erected first. It is in brick, with a
circular-ribbed wooden roof, on the plan introduced
by Phil. de l'Orme, whose well-known book was
published in Paris in 1567. He introduced a construction for roofing that is both cheap and efficient,
and one that while plenty of light and ventilation can
be obtained, gives the largest space in the interior of
the room.

The walls of the riding-house were two bricks thick,
laid English bond. As the foundation rested on the
stone no concrete was used, but the rock, which was
on a steep incline, was levelled in step-like fashion, to
receive the walls. Buttresses were placed where the
circular ribs of the roof were situate; two lines of
iron-hoop bond, 1 in. by $\frac{1}{16}$ in., tarred and sanded,

were laid in all the walls, piers, and buttresses; there
were 13 courses 2 lines in side walls, 16 courses 2 lines
in gable walls, and 7 courses 2 lines in buttresses.
The walls were covered with brick copings formed of
two courses of moulded bricks cut to lengths and
mitred, and set and jointed in cement to gable ends:
the flaunches of the angle buttress were formed with
stocks, the upper courses set and pointed in cement,
and the angles of parapets cut and mitred to the
same.

Ragstone moulded corbels were placed over the
piers inside the building, from these the circular ribs
sprung and into which they were stubbed. The roof
was thus described in the specification :—The roof will
be formed of circular ribs placed two and two, each
$7\frac{1}{2}$ inches apart, screwed and bolted together, each
single rib to be in three thicknesses, the inner one of
oak and to consist of twenty-six pieces of $1\frac{1}{4}$ inch
deal and ten of $1\frac{1}{4}$ oak, each separate piece 1 foot in
width, and to be as long as the scantling of the
timber will allow, the ribs to be wrought and glued
together, and at each joint to have two hard nails or
$\frac{3}{4}$ inch screws having a good thread; the top and
bottom edges of rib cut fair for linings, the side finished
for paint. Cross pieces, $7\frac{1}{2}$ by $2\frac{1}{2}$ inches, twelve to
each pair of ribs, the whole to be bolted together.
To prevent the ribs from being at an unequal distance,

the two outer ribs to be sunk half-an-inch at the places where the purlins notch in them.

The purlins, eight in number, to run the whole length of roof, notching in the rib arches. The purlins to be placed in pairs and to have small cross struts either notched into them or securely nailed to prevent them from buckling or twisting.

All the horizontal timbers of roof, such as the purlins, poll plate, sill, and heads of skylight, to run 9 inches in end walls, and to be cogged on template. Each purlin, if not in one piece, to be properly scarfed. An oak wall-plate, 9 in. by 6 in., was laid the whole length and width of the building, running 6 in. in the wall at angles, where it was pinned and lapped. The plate in the arch over the entrance formed the upper part of the railing in the gallery.

This plate served as the abutment for twenty-four oak braces or struts, each 7 in. by 4 in., placed in the lower portions of the roof on each side, each strut to be stub-tenoned either into purlin or cross piece between rib, and the whole to be securely fixed.

The framing to support curb or sill of skylights to be in one piece, to run over the wood arches, and to be securely fixed to purlin.

Each pair of circular ribs moneyed out 22l. 4s. 6d. The more modern French style of forming this kind of roof would have been by bent ribs composed of three ten-inch planks, 12 inches by 3, cut true at the saw-mill, jointed with glue, planed all round, chamfered to edges, with 20 half-inch bolts. These would have cost only 13*l*. 16*s*. 8*d*. each, but they would have caused considerable lateral pressure against the side walls.

The roof of the riding-house is correctly shown in the small view, p. 389, which serves also to show the section. Fig. 1 of the accompanying cut shows one

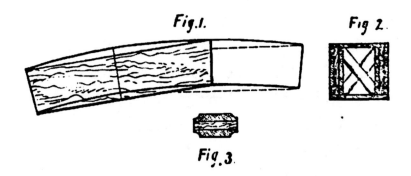

Fig. 1.   Fig 2.

Fig. 3.

of the circular ribs, fig. 2 the section of the pair joined together, and fig. 3 the section of the more modern French method of bent ribs. A roof in this latter construction was put up by Mr. Charles Fowler, architect, at the sale-room, St. Paul's Churchyard. The circular ribs of the roof were formed in three thicknesses of 1¼ deal, footed into iron sockets or corbels let into stone templates. As a precaution until the perfect set and settlement of the work, three of the roof-frames had iron tie-rods, which were removed when all fear of lateral thrust was over. A print of the room was given in the *Builder*.

The first construction described could be much improved, strengthened, and lightened by introducing an iron bar in lieu of the oak rib; and this has been done in several instances, resulting in the roofs standing well.

The chief portion of the bricks used in the construction of the riding-house were provided from the estate, and were carted on the ground for the use of the builder. His account came to 920*l*.

The elevation of the stable shows the entrance to the coachhouse in the centre, between coupled columns. These were in iron, of slightly Elizabethan character as to style. Two gabled buildings are on each side, one forming the entrance to the riding-house, the whole flanked by two towers; that on the left contained the staircase leading to the gallery of the riding-house seen in the view, the other is the prospect tower, overlooking the park. These buildings were commenced and finished in 1848. The builder had to take down the old coachhouse and stabling which stood upon the site, and was permitted to use the old materials as far as they would go; one roof was re-used. The cost of the new building was 1107*l*. The whole length was 95 ft. One of its principal features was the prospect tower, a view of which and

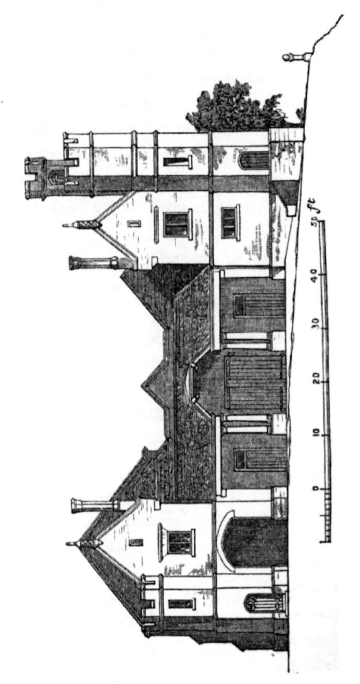

Elevation of stable.

a representation of the back front is on p. 398; this was 60 ft. in height above the foundations.

An iron staircase led up to the small tower, which had a staircase leading to the roof or lead flat, upon which was a seat and flagstaff. The battlements of

Cap of iron column.

this small tower and its doorway were constructed of ragstone. This turret was corbelled out from the building as seen in the view; its plan and that of the corbelling is given on p. 399. The corbels were two bricks in height, each course; the arch is covered with

Perspective view of prospect tower.

a stone landing upon which the small turret stands. It has a lightning conductor. This, the three iron staircases, and the columns, cost 200*l*., which, however,

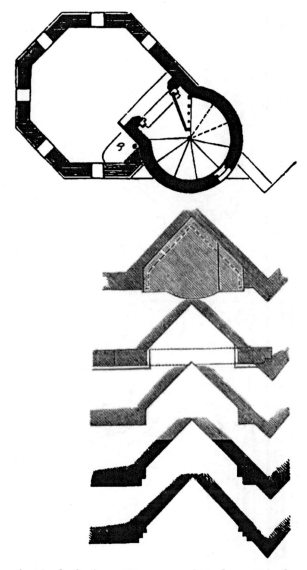

was included in the previously stated amount of 1107*l*.

It was proposed to give the terrace-walk an ornamental stone. The balustrading and one of the bays of this balustrading are illustrated below.

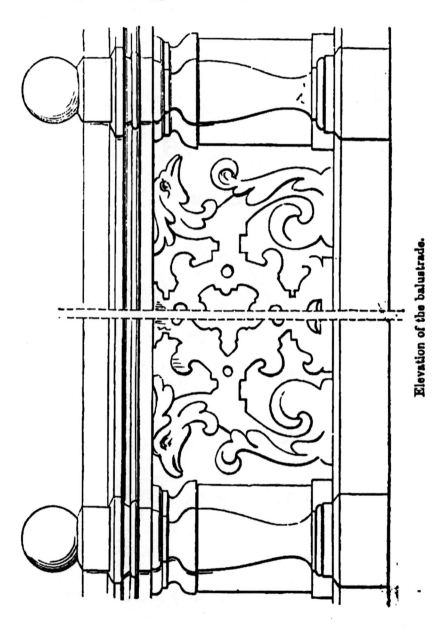

Elevation of the balustrade.

A BACHELOR'S HOUSE.

THIS building was intended to have been erected on an estate in the neighbourhood of London, for the solicitor acting for the lessee, a builder who was erecting numerous first-class houses upon the property, and who required his solicitor to be often with him. The gentleman was a bachelor, and this was, for a time, to have been his private town dwelling. It was only to consist of a basement and ground floor, but the walls were to be made sufficiently thick to enable the structure to be carried upwards when the estate was fully covered, and the house would be required for a family.

The plan was arranged after the legal gentleman's own directions: *a* is the small entrance hall, leading to the inner hall, from which the living room *b*, and the picture gallery *f*, are gained; the gallery contained a choice collection of cabinet pictures, hunting subjects by a celebrated painter; *c* is a small bedroom, which could be enclosed or shut off from the living room by a lifting-screen, worked somewhat similar to a lifting shutter. The screen was to be covered on the side next the living room with paintings; *d* is the bath

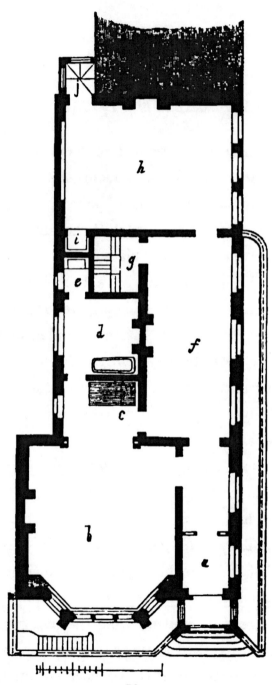

Plan.

room, *e* the closet, *h* is the dining-room with its lift, *i*, from the pantry in the basement; *j* was a small iron staircase leading down to the stable, where some valuable hunters were to be kept. Under the dining-room was the coachhouse; no rooms were over the stabling. The servants' entrance was in the area. The exterior of the building had a plain Gothic Tudor front.

The vignette shows a corbel in the French cut-wood style.

THE FIREPLACE.

FLUE CONSTRUCTION AND SMOKE PREVENTION.

AN especial love for home comfort has always been an English characteristic. It has formed a species of national taste and pride even among our working classes. The constant changes of our climate are injurious to every class; the chief point of attraction in the English dwellings, during winter's wet, cold, and fog, is centred in the fireplace. This has long been deemed the favoured spot where

> " Social mirth
> Exults and glows before the blazing hearth."

The fireplace suits our climate; it is cheerful and attractive, but it gives its heat only by radiation. We are warmed on one side and chilled on the other, but neither the warmth nor the chill is too great to bear, and the occupant of the room can move into any temperature that suits him. In more northern climates the use of the fireplace would not be tolerated; there the cold is so excessive that an equal warmth must be diffused throughout the apartments, and flues in hollow walls, and closed stoves either in iron or brick, are in the ascendant, as already mentioned in an earlier part of this work. But such means, by which the air is heated, and not merely warmed—and there is a great difference between warmed air and heated—would not be tolerated here. A puff of air from a closed stove caused by a back draught is not pleasant, and is very different from the honest puff of smoke from an English fireplace, that gives, as a natural product of combustion, carbonic acid gas. But not one of these stoves, nor those that are called " smoke-consuming stoves," make a good companionable fire—and this is not liked.

The common open fireplace has held its own, and will continue to hold its own, against the best-contrived stove that can be introduced in lieu of it. But it still remains to find such a construction as will remedy its serious defects. These are chiefly such as pertain to the flue; it is not to the stove that these belong, for that, thanks to our excellent makers, is quite perfect.

In our sluggish winter atmosphere the smoke leaves the open flue with tolerable certainty unless the flue is foul with soot; but when high winds prevail and the atmosphere is anything but sluggish, it teaches us the faults of the open flue, and volumes of smoke descend into our apartments. There are few occurrences in domestic life more vexatious and annoying than this; the numerous unsightly appendages in the form of cowls, turncaps, and windguards which appear alike on our houses, churches, and palaces, whilst they exhibit the ingenuity of our builders and workmen in remedying the trouble of smoky chimneys, demonstrate also the frequency of the misfortune.

When flues are carefully constructed, with the best modern improvements, and a due supply of air is admitted into the stove, a smoky chimney is an exception; still the flue forms only a simple open funnel for the passage of the smoke, and failures will inevitably often happen. A construction on a good principle should render these defects as trifling as possible. In our best houses—those constructed within the last twenty or thirty years—two kinds of the common brick flue are mostly in use. One is of the old-fashioned kind, having a section of 14 by 9 in., which was made originally of that size for the accommodation of the poor sweeping-boys. This is now retained only for the kitchen fire, which makes a large quantity of smoke, and for the rest of the fireplaces the flue known as "Cubitt's" flue is employed, which has a diameter each way of 9 in. The author prefers the small flue, and always uses it in the buildings he has constructed. There are many persons who still maintain that the old-fashioned flue is the correct one, and it is still very generally used. There is an old saying about the proof of the pudding. In Belgrave-square, all the houses first designed and erected have the old-fashioned flue, and there are scarcely a dozen of the old chimney-pots left; all have been changed for tall-boys and other similar contrivances; one house has about 24 in one stack. No. 49, built by Cubitt about 35 years ago, and having the descending or sweeping flue, has the stacks exactly as at first constructed, with the exception only of a little doctoring to the kitchen flue. In the house opposite, No. 48, one of the first, the external stack alone, next the street, has no less than 17 tall-boys, two of which appear to be broken off. On the opposite side of the Square, in Chesham-place, is No. 38, built by Cubitt about 30 years; it has all the original stacks untouched.

The Cubitt flue can be recognised by the small peculiar cap on the chimney-pot, and several of these stacks remain in their original state. In Eaton-place and Eccleston-square, where this flue is used, the roofs tell the same story. In the first buildings erected by the author he used the large flue, and he now finds several specimens of chimney-doctoring on the roofs. In some large houses he lately erected at Queen's Gate, in which the sweeping flue is used, there are several houses together without any disfigurement at all on the roof. He considers that the appearance of a tall-boy on one of them would be rather a proof that there was something wrong about the servants' management of the fires, than an error in the construction of his flues.

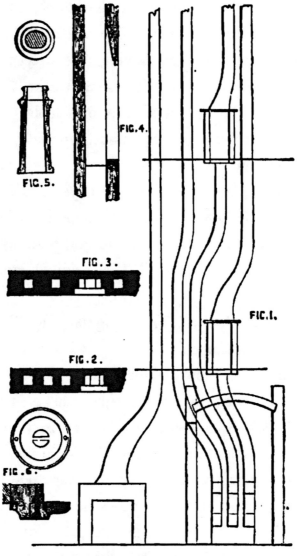

FIG.4.

FIC.5.

FIC.3.

FIC.I.

FIG.2.

FIC.6.

Flue construction.

A representation of this flue, and the manner of introducing it into a building, is here given.　Fig. 1

represents a portion of the chimney-flue construction of a first-rate house; the lower chimney opening is in the basement, and above it are two others, one on the ground floor, and one on the first floor. It will be seen that there are three flues descending or taken down to the basement. The third flue belongs to the room on the second floor. The wall is two bricks thick, the flue 9 in. in diameter, and contained within the wall with no chimney-breast projecting. Fig. 2 is a plan of the flues on the ground floor, and fig. 3 of those on the first floor. Fig. 4 is a section of the fireplace opening; this is 3 ft. in height from the floor-line, the brickwork at top is splayed, and supported by an iron bar; these openings are always filled up with 4½ straight joint work, to be taken out when the mantelpiece is fixed. Fig. 5 is the chimney-pot and its cap, the latter opening at top 7 in. by 9 in. only; fig. 6 shows one of the sweeping doors, in which there are two to each descending flue. The latter three figures are twice the scale of the former. A plan and section of the chimney complete, with its marble mantel and stove, is given in figs. 7 and 8. The flue passes completely down at the back of the stove, the front is closed by an iron plate to a height of 2 ft. On this is fixed the moveable door or register, shut fully or partly over the flue when the stove is in use, and closed over the stove when the flue has to be

swept.   The arrows show the mode of admission of
air to the front of the fire; it is brought through the

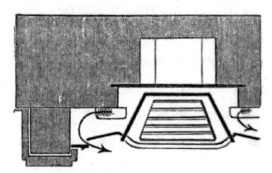

Fig. 7.—Plan of stove.

floor and two openings in the back hearth from the
outside of the house.   This is generally kept concealed,

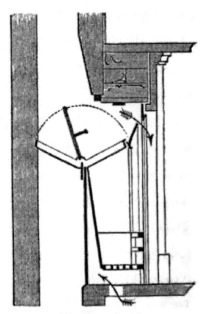

Fig. 8.—Section.

and in order to ensure a supply of air to the stove the
room should be kept completely closed.

To cause as full and perfect a combustion of the fuel as possible, a draught or current of the external air should be always admitted to the stove, and it could easily be placed under open management, so as to admit either a large or small supply of air, as required. Numerous patent processes to effect this are in use, but the most effective way of doing it is that shown in figs. 7 and 8 : it is too simple for a patent.

Fig. 9 shows a method of admitting air above the architrave of the entrance door of the room. The opening is made about 2 ft. in length; this, after a little time, becomes marked by the blacklets coming in from the passage. The sweeping flue when the fire is lighted becomes very hot; the smoke ascends speedily and soon leaves it. The flue requires the

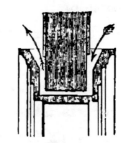

Fig. 9.

stove to be formed expressly for it. Mr. Cubitt made the stoves only for his own houses, and the author had some difficulty at Queen's Gate, in procuring stoves of the right pattern, for manufacturers prefer their own shop patterns, and some of these would have covered up half the descending flue. Those he used were supplied by Messrs. Feetham of Clifford-street, who are well acquainted with the use of the flue and stove. The flue is considered an excellent one; it is a builder's flue, constructed solely of brick, and is certainly the best of the brick flues. The same attention was paid to it as was given to every part of Mr. Cubitt's buildings. It may be asked, " Are there no other kinds of flues constructed of superior materials?" Yes, certainly there are; particular attention has often been paid to the flue. There is Hiort's circular flue, formed in each course of four wedge-formed bricks. Mr. Hiort held a very important position; he was Treasurer of the office of Works at Whitehall, and his flue was extensively used in some of the Government buildings and the houses in Carlton Gardens. It did not bond well with the brickwork, so we have Mr. Moon's improvement upon it. This was considered not sufficient, and another patent was taken out in 1844 by Messrs. Clark and Reed for its further improvement. The flue was an excellent one, but on Mr. Hiort's retirement from the Government Board, it went out of use.

There is Seth Smith's metallic chimney lining, which makes an excellent flue; the lining is a pipe of from 5 to 10 in. in diameter, built in the brickwork. About 150 of these flues are at the Pantechnicon. Mr. Smith announced his determination of never building any house above the value of 30*l*. per annum, without using them. They could be introduced, to form perfect linings to chimneys in buildings already erected, and allow the stack to be reduced in height, without having the unsightly appearance of contractions made above them. The drawback to the use of these tubes by builders was the price. Without any royalty, the 9 in. tube cost 3*s.* 4*d.* per ft. run, the curved tubes 4*s.* 3*d.*, the starting tube 3*s.* 8*d.* The tubes were of the exact form of drain pipes, and they were cheaper, and as effectual.

If Mr. Smith's metal tubes had been introduced into a large brick flue, they would have rendered the latter an efficient shaft for ventilating every room in its upward course, openings being made for the purpose at the upper part of the rooms. This mode of ventilation was applied to hospitals on a large scale by the late Mr. Jacob Perkins several years ago, with perfect success.

Denley's flue, introduced in 1843, is believed to have been the precursor of that used by the late Mr. Thos. Cubitt at Belgravia and Pimlico, and there is a great resemblance between the two; but Mr. Denley's flue has nothing like the simplicity nor ease of construction of Mr. Cubitt's. The downward flues were merged into one at the basement, and all the soot and cinders were collected or thrown down into a fire-proof box, which must have stood out in the lower rooms, from which they had to be removed. The flues were swept from the roof, the register doors of the stoves being closed, and there was no provision for sweeping the flues between the basement and the stoves. Joined to his system for sweeping, was one of air flues which brought a current of air direct from the exterior of the house to each fireplace.

We have several flue systems which have ventilating flues in connexion with them. Boyd's flue forms the wythes, or half-brick spaces between the flues, of iron plates, and the open spaces thus gained make ventilating passages. Mr. Doulton's combined smoke and air flues are manufactured in terra-cotta, in three sizes; the air flues follow the line of the smoke flue, the passages being quite distinct, as in Mr. Boyd's. The heat from the smoke-flue causes a current in the air-flue which carries off the vitiated air admitted by openings near the ceiling. The common drain pipes and the glazed fire-clay pipes make good flues; the use of these pipe-flues has greatly increased during the last few years; they improve the draught, and clean easily. Flues for ventilation from rooms should, like Arnott's ventilator, enter into the smoke or a hot ventilating flue. Arnott's ventilator requires careful adjustment, to be balanced in such a way that it should stand closed on a calm day.

The superior patented flues, as they are of considerable cost, and take extra time in construction, are only used in the better class of buildings, or in those erected under the express direction of the owner.

In speculative buildings they are never used. The time required for their construction beyond that of the common brick flue, being regarded by the builder as so much money lost.

The great desideratum in a flue is to make it pass off its smoke quickly, and this the small size flue effects more certainly than the larger one, as it warms sooner and keeps its heat longer.

An enthusiastic admirer of the descending or sweeping flue once told the author that with a good fire in the grate, if a kettle of water could be placed on the top of the chimney-cap the water would soon boil, even if the flue were fifty feet high. The flues constructed of metallic or earthenware casings retain also the heat longer, and keep hotter. It may be imagined that with these flues, and the large quantity of gas lamps in the streets, why the temperature of London should be always some degrees higher than that of the country. In winter snow may be seen in the suburban fields, but none is found in town.

Architects have often been blamed for not inventing a good system of flue-construction, not only for the prevention of smoke in our dwellings, but for the hindrance of its presence in the atmosphere. Several, and most excellent attempts, have been made for the former, but very few for the latter, which is one of far greater difficulty. Yet this is one that admits of a cure, great as the evil is. The chimney flue might be so improved as to effect a more certain and larger ventilation of our houses, without any addition of ventilation flues. The introduction of the French Mansard roof with us, one from a country where coal fires are not in use, renders it almost imperative for the chimneys belonging to such buildings to have a different construction, for chimneys when placed against a building or roof that overtops them, are sure, as they are at present made, to become smoky : the wind returning owing to the high construction, and descending in the flues. The following few designs are offered to cure these various evils.

Accepting as a fact that tall-boys, and the other iron and zinc constructions, are useful appendages, there can be no reason why they should be so used as to disfigure our buildings. Some of the finest specimens of architectnre in the Metropolis serve only as pedestals to an ugly collection of cowls.

The author proposes to form the upper part of the flues in a building, for a length of about 15 to 20 feet, entirely of iron or other tubing, in square, round, or oblong sections, of a less diameter than the brick flues to which they are attached. This tubing is gathered up in groups, and carried out at an angle of 45° towards a centre stack : the tubes in direct contact with each other, having no brick wyths, except one or two to strengthen the stack.

It is obvious that if only one of the flues be in use, it would moderately warm those next to it; and if the whole of the flues of a building were constructed on this plan, and two or three were in use, such a power would be obtained as would effectually ventilate every room; the action would be continuous and imperceptible, and a fire could be lighted in any one without the risk of return smoke from a cold or damp flue.

Thus the heat now wasted in the atmosphere by the action of the common flue, would be partly retained and turned to use, and the draught of the flue very much improved.

This tubing could be readily introduced into either old or new buildings, as the introduction does not involve taking down more than twelve feet of the brickwork, measuring from the top of the coping. The tubes could never become sufficiently heated to be dangerous, and less brickwork would be required.

They might be made either of zinc or earthenware; cast-iron would be objectionable on account of its weight. It will be seen that they admit a better mode of sweeping than that now practised, and they could easily have some kind of capping to prevent down-draughts.

These " stack flues" should commence from the attic
or upper story of a building, at about six feet from
the floor; sweeping doors should be placed beneath
them, so as to give the sweep command of the flue
beneath as well as above.

Each flue should be composed of three separate
forms of tubing, by which the various directions and
turns necessary for the construction might be obtained.

Fig. 10 gives the representation of the three forms;
1, is the first; this is placed directly over the brick

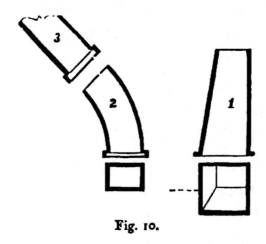

Fig. 10.

flue, and gathers it up to a size having an internal
dimension of $6+4\frac{1}{2}$. It is 21 inches in height.   2,
the second piece, is on a curve; the top and bottom
lines, if carried on, would form an angle of 45°; it is
about 18 inches in height, and internal size $6+4\frac{1}{2}$.
The third, 3, is a straight piece, internal size $6+4\frac{1}{2}$,

the lengths various. Fig. 11 gives a plan of four
flues and an elevation of the commencement of two.
The sweeping doors are shown below. The flue without a door is the ventilating flue for the basement.
The ease with which this tubing can be grouped is
shown in fig. 12. The stack consists of five flues;
the tube, 2, connects them together below, and

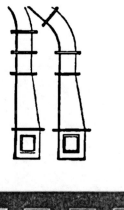

Fig. 11.

separates them above. The stack above the roof is
4 feet 9 inches in length.

Fig. 13 shows, in the upper plan, how the flue wall
could be reduced in thickness, made a brick and a
half only, with a two-brick block at each end; it contains coupled and tripled sets of tubes.

The middle plan shows nine flues grouped together,
the centre being that belonging to the kitchen. The

last plan shows a group of six in a two-and-a-half-brick wall; by the side of this are two flues of the common construction, 14 inches by 9, made of this

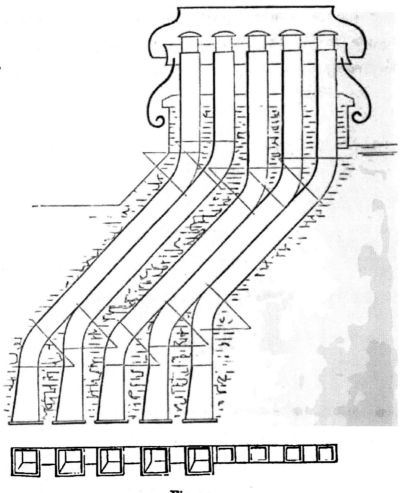

Fig. 12.

size to enable a boy to get up to the top and place his head out of the chimney-pot.

The tube 1, fig. 12, can have its position reversed,

as shown in fig. 14; six flues can thus be grouped together, as shown in the third plan, fig. 13. The elevation of this stack is given in fig. 15.

Fig. 13.

For a covering to these tubes figs. 16 to 20 show ornamental pots and their sections. The only merit

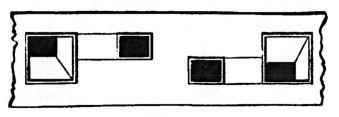

Fig. 14.

in these may be that they are of a more ornamental character than any that have ever been introduced;

they are formed of zinc, supported by a stout dwarf
iron railing.   The intention is to permit the smoke
to escape in any direction, either upwards, sideways,
or downwards, sheltering it as far as possible from any
action of the wind, and rendering of little consequence
whether the stack is high, low, unsheltered or other-

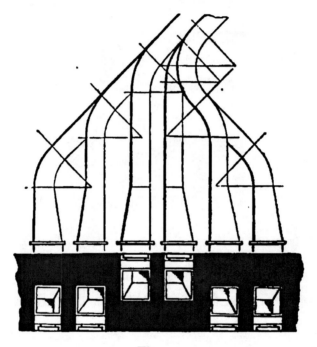

Fig. 15.

wise.   If any sudden gust of wind take place and the
smoke be driven back, the capping provides larger
outlets for its escape than the small aperture of the
flue itself; in other words, it is easier for the smoke
to pass in any direction rather than return down the
flue.

The stack flues are only, in fact, tall-boys boxed up and not put out in the cold, and it is presumed they would be sufficiently powerful, from their warmth, to ensure a good passing off of the smoke, and secure ventilation to the building.

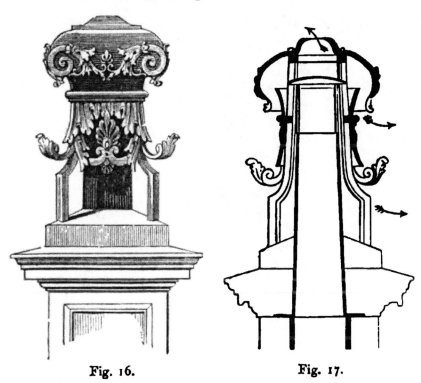

Fig. 16.   Fig. 17.

A forced ventilation to our dwellings, in ever so slight a degree, is a matter of importance. By the proper construction of these proposed stack flues it is presumed that any amount of ventilating power, self-acting and continuous, could be obtained. Their introduction alone would be beneficial; combined with the flue pedestal, to be described, the tubes could be led into one general upward shaft; by either plan we should have some command over the smoke, while the roofs of our buildings might be made ornamental and picturesque. It would be a treatment of bituminous coal alike artistic and novel, surprising to foreigners and creditable to ourselves.

Fig. 18.

It remains to show how the open character of the flue could be taken away (this forms its chief evil), and how a chimney-stack may be formed without chimney-pots. The late Lord Palmerston, when Home Secretary, proposed the abolition of chimney-stacks, and the use of only one chimney-stalk for each separate dwelling. In 1856, a commission was appointed to

inquire into the best modes of warming and ventilating the apartments of dwelling-houses and barracks.
Their report, given to the General Board of Health,
was published in 1857, and it afforded a section
illustrating " the principle on which it was proposed
to construct dwelling-houses." There was only to be

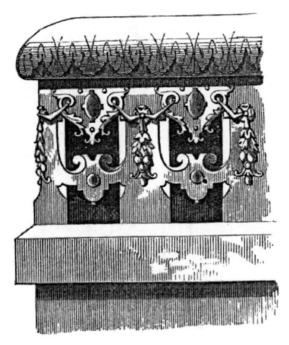

Fig. 19.

one flue, and this of metal 10 inches in diameter,
enclosed in a large brick flue, which was to serve for
ventilation. In the metal flue were to be inserted the
flues of the several fireplaces; these were placed back
to back, and if the register doors of the stoves were
open, a person in one room might both see and con-

verse with another in the next; the music of a pianoforte in one room could be heard in them all; this
construction was taken up through four stories, there
being eight fireplaces. For one fireplace alone it
would have been perfect, but the smoke from the two
kitchen fires would have been sufficient to have choked

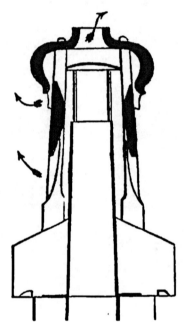

Fig. 20.

the flue and caused the smoke to enter into the whole
of the eight rooms.

The chimney-stack might possibly be lowered, and
it certainly could be constructed without chimney-
pots, but each separate flue must have its own outlet.
A design for this, one that should take away the open

character of the flue, and fit the stack, possibly for the Mansard roof, is here given.

In fig. 21, *a a* are the flues, delivering their smoke into a large ventilating flue, *b*. The warm smoke would induce a current of air to enter at *c*: any current will have a tendency to draw another with it, so that the smoke leaving the flues *c c* would be taken out at *d* by the current of air at *c*.

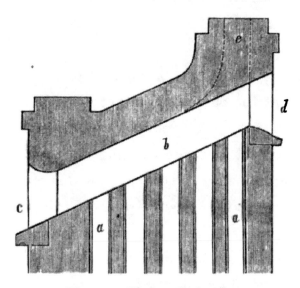

Fig. 21.—The ventilating flue.

This is the principle upon which all the best ventilating chimney-pots, tall-boys, and cowls are made, and it is a very sure one. The jet of steam in the funnel of the locomotive, drawing the smoke from the fire, and creating a draught, is adopted on the same principle.

In scientific language, the established law both of pneumatics and hydraulics is that when two currents of fluid matter passing in the same direction, but in separate channels, arrive at any point of confluence, the stronger current draws the other along in its course, and with a considerable portion of its own velocity. Thus the force of the wind, which checks in other instances the action of a chimney-draught, is made to produce a stronger draught, exactly in proportion to the violence with which it blows.

Returning to fig. 21, a current of air, instead of coming in at the opening *c*, might come in at *d*. It would then have a tendency to blow down the flues *a a* : to prevent this, the opening *d* could be closed, and an upright stalk placed at *e*,—this should have a downward shaft, a place for soot, and a sweeping door.

There is still another mode of treatment ; fig. 22 represents the flues grouped, each with a separate ventilating flue, the smoke delivered being at the side of each.

The stack might be covered with zinc in the ornamental style with which that metal is now treated.

It is probable that if a stack on this principle was placed parallel to the side of one of these Mansard roofs, it would be secure from the ill-effects of any wind returning against it. The author will not vouch for its success, but it is offered here to the attention of architects and builders as an experiment worthy of trial.

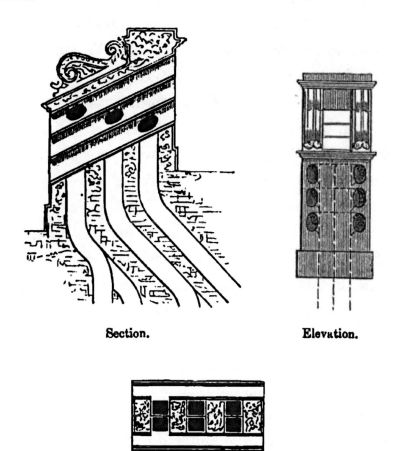

Section.   Elevation.

Fig. 22—Plan.

It has been affirmed that the smoke of towns, however disagreeable it may be to the inhabitants, neutralizes the poisonous effect of the gases caused by sewers, &c. If it was possible wholly to remove

carbon evolved by smoke, our towns would almost
be uninhabitable, and they represent that any scheme
for getting rid of smoke must be combined with one
for getting rid of the exhalations from sewers at the
same time. If the two evils were brought together,
they would neutralize each other, and both could then
be got rid of at one operation. The best scheme for
this is a matter of important consideration, but few
have been proposed.

It may be asked, what has a work on Picturesque
Architecture to do with either smoke or sewer gases?
The author in reply considers that buildings never will
look picturesque while they are covered with great
patches of soot. An eminent sculptor once affirmed
that the statues of London were improved by their soot
covering, because it made them stand boldly out
against the sky. But those beautiful decorated smoke
towers which stand on the roof of the Houses of
Parliament, and which are as black as Erebus, look
anything but pleasing, standing amidst the whiter
front of the rest of the building. Besides, tall-boys
are beginning to make their appearance on the roof
under the Victoria tower, and these certainly form no
part of the architecture, but appear monstrously ugly;
consequently smoke and its abolition are clearly questions to be considered in relation to Picturesque
Architecture.

A plan for removing smoke from the atmosphere of towns, and at the same time ventilating buildings and sewers, was proposed in 1849 by Mr. Flockton, surveyor to the town trustees of Sheffield,* a town as much begrimed with sooty smoke, only in a smaller way, as the Metropolis.

The proposal was, that under the footpaths along the side of every street and lane, flues should be constructed of sufficient capacity to carry off all the smoke and other atmospheric impurities, these flues all converging, upon a general plan, to tall shafts or chimneys at some distance from the town, and supplied with furnaces. These, when the fires were once ignited, would give a fire produced by the combustion of the inflammable gases accompanying the smoke, and which would burn spontaneously in a similar manner to the combustion of foul air from old shafts connected with coal mines. The combustion might be assisted by jets of coal gas, in a fire of coke.

In very large towns it would be necessary, Mr. Flockton added, to divide the whole into districts, and to erect towers in the centre of each, to which all the flues should converge. He published a plate, showing

---

* " Plan for Purifying the Atmosphere of Towns." (Hamilton, Adams, & Co.)

two large dwelling-houses, with a street between, the common sewer in the middle of the carriage way, and the smoke flues on each side under the footpaths, also showing the connexion between the sewer and flue. The alteration proposed to houses already erected consisted in converting ascending into descending flues; turning the smoke from the chimney-top into the latter, and from thence into the street flue. This operation would have necessitated the pulling down and rebuilding of the flue walls. The street smoke flues, in order to carry off the smoke from a few thousand chimneys, would require to have been made of a size even larger than the sewer itself. Provision must have been made for clearing out the soot, for the smoke would have been cooled and the soot would accumulate in large quantities in them.

The same scheme, with similar constructions, was proposed by a foreign gentleman, who took out a patent for it in 1850 (No. 13,061). His plan was a very grand one; he did not propose alterations in existing buildings, but pulled them down and gave designs for a new city.

A more practical plan was proposed about 1851 by Mr. Devey, a surveyor of Furnival's Inn. A model of his invention was in the Great Exhibition of 1851, and it is described and an engraving given of it in the illustrated volumes published by the Royal Exhibi-

tion Commissioners at the close of the Exhibition.
The model is now in the Museum at South Kensington.
Mr. Devey's plan was to make only one descending flue
to each building, to which the flues at the top could
be either connected or not, at pleasure ; the descending flue was carried to the sewer in the middle of the
street, and the action of this was to be assisted by the
heat of the kitchen fire. He says, " The smoke would
be drawn down by the current produced by exhaustion
in the sewer, the action being assisted by the kitchen
fire." Mr. Devey did not propose to have furnace
shafts, but depended entirely upon the sewer acting as
an exhaust.

In this scheme the objections were, that one
descending flue was not sufficient to carry off the
smoke from several chimneys, and the sewer certainly
would not act as an exhaust without its being connected with upright furnaces. Our sewers generally
have ventilating openings which permit their odours to
ascend into our streets. Soot would no doubt neutralize these odours—this, a paper in a late *Quarterly
Review* (April 1866) admits. First, speaking of the
sewer gases, the reviewer says : " These offensive gases
have often engendered formidable diseases, and have,
in several instances of late, been clearly shown to have
caused the outbreak both of typhoid fever and cholera."
Of this the author has had proof during the outbreak

of cholera in London in 1849. He was superintending the construction of a mass of buildings in one of the worst dwelling districts in London. This builder, who had just finished the erection of Harrington House, a description of which is given in this volume, died the first night of the outbreak in the greatest agony; he was a strong robust man; from one to three deaths took place in every house in the locality; a black flag was put up in the streets, and the foul fiend reigned for a while supreme. A large mass of the worst buildings have been cleared away, and model lodging-houses erected, but a considerable portion of the rotten old structures remain, the sewers are untouched, and the visitation of the cholera forgotten.

The *Quarterly Review* says there is no reason why ordinary sewers should not be made to serve the double purpose of carrying off smoke and sewage at the same time, provided they were connected here and there with high shafts rendered powerfully expansive by furnaces; and adds, " sewage would be improved for agricultural purposes by admixture with soot, which is an excellent manure, and the noxious qualities of the sewer gases would be destroyed." Whether soot would increase the value of sewage or decrease it, is a question for chemists to decide; a generally increasing opinion is, that our method of using sewage by liquefaction and sending it away, is a mistake, and renders it quite worthless, and that the system of dry earth-closets is more conformable to Nature's laws.

The subject was taken up in 1857 by Mr. Peter Spence, of Manchester, a large alum manufacturer.* This gentleman states that the " blacks," the horror of the Londoner, are guiltless of any deleterious effect to human health, as carbon is one of the most anti-putrescent of bodies, and while floating in the atmosphere over everything, arrest and destroy noxious and miasmatic vapours. Perfect freedom from smoke would, if accomplished, only increase the evil arising from the purely gaseous results of combustion. He proposed a system of *atmospheric* or *gaseous sewage,* and the complete removal of all their gases to a safe distance from our towns. He would combine this gaseous sewage in such a form with town drainage as would bring all the liquid sewage into contact with the gases from our furnaces and house fires, the liquid sewage being kept from all surface drainage. The same liquid and fœtid mass of sewage he would con-centrate in an innoxious form, to be converted, in a convenient place, where it might with perfect safety be manufactured into manure more valuable than the richest guano.

---

* " Coke, Smoke, and Sewage." (Cave and Sever, Manchester).

For effecting this all the gases from our coal combustion would have to be conveyed along the same tunnel with the sewage to centralizing conduits converging to a point, where an immense chimney, 600 ft. high, should be erected, to discharge these gases into the atmosphere, the ascensive power being obtained either from the retained heat of the gases, which would probably be found quite sufficient, or if not, artificial heat could then be applied to effect the object. The chimney should be of the internal diameter of 100 ft. at the top, and 140 ft. external diameter at the bottom. This would take the smoke from 500 chimneys and every particle of foul emanation from the sewer, and every leak or opening to the upward air from these sewers would not then emit foul gases, but draw in fresh air with a pressure or suction of three and a half pounds per foot, and with a velocity of 40 feet per second. This gentleman says : " It is idle to talk of trapping, and thus confining gases evolved under ground ; exit they must and will have, and when you imagine you have secured them in one place, you will find them pouring out in another." He makes this plain by an illustration. He took an old-fashioned detached house; after entering into possession he found frequently very disagreeable smells, especially after rain, a change of wind, or a fall of the barometer ; it may be remarked here that

it was not necessary to take an old-fashioned house to
find out this ; in more modern-built houses in London,
after a fall in the barometer or rain, such a thing
repeatedly occurring.   Mr. Spence, to cure the evil in
his old mansion, exhausted all the remedies which the
philosophy of London schemes acknowledges ; he
trapped all the exits from the sewer with the most
approved patent girds ; all slopstone pipes were cut
and water-luted.   But this was of no use, the smell
came through the very walls and floors, and one bedroom on the first floor, which showed no connexion
with the sewer, was quite uninhabitable.   He adopted
a plan which succeeded : a branch from the main
sewer was brought right under the kitchen grate, from
that a pipe of cast iron, four inches in diameter, was
carried up through the brickwork, and the open top
projected into the chimney a yard and a half behind
the kitchen fire, above the fire.   When this fire was
again lighted, in a few hours the house was perfectly
sweet, and the distant bedroom, uninhabitable before,
has been slept in ever since.   When this nuisance
occurs in a London house the only remedy is to open
the doors and windows to get rid of it, as we are not
allowed to meddle with the sewers.   Disagreeable
effluvia in dwellings often occur, and baffle every
endeavour to trace from where they proceed ; in
every case it is from choked-up drains or the sewer,

and the decomposition of animal and vegetable matter therein retained.

As for Mr. Spence's scheme, its grandeur almost stops its execution. It is well known that in all large manufactories, and in gas works, a tall chimney serves to draw out the smoke from the numerous fires, and it forms a smoke-outlet for them all. In most of these places the fuel is used up so completely that it is only the gases of combustion that are drawn away. Mr. Spence's scheme has been successfully tried in its application to private residences, and also on a large scale to the new Assize Courts in Manchester. It was adopted by one of the architects in the competitive designs for the New Law Courts in London.

If these tall shafts and furnaces were applied in London, it may be questioned whether the smoke in cooling would not deposit the soot in the sewer, and this must be removed, if not run off by water. The flues connecting the house fires with the sewer would be partly horizontal, and these would certainly fill with soot, and no machines we have at present in use could clean out these flues from above. The operation must be performed from within the sewer, and then these flues being unsupplied with drain-eyes at their entrance to the sewer, would form so many open channels for the passage of the sewer gases into the houses. This would be the case in a very great degree where there were no fires in the stoves and their register doors were open. It would require an immense consumption of fuel in the high stalks to cause a current to prevent it, and the furnaces must be close together to lessen the cooling effects of cold currents of air from flues not in use.

As to the mere ventilation of the sewer itself, it could easily be effected by single drain pipes 6 inches in diameter, placed at intervals, from the sewer to the ash-pit of any neighbouring furnace. It would be probably to the advantage of the furnace itself, as even the tall stalks must sometimes make black smoke. A legislative enactment should require their owners to let them perform this service. It might require strong furnaces and plenty of them to effect it. A suggestion for getting rid of that "monster nuisance, London smoke" was made known in the *Builder* about 1859, by Messrs. Bruce Neil. It is thus described : "The plan consists in placing small tanks containing water over the chimney (the chimney-pots being fixed inside the tanks, and made of a spiral and bent form). The chill of the water gradually condenses the smoke, which becomes decomposed and destroyed, being precipitated at the bottom of the tank in the form of mineral tar. The water is turned on and off daily. It will be here observed that in the event of a fire in the chimney the flames cannot spread, as they are immediately quenched by the water in the tank. According to Mr. Bruce Neil's calculation, the smoke of 80 tons of coal, if collected, will yield upwards of 28 barrels of tar, of $2\frac{1}{2}$ cwt. each. He proposes that the Legislature, or the Society of Arts, should offer a premium to the person who will undertake to rid us of this monster nuisance and convert the smoke into tar, so as to make it applicable to commercial purposes. In the adoption of the above plan a slight alteration in the mode of ventilating our apartments is all that is required, he tells us.

As to the possibility of converting smoke into tar by such means as are above described, some doubts might be expressed if it could really be done; the remedy would be worse even than the disease, every household using yearly 20 tons of coal would have in that time to remove 7 barrels or $17\frac{1}{2}$ cwt. of tar from their roof. The *Builder*, in publishing this suggestion, did not give any diagram or sketch showing how the process was to be effected. Mr. Bruce Neil no doubt made one, as he speaks of the alteration required in the ventilation of our apartments; a drawing would at least have explained how the water was to collect the soot, and how it was to have access to the flue in case of its being on fire.

The suggestion of collecting soot at the chimney-top by means of water was a valuable one, and there

is no doubt it could be done to some extent, but not
by encircling the pots with cold water, which would
chill the smoke and prevent the soot from rising.   A

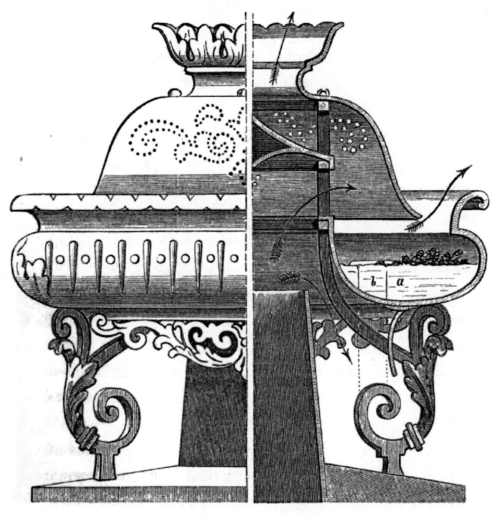

Fig. 23.— Water chimney-vase for collecting soot.
Half elevation.   Half section.

design is here given, fig. 23, to show how it could be
effected.

It will be seen that the chimney-pot or funnel has a zinc cover carried by stout ironwork surrounding it; *a* is the water, *b* the pipe to convey it away; it would be self-acting, and being washed by every shower would not be likely to get out of order. The rain-water must be looked for as to supply—to pay for high service for the roof of our houses to the water companies would not do.

Our climate is more damp than cold, and a considerable quantity of rain falls on our roofs. The zinc cover is spread out, so as to retain as large a portion as possible of the rain-fall. In winter, when there is most smoke, there is most water, with little or no evaporation. A pool of water could be thus collected, and the smoke projected over it would lose some portion of its soot, which could be floated away by the pipe into a receptacle provided for it in the back yard. The water might be sent into the drain and the soot left; or it could be sent into the drain as well.

The arrows in the diagram show the direction of the smoke, and the cover is so spread out and curved as to render it unlikely for any violent wind to flow out both water and soot into the street beneath.

Certainly coal smoke is a great nuisance: it is yearly pointed out as such by our paper the *Times*, in one, probably two, very excellently written leaders.

Even the youngest member of the press, the *Echo*, in one of the common London fogs occurring in April 1868, thus remarks : " The most sad and remarkable circumstance about the fog of yesterday was that the newspapers and people in the streets spoke of it as a ' visitation,' as a ' gigantic pall,' as if, indeed, the black darkness was something as strange and unaccountable as a fall of frogs or fishes from the sky. Of course it was nothing but our own familiar coal smoke which stopped the way of the sunlight. It is most lamentable that Londoners are becoming so used to this filthy nuisance that nothing more than a passing exclamation is uttered when it is forced down upon them in such volumes as to produce almost the darkness of midnight at midday. If ' cleanliness is next to godliness,' then the people of London must have been yesterday the most ungodly people in the world, for nothing would remain clean which was exposed to the fog of that morning. A plague of locusts would not create more terror and sense of ruin in any foreign capital, where every article of dress and furniture and house decoration, both external and internal, would have been regarded as spoiled by the loss of freshness. But London received its coat of dirt yesterday, and to-day only wonders with the remark ' how dark it was !' Will nothing move us to abate the nuisance ? Is there no hope but that distant one of the exhaustion of our coal-beds ?　Must we inhale coal-blacks, and always contemplate dirty houses and grimy furniture ?　Is it not possible by smoke sewers, or some contrivance or machinery, to relieve us of this plague." It is very possible it could be done with the greatest ease, but at some first expense ; and in some generation or other it will be written that it found London foul and left it sweet, and there will be a time when this will be appreciated ; and the man who gives the city the pure atmosphere of a small country town will receive all due honour and ac-knowledgment, that is, when he is in his grave and securely buried.

The public have so long been accustomed to be choked with smoke, and their health affected by dele-terious gases, that they look upon the proposal of any scheme to secure pure air as the hallucinations of dreamy philosophers or inexperienced Utopians.

None of our present flues can, in the very slightest degree, stop these aqueous vapours from ascending into the atmosphere, neither can they effect any puri-fication of the smoke, or retain the blacks for any useful purpose ; and it is of no use disguising the fact that any contrivance or appliance, to effect either of these most desirable objects, must consist of an additional construction to the flue, which will be attended with additional expense, and require extra attention. Therefore any such appliance, if introduced, should be effectual, and repay such additional cost to its owner, by a saving, or at least a more economical use of fuel.

The appliance to the flue the author has to recommend, he considers will not only cause an economical use of the fuel by not permitting the present waste of heat, but it will purify the smoke, and retain the blacks for any useful object to which they can be applied.

The principle of the best-constructed flue at present is to get rid of all vapour, smoke, and soot as soon as possible, without the slightest consideration for the people outside. That the smoke should not return to annoy the occupants within the house is the aim of the constructors, and to secure this, the waste of heat in the chimney, and the consequent waste of fuel, is considered of no importance, for is it not the hot smoke that carries up the soot and ventilates the apartment?

This operation of the flue could be taken advantage of. In the construction of chimney-flues in a wall they are often turned at an angle to the right or left to pass an obstruction, such as a fireplace or timber placed within or against the wall. A flue could easily be taken out of the wall and returned, and if the part so taken out was formed in cast iron with a small

cistern of water at top, it would become a warm-
water pedestal, and could moderately warm or air an
apartment in which it was placed; the author calls
this the flue pedestal, and it is represented in the
following cut.

Fig. 24.—The flue pedestal.

It is about three feet six in height, not much
higher than a small cabinet. The door could open,
and a small tap supplying warm water for domestic
use would be seen. Thus the upper rooms of a house

could be warmed or aired by the fires below in perfect safety, and the present waste of heat in the flues prevented. This would be economical, as in most cases no fires would be necessary in the upper rooms.

The flue thus brought out in iron could contain a fine spray of water, that would draw up the smoke, and take down its vapours and soot at the same time into the sewer.

Fig. 25 shows a section of the flue thus brought out. The wall is two bricks thick, the flue *a*, is 9 inches in diameter, *d* is the cast-iron flue, and another, *e*, shaped like a funnel, is placed behind it, to collect the soot and water, and pass it off through the pipe *h*. The cistern is partly within the walls and partly covering the two flues. It is not necessary that the water in the cistern should supply the spray: that might be done by a separate pipe with a tap to turn off and on as desirable; *b* is the moveable pedestal covering the whole.

The adaptation of this simple contrivance to any kind of domestic chimney-flue is not a very difficult operation. It is only necessary to take out the brickwork in front of a flue of a height of 4 to 5 feet, and then introduce the iron flue, gathering up the brickwork beneath it; the section, fig. 25, supposes the iron flues to be in an external wall; should it be required in a party wall the soot goes off at *g g*, to be conveyed

outside the building in the nearest way; doors are
provided for the purpose of sweeping; any down

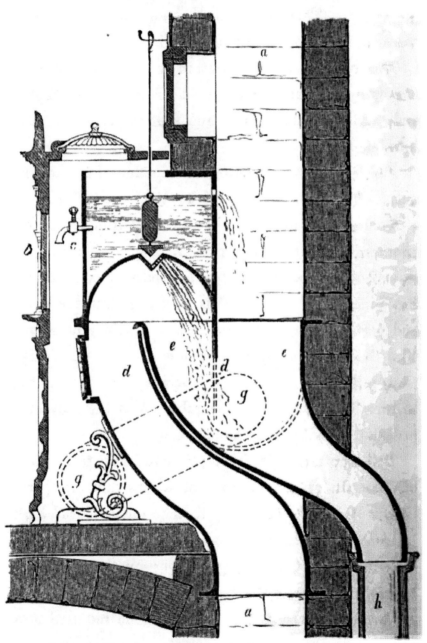

Fig. 25.—Section of the flue pedestal.

draught of air in the chimney might expend itself in the soot flue, and the smoke having passed the spray could not return. The spray of water should be equal to the whole width of the flue, and proportioned in strength to the work it has to do; the smoke from a whole group of flues might be conducted to one powerful spray, one upper flue or chimney would then suffice for the roof, while the soot and flues in any number might be formed into one before passing to the sewer.

The pipe *h*, shown in fig. 25, would not form an open communication with the sewer; it would be supplied with a flap-cover or drain-eye, like the common house drain at its extremity. This would open only when sufficient water and soot was behind it, and close when it was passed. It would not require sweeping, the water keeping it clear. It should have another kind of drain-eye to that at present in use, the lid, or flap of which is hinged from the top, the soot floating on the surface of the water, would require the flap to open from below. Fig. 26 shows the kind of drain-eye that would be required.

If it was not for the difficulty of the present form of drain-eye to our houses, the soot flue might discharge its contents into the house drains at once, below the trappings; there is probably no absolute necessity at all for drain-eyes at the termination of

G G

house drains, their use is to make precaution doubly sure, to prevent the rising of the gases from the sewer, and to keep out the rats, to prevent them, by getting through the traps, from entering the house.

Fig. 26.—Drain-eye.

Experiments were made with a shower of water in Mr. Cubitt's descending flue. It will be seen by inspecting the figures 1 to 8 that these flues could easily be formed into one, and taken into the drain; the experiment did not succeed, as none will, that brings heavy smoke in opposition to a water-fall. The smoke must go with the current or water-shower, and not against it.

The flue pedestal, with its water-spray, is the whole of the contrivance by which the author believes the smoke of the domestic hearth could be got rid of, or rendered inoffensive. What the action of the water would be on the gases that escape from the fuel he cannot say, but he presumes it could not be other than beneficial.

He experimented on the subject a few years ago, and had a stove and flue erected about ten feet in height; the lower part of the stove was of brick, the upper part with the cistern of zinc. The coal fire was lighted, and as soon as black smoke appeared at the chimney-top, the water-valve was lifted and about 16 fine jets of water were sprayed against a piece of loose perforated zinc, suspended in the flue; this zinc is shown in fig. 25; in the second flue *e* (it should have been marked *f*, but by a mistake in the cutting it is made *d*), the smoke had to pass through under this perforated zinc to get to the chimney above. On the instant the water was applied, the smoke appeared at the chimney-top of a light colour, and it came out of the soot receptacle, placed a little height above the ground, nearly as much as it did at top, and of a similar light vapourish character,* a sure sign that it was drawn down by the current of water. Soot in large quantities was soon seen in the receptacle; the author has not ascertained the quantity of soot which would be obtained by this process from a ton of coals, but he believes it would be very considerable, possibly two sacks or more. As clean unmixed soot is worth

---

* A print of the stove is given in the author's pamphlet entitled "The Smoke Nuisance, and its Remedy; with Remarks on Liquid Fuel." Price 1s. (Atchley & Co.)

in London 2s. 6d. per sack, if this soot were retained it would pay for the extra expense of the water, and the retaining of it, and to carry off the water would be an easy operation.

The "blacks" are good things at present in their wrong place; they could in the way proposed be very easily got rid of, and if it were possible to cut into all the chimneys of London and apply the remedy, the whole of the soot, which at present escapes into the atmosphere, might be caught and passed into the drains; it would there probably fully deodorize them. It is certainly not possible, from the herculean nature of the task, to disturb the whole of the chimneys of London, but the worst only might be operated upon, such as the chief kitchen flues of the great establishments, which are continually sending out black smoke.

Among the chief offenders are our bakers, nearly twenty of them being fined weekly for this by the magistrates, and for fires occurring in their chimneys. It appears that the Smoke Nuisance Act bears hardly upon them; the smoke-consuming apparatus forced upon them by the Act has utterly failed in its purpose, and it is impossible for them to comply with the requirements of the Act, and carry on their business in a satisfactory manner either to themselves or the public. They have applied to the Home Secretary for relief, and a bill to repeal so much of the Act 16 and 17 Vict. that relates to bakehouses has been in contemplation.

There would be no difficulty in placing a flue pedestal in their flues at any height above their oven fires; it would not only relieve their neighbours from the annoyance of black smoke from their chimneys, but it would secure the chimneys themselves from taking fire. The water need only be turned on when required, when black smoke was being made, and if they chose to collect the soot the expense of the operation would be trifling, if anything, beyond the first expense of the flue pedestal, in the end.

In large country houses the flue pedestal would warm the upper rooms or passages, and cause a more equal temperature in the building; this, together with the practicability of collecting the soot for agricultural purposes, might be an inducement to its introduction. Water could be lifted to the roof of a country mansion by that ingenious contrivance the hydraulic ram, and passed off to its original source when done with, the soot being left behind.

The beautiful self-acting machine, known as Gwynne & Co.'s improved hydraulic ram, is peculiarly adapted for raising or lifting water to any required elevation. It is necessary to have a fall of water to work it, and the greater the height of the fall, the more effective will be the machine. In favourable cases it will raise water thirty times higher than the fall working it. The greater the height of the lift, of course the less will be the quantity raised in a given time. This machine can be made to deliver comparatively large quantities of water, either in tanks on the roofs of houses, or in farmyards for filling ponds. It will work day and night without any attendance or expense after it is once fixed. Two or more rams may be used to force through the same pipe, or rising main. Where a continuous stream of water to work the machine cannot be obtained, a spring, or even rainfall, or drainage may be stored up in a reservoir or dam, and made to work the ram.

The expense of these machines is not excessive, as the following table will show :—

Diameter of Feed Pipe.	Diameter of Delivery Pipe.	Approximate Number of Gallons of Water raised in a day of 24 hours.	Price of Ram, complete, with all the accessories, but exclusive of Pipes.
Inches.	Inches.		£
2	1	800 to 1150	12
3	2	3000 to 4000	24
4	2	4000 to 5000	34

A small room or enclosure must be erected to contain the machine.

The question of how far the removal of smoke from the atmosphere would affect the various gases of combustion floating therein is a question for the chemist.

The plan that has been here proposed is founded on the supposition that Nature's law, relative to the diffusion of gases, permits only carbonic acid gas, the chief product of combustion, to remain in the proportion of 1 in 2000. The introduction of so much water in the sewer, where its presence already is considered an injury to the sewage, is an objection, but the present system of drainage requires a plentiful supply of water, to prevent stoppages or choking. Should the dry earth system ever be generally introduced, the present sewers would serve to remove liquid sewage and all products of combustion. The operation of the sewer in any way in receiving this smoke and soot, would permit the full and cheering light of the sun to shine alike in country and town.

DESIGN No. 36.

A LECTURE HALL, OR LITERARY INSTITUTION.

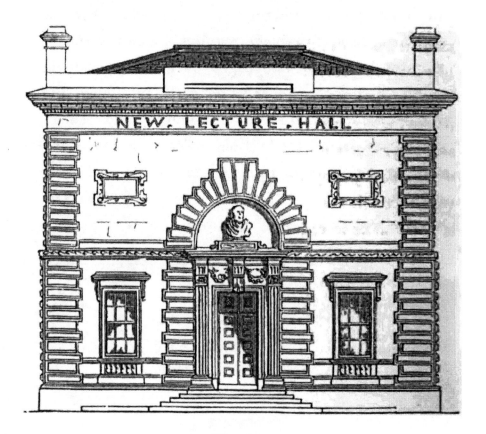

Elevation.

THIS design was made to refront an old chapel in
the country which had been purchased for the
purpose of forming a Literary Institute.   The interior

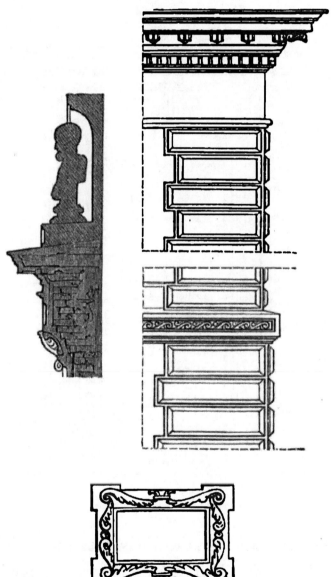

Tablet in front.

was one large room, the lecturer's table at the back, a recess and fireplace behind, a large gallery in front, under which were formed two small rooms, with a

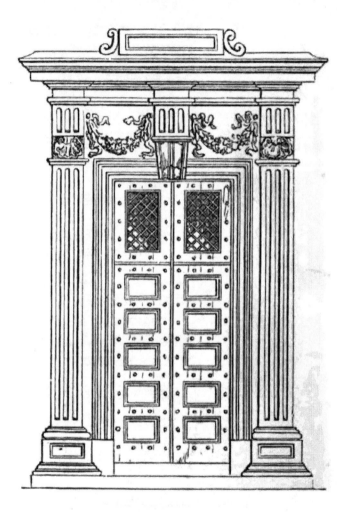

Elevation of entrance-door.

passage from the grand entrance between. The entrance-door with a bust of Socrates over it, under the arch, was made large, to give an important character to the front.   A section of the niche over the door-way is given, some details of the angle rustication, together with an elevation of the entrance-door.

ENCAUSTIC TILES.

A SLIGHT digression from the subject-matter of the preceding pages may serve to break monotony, and introduce to the notice of the reader an ornamental object—the encaustic tile. They are

Design for a floor encaustic tile.

now of universal use, both for floor and wall decoration, and have become general favourites for such purposes. A few suggestions, therefore, for the purpose of making them more artistic and pleasing will not be out of place.

The present patterns are almost entirely of a conventional kind, or according to strict geometric forms. The same pattern is repeated all over the surface, without variation, and however excellent the pattern may be, it is designed on the same principle as that of a printed wall paper.

The design just given puts all geometric forms aside, and introduces a free-hand treatment, allowing the pattern to be varied on every surface laid down.

Design for wall encaustic tile.

The first tile shows eight points in which the stem of the pattern (suppose that of a flower design) meets in them all. The second tile shows the stem; the third and fourth the flower pattern varied. One tile might have more flowers than leaves, another all leaves or buds, and as all the tiles would fall in their right places, they depend only on the care of the workmen who place them; the pattern might be varied according·to the number of tiles of different pattern.

For wall linings a trellis work might be shown on the tile, having a blue ground; some tiles might be without either leaves, stems, or flowers, and the design would show a flowered trellis against the sky. The figure given on page 461 shows this.

These tiles are beginning to be used on columns. Some good examples are to be seen in the .South Kensington Museum Galleries. In columns with trellis work a white marble ground with leaves and roses twined round it naturally, would look a great deal better than formal lines of stiff ornaments.

Some of our latest Gothic architects who were at the same time artists, did not trouble themselves to draw out according to rule the geometric lines for the foliation of their Gothic windows. They knew the principles thoroughly, but merely made the vertical lines correct, and then sketched in the foliation with a free hand. This gave an outline greatly superior to the usual stiff conventional forms. Some examples of this may be seen in one of the author's books, now in the Fine Art Library of the South Kensington Museum, in which the free-hand designs (rubbings) are placed by the side of the same patterns drawn out geometrically.

The vignette shows foreign cut-wood patterns for roof ornament; the section the method of forming the zinc gutter.

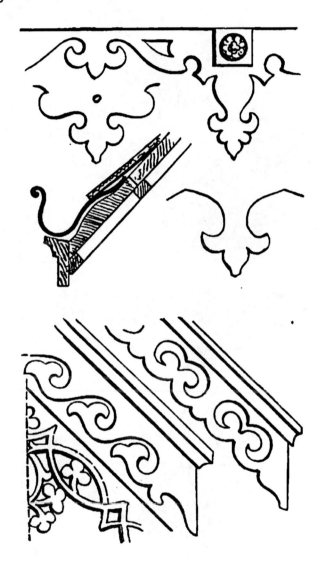

DESIGN No. 38.—RESTORATION OF CASTLE GUNNARSTROP, SWEDEN.

IT has been remarked in the Introduction, that the localities in which a residence can be placed greatly affect their picturesque appearance. The north and west Highlands of Scotland, in our own country, and a similar class of scenery in Sweden and Norway, greatly aid by their natural beauties the best effects of the architect, and generally in northern Europe, including Denmark with the above-named countries, those accessories can be largely taken advantage of. An instance of this can be found in the design now under consideration. In this castle the gables are carried up to a greater height, and made more ornamental and of greater importance than with us. In the year 1852 the author was making a design for a villa for the Count de Bark, a Swedish nobleman. It was to be erected on the heights bordering the Sound near Copenhagen, and was seen from the sea in passing, peering above the trees. The upper part of the villa was made as picturesque as possible, with a tower, battlements, and turrets. The lower part of the building was very plain, and the plan merely contained a few living rooms and servants' apartments; it was much unlike our style, and is therefore not given here: only the view from the vignette is afforded in this description. The Count's uncle occupied the old castle, the Vrams Gunnarstrop in Sweden, then very much out of repair and

unfitted for the requirements of modern domestic
life.

It was planned originally on a grand scale; the
fronts had high triangular gables in steps, and decorated with cut granite ornaments, but the whole was

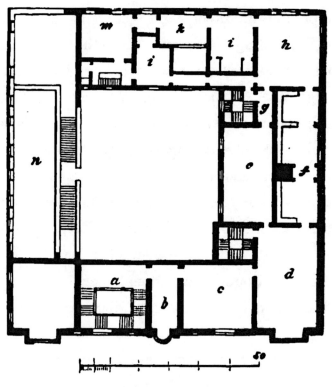

The one-pair plan.

very plain.   The north front was in two floors, and
the angle towers of the building had only two floors.
The portions between one story—that of the ground
floor—thus had to be raised.   The ground floor was
given to the servants, and the southern portion of the

building was to remain for a time in its then existing
state.   The plan shows *a*, the grand staircase, adorned
with columns supporting the upper landing.   It was
27 ft. in length by 26 ft. in width, and led up to an
ante-room *b*, in the centre of the building, 26 ft. in
length by 12 ft. in breadth.   It opened into the first
and second drawing-rooms, *c* and *d*: one 30 ft. in
length, the other 40 ft., and both of a width of 26 ft.

Perspective view of the Count de Bark's villa.

The dining-room *e*, entered from the chief drawing-
room, was 40 ft. in length, with a width of 22 ft.; *f*
shows the gallery or library filled with book-cases, and
leading to the day-room *h*; the chief bedroom is shown
at *i* adjoining, *k* is the lady's dressing-room, *l* the
gentleman's dressing-room and bath; *m* is the nursery,

with a servants' staircase and closet adjoining; *g* is the servants' serving-place at the entrance of dining-room. The light portions of the plan show the additions made; the black, the old portions of the castle. The two towers contained staircases to the attics which were formed in the high roofs.

The principal elevation faced the west. The perspective view of this front is given. Its length is 130 ft., and the height of the principal entrance from the ground to the top of the gable is 60 ft.

The south and west sides were of an equally picturesque character, but neither had any central gable. The south had triple dormer windows joined in the centre with one dormer window at each side. The two towers were seen rising above the roof, and a wide terrace with open stone Elizabethan balustrading extending the entire front, with steps down to the garden in the centre below. The terrace was 130 ft. in length. The west side had the two gables, one at each end, with three tall dormer windows in the roof; these were connected by wood balustrading, and a window with three lights was placed below each. The granite-stone ornaments in the old fronts were replaced in the new fronts.

The vignette gives a view of a small garden fountain, designed from one in the old garden at Blickling in Norfolk. The plinth is hexangular in plan, with the scrolls projecting on the three sides. To the top of the jet its height is about 9 feet.

DESIGN No. 39.

SUMMER VILLA FOR THE COUNT KINSKI, AT TEPLITZ.

Perspective view of Count Kinski's summer villa.

THIS villa was designed about the year 1852, for an Austrian nobleman, who wished to have a villa in the English Elizabethan character. The plan was arranged after his own figured sketches, and it is given here as showing the requirements considered desirable for such a building in a summer place of

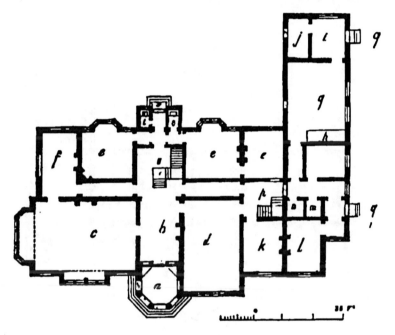

Ground plan.

retirement, or palace for a foreign nobleman's occupation. The porch was approached on four sides by flights of steps 12 ft. 6 in. in diameter; it opened into a hall *b*, 20 ft. in length by 14 ft. in width. The drawing-room *c*, of noble size, with two bay windows, was 36 ft. in length by 22 in width. The dining-room *d,* in the opposite side of the hall, was 28 ft. in length by 18 ft. in width. The butler's pantry, *k,* and the servants' offices and kitchen *g,* with a large store-closet *h,* and scullery *i,* adjoined. A bread room is shown at *j, l* is the servants' hall, *m* a china-closet, *n* a store-room, and *o* the servants' staircase, *q q* are the servants' entrances, and *r r* the closets.

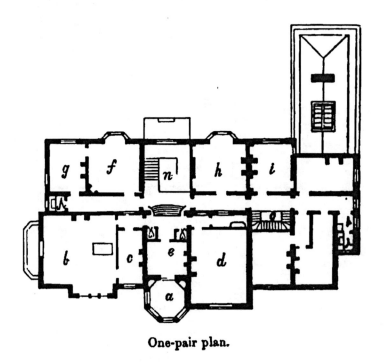

One-pair plan.

Returning to the principal portion of the building, the chief staircase, *v,* opens from the entrance hall, *e e e* are nurseries, and *f* is the library. On the first floor, *a* is the balcony over the porch; this was to be used for smoking, &c., *b* is the best bed-chamber, and *c* the boudoir to the same, *d* is the second best bed-chamber, and *e* its boudoir, *f* is the third best bed-chamber, and *g* its boudoir, *h* is a bedroom without any boudoir, *i* is the housekeeper's bedroom, *k k k* the men's sleeping room, *i* housemaid's closet, *j j* closets, *l l* linen-closets, *m* a closet or bath-room, *n* the principal staircase, and *o* the servants' staircase.

The attic plan was devoted to the sleeping rooms, *b b b*, of the female servants.   Here plans are made

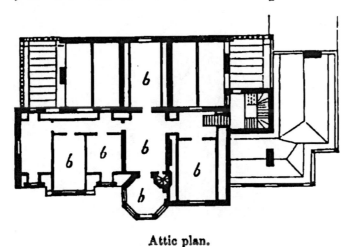

Attic plan.

(the building being so large) on a smaller scale than the other plans in this volume.

The perspective view merely exhibits the common forms of Elizabethan character.   The tower which formed the entrance was 70 ft. in height from the foundation to the top of its roof, the height of the ground-floor rooms was 14 ft. 3 in.   They had rich plaster friezes, and the staircase had carved oak Elizabethan balustrading.   The second-floor rooms were 12 ft. 3 in. in height, and were very plain in character. The upper floor of the tower was open, but could be closed by sashes; this was intended for a smoking retreat. A small detail of one of the gabled windows in front is given below. Altogether, the design had a most picturesque effect, and its style met with approval. It combined utility with elegance,

Gable window.

and completely answered the objects for which it was constructed.

Another villa was designed for an Austrian noble-man, the Prince Clary: a view of it is given in the first illustration of this volume, through the window of the architect's study. It was intended as a summer retreat for the Prince and his friends when engaged in a fishing-excursion on the noble river the Elbe, on

the banks of which it was placed.   It contained a
large centre dining-room, 48 ft. by 22, with a saloon
or drawing-room, 40 ft. by 20 ft., and extensive accommodation for the kitchen and servants' departments.
The upper story contained 14 best bedrooms, each
with an ante or dressing-room, besides bath-room and
the sleeping apartments for the domestics.

DESIGN No. 40.

HARRINGTON HOUSE, QUEEN'S PALACE GARDENS.

Perspective view of exterior.

THIS building, with which the present collection of designs closes, is probably the most unpicturesque example in the volume. Its exterior has been frequently criticised; whatever its merits or demerits may be, it certainly is wholly unlike, while at the same time it is not inferior, to the strange style at present so popular with the younger branch of architectural professors, which appears to be a

Elevation of principal staircase.

mixture of the Byzantine and Romanesque styles, joined with the Roman Gothic. Some call it the Missal style, others the Northern Italian. The sole recommendation of it is that it comes more expensive to carry out than any other. This house has at least the reputation of being a very comfortable one, and as more than usually adapted to receive large assemblies and fashionable parties. Indeed the noble Earl who erected it was so pleased with it, that on entering, on its completion, he addressed the following note to the author :—

H. H., Kensington Palace Gardens,
31 *May*, 1854.

My dear Sir,—

I take this opportunity of expressing to you my thanks for having constructed a house, in my humble judgment, *without a fault.*

Believe me most sincerely yours,
(Signed)   HARRINGTON.

To C. J. Richardson, Esq.

And after having resided in it nine months, he again wrote as follows :—

H. H., Palace Gardens, Kensington,
2nd February, 1855.

My dear Sir,—

I pray you to accept my cordial thanks for your most able architectural skill in the construction of my house.   I have lived in it one season, and have not discovered in it a single fault.

Believe me most truly yours,
(Signed)   HARRINGTON.

To C. J. Richardson, Esq.

The site upon which the house stands was taken by the Earl from the Commissioners of Her Majesty's

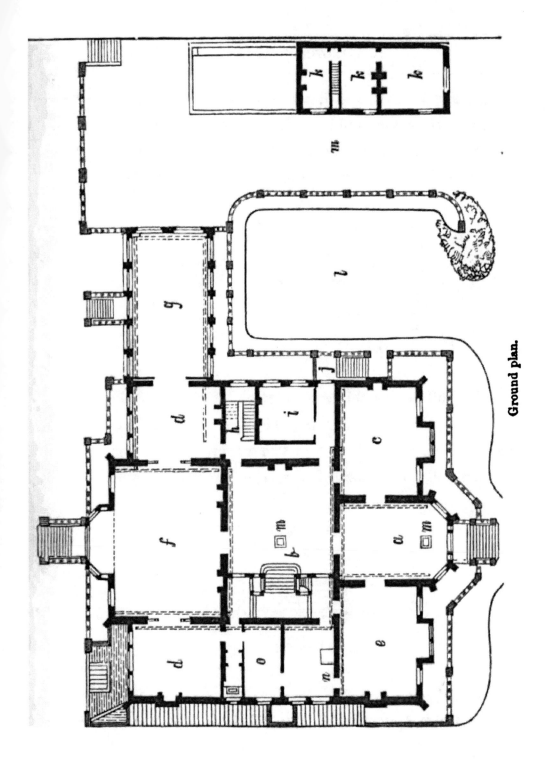

Ground plan.

Woods and Forests, and it certainly is, or was, one of the best sites for building in the metropolis. It adjoins Kensington Gardens, looking on the old winter garden of Queen Anne. Agreeable and admirable a

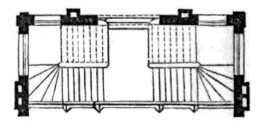

One-pair plan of staircase.

site for building as this was, in 1853, it remained for some time utterly neglected. The first speculator had been ruined, and only one or two of his houses (one erected by Mr. Owen Jones, the architect) were

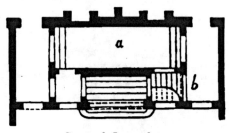

Ground-floor plan.

standing in the road. Soon after the Earl of Harrington acquired the land, and erected this building, the whole of the road, on each side, was covered with first-class mansions.

The terms of the agreement were, that the Earl should take plot No. 9 and the northern portion of plot No. 10, having a frontage of 196 ft. to the Queen's-road, and a depth of about 260 ft., for a period of 91¼ years, from the 5th July 1851, at a peppercorn rent for the first year, of 73*l.* 10*s.* for the second year, and of 147*l.* a year for the remainder of the term, also a rent of 5*s.* a year in lieu of land-tax for every year except the first.

The Earl was to expend a sum of not less than 6000*l.* in erecting upon the ground a dwelling-house of the first-class style of building. The house was to be insured in the sum of 6000*l.*, and the Earl was to pay jointly, with the adjacent occupiers, the expense of lighting and keeping up the road, which was a private one, and to pay the gatekeepers at the lodge. The rest of the covenants of the agreement were such as are usually found in such documents.

The house was, until the present year, the only Gothic one in the district, the Earl insisting upon having this, his favourite style, admitted. It stands in the centre of the road at the highest level, and is well up out of the ground. The principal floor is 7 ft. above the outside road of approach, and 14 ft. above the level of the public road. The whole of the walls stand on a basement of concrete, and the lower flooring is 5 ft. above the level of the foundations.

The basement story is 14 ft. in height, and of entirely
fireproof construction.   The best rooms on the
ground-floor are 17 ft. 6 in. in height, the secondary
rooms are 15 ft. high.   All the principal staircases
are of stone; the ground plan on page 479 shows the

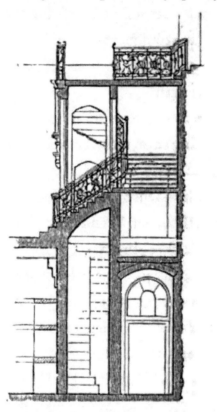

Section of principal staircase.

entrance hall, *a*, approached by 12 steps; it is 30 ft.
in length, by 21 ft. in width; *b* is the principal staircase, situated on one side of the saloon in the centre
of the building; the latter is 41 ft. long by 21 ft. wide.
The dining-room *e*, and the library *c*, on each side of

the hall, are respectively 30 ft. by 22 ft. The great room, with the bay window, entered from the saloon, is the picture gallery *f*. This room is 41 ft. long by 30 ft. wide, without the bay. The drawing-rooms *d, d*, on each side, are each 25 ft. by 20 ft.; *g*, the conservatory, measures 40 ft. by 21 ft.; this, with the two drawing-rooms and the picture gallery, can in less than half an hour be thrown into one by the removal of the large folding-doors in the picture gallery, which

Ornament for stairs.

can be taken away, frames complete, by simply removing a few screws. A length of drawing-room is then gained of 125 ft.

The principal staircase is shown in elevation on page 477; the plans are here given to a larger scale.

The lower plan shows a portion of the first flight and the servants' passage, *a*, under the first landing; *b* is their staircase down to the basement, this should

have been shown on the left-hand side. It is the
footman's staircase, adapted for him to ascend and

Iron railing on staircase.

descend readily from or to the basement, and the
passage *a* permits him to enter either side of the

house without being seen. The upper plan shows the two flights, right and left, rising from the principal landing. Each of these has 22 steps. Three more in the centre lead up to the gallery round the saloon; the section of the staircase, given on p. 482, clearly shows this arrangement. The staircase front is in Bath stone. The only ornaments are the decorated corbels supporting the small angular projections or buttresses necessary to receive the iron standards of the railing above. One of the corbels and a panel of the iron railing is given. This is carried up the stairs on both sides and round the gallery, and is richly coloured and gilt. The only remaining portions of the ground plan to be described are the secondary rooms. A side entrance is at *j*, and the waiting room, *i*, is also at the side ; *h* is the servants' staircase, going from the basement to the attic. On the other side of the building *o* is the Earl's dressing-room, with a study or writing room by its side. This has a lift, *n*, from the kitchen, enabling it to be used as a serving room. The picture gallery has a flight of steps descending to a large ornamented garden at the back of the house, *n n* is the stable-yard, and *k k k* rooms over the stable.

The section through the complete building, given on page 486, shows the general character of the interior. The rooms are wholly without ornament; all have plain cornices formed of running Gothic mouldings. The

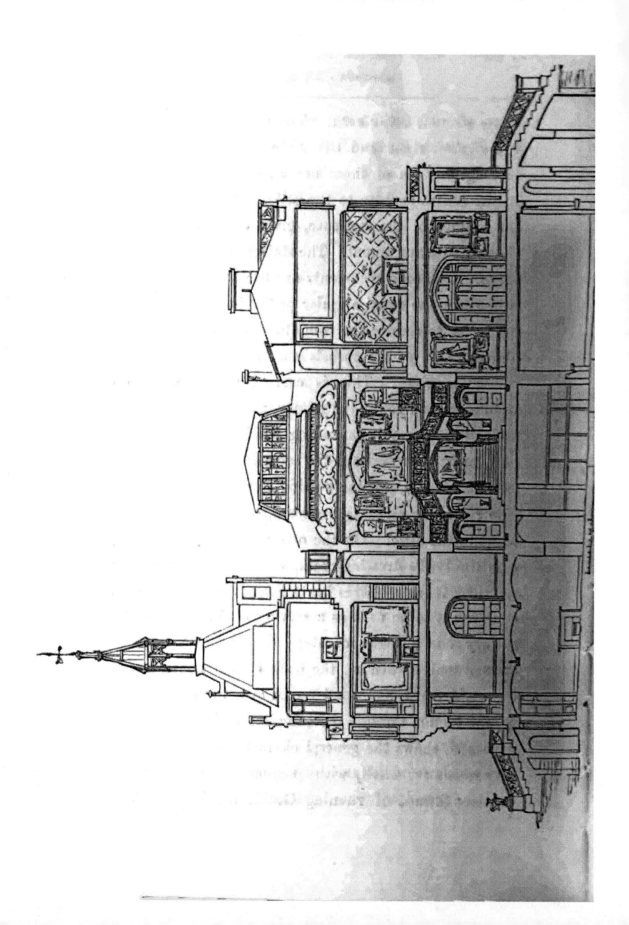

only decorated portion is the saloon (*inf.*), the coved ceiling of which has the shields of painted and gilt coats of arms of family connexions, together with mottoes and

monograms. The skylight is filled with richly coloured embossed glass, every pane having a shield of arms, its ceiling being panelled with painted enrichments on a blue ground. A view of the saloon is given on p. 487; it contains in the centre a statue by Theed, of

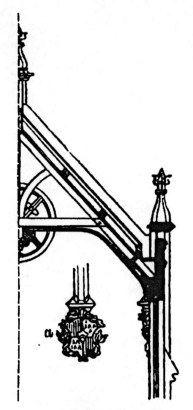

Half-section of roof of conservatory.

Lady Chandos Pole, the eldest daughter of the Earl. The statues are shown in the plan by the letters *m m*. The ground floor is supplied with warm-water pipes; these are shown by the dotted lines. They are sunk in the brickwork forming the substructure of the flooring, and covered with open ornamental ironwork. The hall has two warm-water pedestals. The whole of the rooms and conservatory are so warmed.

The latter part of the interior resembles in some respects a small chapel. A half section of a portion

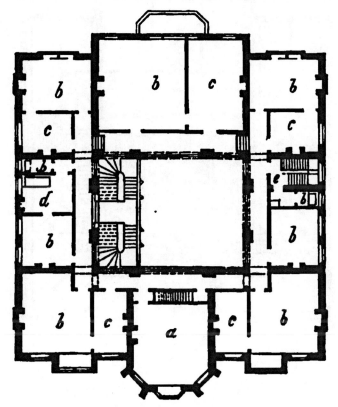

Plan of one-pair.

of its roof is given on p. 488 ; it measures 22 ft. from the floor to the collar-beam. The corbels, from which the roof springs, are decorated with shields of arms, surrounded by a garland of strawberry leaves.

In the plan of the one-pair floor, *a* is the boudoir

or morning room; *b b b* are bedrooms; *c c c* dressing-
rooms, and *d* is the bath-room.   The gallery is shown
as completely going round the saloon; its ceiling is
of ground glass arranged in panels, each of which is

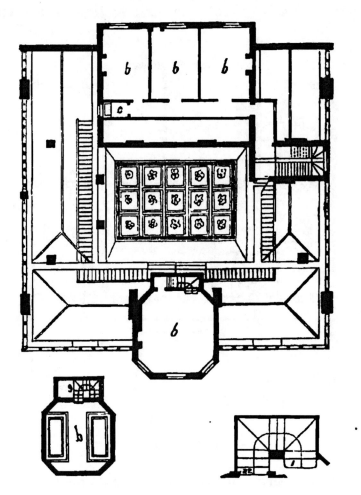

moveable, with a skylight over the whole.   There is
plenty of light therefore afforded for the paintings
with which the walls are covered.

The small attic plan shows these skylights on three

sides only, likewise the sleeping-rooms *b b*, and the housemaid's closet *c*. Under this plan is that of the upper room in the tower with its two slate cisterns, each capable of containing 800 gallons of water. They are supported by strong trussed girders fixed in the walls.• This upper room is approached by a

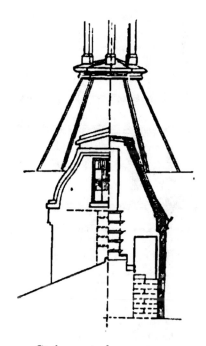

Staircase to lower rooms.

cottage staircase, the plan of which, with its 22 risers, is shown in cut on p. 490. It enables the room to be approached without any structural appearance being seen from without. A half elevation of the exterior, and another of its section, is given above. It is well supplied with light.

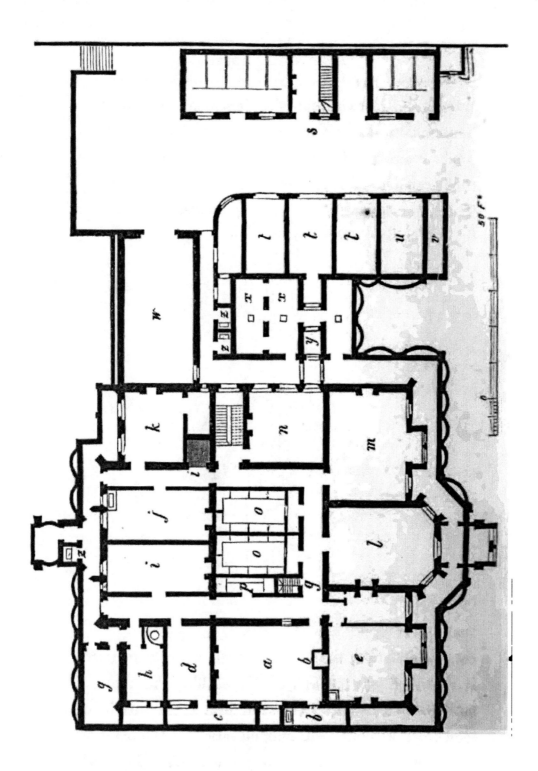

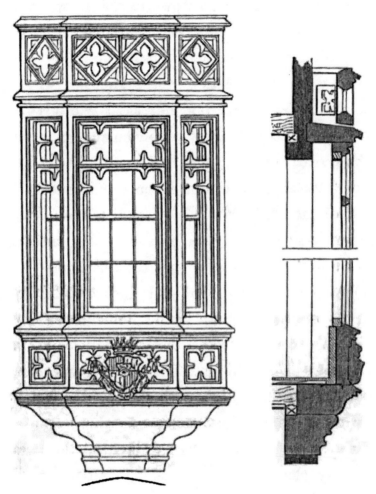

Elevation of bay window.   Section.

Plan.

The building contains upwards of forty rooms;
the basement is very large, and contains considerable
accommodation.   The mere enumeration of these
would require every letter in the alphabet to point
them out in an engraving, but as it is desirable to
show how closely a large establishment of servants
can be packed together, the basement plan is given.
a is the kitchen, *b* the scullery, and *c* the larder.   The
kitchen is provided with a lift *f*, and a small service
window; *d* is the pastry-room, and *e* the still-room,
with the lift; *g* is the dairy, *h* the washhouse, *i* the
laundry, *j* the butler's pantry, *k* the steward's room
with its strong closet; *l* is the housekeeper's, with
the cook's room between it and the still-room; *m* is
the servants' hall, *n* the men's sleeping room; *o o* are
wine-cellars, *p* the butler's wine-cellar, *q* the footman's
stairs under the principal staircase, *r* the warm-water
furnace, by the steward's room, placed at the back of
his strong closet; *s* is the stable, containing eight
stalls, one loose box, and a harness-room; *t t t* are
cart-sheds, *u* is the cowhouse, *v* the dung-pit, *w* the
coach-house, *x x* two of the three coal-cellars, *y* the
dust-pit, and *z z z* are the closets.   The carriage-road
to the side entrance is formed over the cart-sheds and
coal-cellars.   These are arched over in brick and
covered with a thick layer of Brown's metallic lava,
and are provided with proper drainage.   The boot-

cleaning place and that for lamps are between the coach-house and the cart-sheds.

The exterior of the building has been censured on account of the Gothic outline being too flat, the roofs too low, and all the windows having common sash

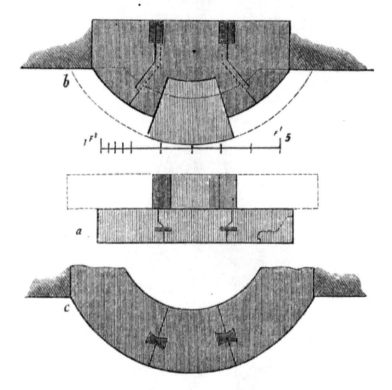

frames. With regard to the latter, it may be considered very probable that if the Gothic race of architects had continued with us to the present day, they would have adopted plate glass for their windows, and put aside their lead-lights and small panes of common glass. One of the greatest improvements that could be made in our cathedrals, not excepting

even St. Paul's, would be the reglazing the windows
in the modern style.

Half-elevation and section of bell-turret.

As a specimen of the architectural style of the building, the centre bay-window of the principal front is given, with its section and plan. It is 9 ft. 6 in. across, and 21 ft. 4 in. high, and stands directly over the chief entrance. The construction of a projecting bay-window coming over an archway requires a short description.

The three diagrams on page 495 show the manner in which such windows are corbelled out. The upper

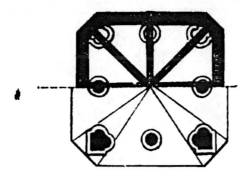

Plan of turret.

one is a plan of the bottom stone course, immediately over the key-stone of the arch; it shows also the centre stone of the second course upon it. The middle diagram shows the two courses from the back. It will be seen that the middle stone of the first course does not bear upon the arch, but is supported by the two end stones let into the wall. The last diagram is a plan of the upper course at top. Slate dowels were used, and an iron bar, shown in plan

under elevation *a*, 3 in. by ¾ in., was placed across
the course tailing into the walls on each side; and
two bars *b b*, each 2½ by ¾ in. and 12 ft. in length,
tied it to the flooring of the room. This is shown
likewise in the plan, the dotted lines dividing the
length of flooring; *d* is the upper course of stones, and
c one of the principal beams of the floor.

Balustrading on top of building.

The bell-turret stands 20 ft. above the roof. This
is carved in oak; an elevation, section, and plan is
given. Only those parts of the building are intended
to be here illustrated which have some peculiarity of
design or construction.

A building of this size would require about 150

working drawings to be made for it, and a considerable number to be given to show its construction.

It was completed in about two years, at an expense of 14,814*l.* ; but this did not include the price of the warming apparatus, nor that of the lightning conductor fixed to the bell-turret.

Front.   Side.

Pedestal to steps.

Whatever opinions may be expressed in regard to the architectural details of this erection, the author at least can plead, as its owner stated in the letters, copies of which have been given, that the essentials of a house, convenience, comfort, and complete suitability for all domestic purposes, were accomplished. These objects being attained, any real or imaginary faults perceived by professional critics may be palliated if not forgotten.

INDEX.

THE END.

VERY IMPORTANT NEW BOOKS.

Special List for 1871.

Charles Dickens—The Story of his Life. By the
Author of " The Life of Thackeray." This day, price 7s. 6d., with
numerous Portraits and Illustrations, 370 pp.

Dickens's Summer House.

"Anecdotes seem to have poured in upon the author from all quarters. * * * Turn where we will through these 370 pleasant pages, something worth reading is sure to meet the eye."—*The Standard.*

——Ib.—— Another Edition. Uniform with The
" *CHARLES DICKENS EDITION*," and forming a supplementary
volume to that favourite issue, crimson cloth, 3s. 6d.

Artemus Ward, Complete. The Works of Charles
Farrer Browne. better known as "ARTEMUS WARD," now FIRST
COLLECTED. Crown 8vo, with fine portrait, facsimile of hand-
writing, &c., 540 pages, cloth neat, 7s. 6d.

₂ Comprises all that the humorist has written in England or America.
Admirers of poor Artemus Ward will be glad to possess his writings in a complete form.

John Camden Hotten, 74 and 75, Piccadilly, W.   1

A TRULY MAGNIFICENT WORK.—"LIVES OF

THE SAINTS." Enriched with Fifty-one exquisite Full-page Miniatures, in gold and colours. Every page of the Text within Engraved Borders of Beautiful Design. In thick 4to, sumptuously printed, and bound in silk velvet, enriched with gold, preserved in a case, £7 7s. ; in morocco, extra gilt, inlaid, £10 15s.

☞ *THIS VERY IMPORTANT WORK, commenced three years since, has at length been completed, and fully justifies the high expectations formed of it during its progress through the press. Taking the text of the Rev. Alban Butler as his guide, the Editor has, wherever practicable, carefully verified the references of that eminent divine. The delicacy and finish of the beautiful miniatures have never before been approached in any similar work in this country. They exhibit a beauty and exquisite softness of colour which have hitherto only been realised by the most expensive miniature paintings. The work must be seen to be appreciated, as it is like no other of the kind. The preparation has been so costly and slow that the book is never likely to decrease in value.*

A VERY SPLENDID VOLUME.—SAINT URSULA,

PRINCESS OF BRITAIN, AND HER COMPANIONS. With Twenty-five Full-page 4to Illuminated Miniatures from the Pictures of Cologne, and exquisitely designed Woodcut Borders. In crown 4to, beautifully bound in silk and gold, £3 15s.

₊ The finest Book-Paintings of the kind ever published. The artist obtained the Gold Prize at the Paris Exposition.

☞ *THE BOOK MUST BE SEEN TO BE APPRECIATED. The illustrations are exact reproductions of the exquisite paintings of the Van Eyck school, and are in finish and beauty far above any similar book-paintings issued in this country. As the preparation of the work has been so costly and slow it is never likely to decrease in value.*

Exquisite Miniatures and Illuminations.—"Golden

Verses from the New Testament," with 50 Illuminations and Miniatures from celebrated MISSALS and BOOKS OF HOURS of 14th and 15th centuries in GOLD and COLOURS. The text very beautifully printed in letters of gold on fine ivory paper. 4to, in a very handsome cloth case with silk ribbons, 30s. ; or bound in a volume, morocco, gilt edges, £2 5s.

Common Prayer. Illustrated by Holbein and Albert

Durer. With Wood Engravings of the Dance of Death, a singularly curious series after Holbein, with Scriptural Quotations and Proverbs in the Margin. 8vo, exquisitely printed on tinted paper, 8s. 6d. ; in dark morocco, Elizabethan style, gilt edges, 16s. 6d.

Apply DIRECT *for this exquisite volume.*

Brunet's Manual du Libraire. 5 vols. royal 8vo, half

morocco, top edge gilt, 25s. only.

2   *John Camden Hotten, 74 and 75, Piccadilly, W.*

Earthward Pilgrimage (The). By Moncure D. Con-
way, the eminent Unitarian Minister, and friend of Emerson. Crown
8vo, 400 pages, cloth. neat, 7s. 6d.

₊ This volume has excited considerable discussion, as it advances many entirely
new views upon the life hereafter. The titles to some of the chapters will convey an idea of the contents of the work :—"How I left the world to come for
that which is."

Dickens's Speeches, Literary and Social. Now first
collected. With Chapters on "Charles Dickens as a Letter Writer,
Poet, and Public Reader." This day, price 7s. 6d., with fine Portrait
by Count D'Orsay, 370 pages.

₊ "His capital speeches. Every one of them reads like a page of 'Pick-
wick.'"—*The Critic.*

"His speeches are as good as any of his printed writings."—*The Times.*

——Ib.—— Uniform with The "*CHARLES DICKENS*
EDITION," and forming a supplementary volume to that favourite
issue, crimson cloth, 3s. 6d.

————— Cheap edition, without portrait, in paper wrapper, 2s.

Madge and the Fairy Content. A Charming
Child's Story. By BLANCHARD JERROLD. Intended to inculcate a
Spirit of Contentment. With nearly 100 Pictures of the Industry
requisite to produce the Christmas Pudding. 4s. 6d.

A Third Supply of Yankee Drolleries, comprising
the best recent Works of American Humorists. A. WARD'S FENIANS;
MARK TWAIN; AUTOCRAT BREAKFAST TABLE; BRET HARTE;
INNOCENTS ABROAD. With an Introduction by GEORGE AUGUSTUS
SALA, Crown 8vo, 700 pages, cloth extra, 3s. 6d.

₊ An entirely new gathering of Transatlantic humour. Fourteen thousand
copies have been sold of the 1st and 2nd series.

John Camden Hotten, 74 and 75, Piccadilly, W.

The Conscript. A Story of the French and German War of 1813. Translated from the French of MM. ERCKMANN-CHATRIAN. Fcap., 1s.

₊ An authorized and unmutilated popular edition of this now famous work. The translations, hitherto published in this country and in America, can b. regarded as little more than abridgments.

Napoleon III., The Man of his Time:

PART I.—The Story of the Life of Napoleon III., as told by JAS. W. HASWELL.

PART II.—The Same Story, as told by the POPULAR CARICATURES of the past 25 years.

Crown 8vo, 400 pages, 7s. 6d.

₊ The object of this Work is to give both sides of the Story. The Artist has gone over the entire ground of Continental and English Caricatures for the last quarter of a century, and a very interesting book is the result.

Bismarck, the Great German Statesman. The Story OF HIS CAREER, told for Popular Reading. By Mr. GEO. BULLEN, of the British Museum. Fcap., 1s.

₊ An admirable account of the "Man of Blood and Iron;" giving numerous very characteristic anecdotes.

Echoes from the French Poets. An Anthology from BAUDELAIRE, ALFRED DE MUSSET, LAMARTINE. VICTOR HUGO, A. CHENIER. T. GAUTIER, BERANGER, NADAUD, DUPONT, PARNY, and others. By HARRY CURWEN. Fcap. 8vo. cloth, 5s.; half-morocco, 6s.

"A pleasant little volume of translations from modern French poets."—*Graphic*, Aug. 20, 1870.

NEW SOCIETY BOOK,
By the Author of "Puniana."

Gamosagammon; or, Advice to Parties about to

Connubialize. By the Hon. Hugh Rowley. With numerous exquisite and fanciful designs from his pencil. Small 4to, green and gold, 6s.

₀ The Quaintest, Funniest, most Original Book published for a long time. Three years since it was announced under the title of "Advice to Parties about to Marry."

Country-House Charades, for Acting. By Captain

E. C. Nugent. With Illustrations by W. R. Snow. Small 4to, green and gold, 6s.

₀ An entirely new book of Household Amusements. An Appendix gives the various Songs set to Music for accompaniment upon the Pianoforte.

Cruikshank's Comic Almanack. A nine years'

gathering of the BEST HUMOUR, the WITTIEST SAYINGS, the Drollest Quips, and the Best Things of THACKERAY, HOOD, MAYHEW, ALBERT SMITH, A'BECKETT, ROBERT BROUGH. With nearly one thousand Woodcuts and Steel Engravings by the inimitable CRUIKSHANK, HINE, LANDELLS. Crown 8vo, 600 pp., 7s. 6d.

John Camden Hotten, 74 and 75, Piccadilly, W.

The Secret Out; or, One Thousand Tricks with

Cards, and other Recreations; with Entertaining Experiments in Drawing-Room or " White Magic." By GUSTAVE FRIKELL, Professor of the Art for twenty-five years. With 300 engravings, crown 8vo, cloth, 4s. 6d.

To make the Pass.

. A perfect Cyclopædia of Legerdemain. Under the title of " Le Magicien des Salons," it has long been a standard Magic book with all French and German Professors of the Art. The tricks are described so carefully, with engravings to illustrate them, that anybody can easily learn how to perform them.

Art of Amusing (The). A Collection of Graceful

Arts, Games, Tricks, Puzzles, and Charades, intended to Amuse Everybody, and enable all to amuse everybody else. By FRANK BELLEW. With nearly 300 Illustrations. Crown 8vo, 4s. 6d.

. One of the most entertaining handbooks for the amusement of Society ever published.

Flagellation and the Flagellants; a History of the

Rod in all Countries, from the Earliest Period to the Present Time. By the Rev. WILLIAM COOPER, B.A., with numerous Illustrations. Thick crown 8vo, 12s. 6d.

. "A very remarkable, and certainly a very readable, volume. Those who care for quaint stories of the birch will find much matter for reflection, and not a little amusement, in Mr. Cooper's 'Flagellation' book."—*Daily Telegraph.*

The Englishman's House, from a Cottage to a

Mansion: a Practical Guide to Members of Building Societies, and all interested in Selecting or Building a House. By C. J. RICHARDSON, Architect (Author of "Old English Mansions," &c.). Second Edition, corrected and enlarged, with nearly 600 Illustrations. Crown 8vo, 550 pages, cloth, 7s. 6d.

. This Work might not inappropriately be termed "A BOOK OF HOUSES." It gives every variety of house, from a workman's cottage to a nobleman's palace. The book is intended to supply a want long felt, viz., a plain, non-technical account of every manner of house, with the cost and manner of building.

An Epic of Women, and other Poems. By Arthur W. E. O'Shaughnessy. With some Original Designs by Mr. J. T. Nettleship. Just out, fcap. 8vo, with woodcuts, cloth, very neat, price 6s.

"What he has given us is remarkable. With its quaint title, and quaint illustrations, 'An Epic of Women' will be a rich treat to a wide circle of admirers." —*Athenæum*, Nov. 5, 1870.

"Combine Morris and Swinburne, and inspire the product with a fervour essentially original, and you have, as we take it, a fair notion of Mr. O'Shaughnessy's poems."—*Dispatch*, Oct. 30, 1870.

Anacreon. Illustrated by the Exquisite Designs of Girodet. Translated by Thomas Moore. Oblong 16mo, in vellum cloth and Etruscan gold, 12s. 6d.

. *A MOST BEAUTIFUL AND CAPTIVATING VOLUME.* The well-known Paris house, Firmin Didot, a few years since produced a very small edition of these exquisite designs by the photographic process, and sold a large edition at £2 per copy. The designs have been universally admired by both artists and poets.

Albert Durer's "Little Passion." As Engraved by the distinguished artist in 1509-10, consisting of 37 inimitable designs upon wood. With a survey of Durer's Works by W. C. Prime. Royal 4to. The illustrations in exquisite facsimile, emblematic binding, 25s.

. Only 100 copies of this beautiful book were printed.

The Champion Pig of England. A Capital Story for Schoolboys. Cloth gilt. With spirited Illustrations by Concanen, coloured and plain, 3s. 6d.

> " He was a pig—take him for all in all,
> We ne'er shall look upon his like again."

UNIFORM WITH MR. RUSKIN'S EDITION OF "GERMAN POPULAR STORIES."

Prince Ubbely Bubble's New Story Book.

THE DRAGON ALL COVERED WITH SPIKES.
THE LONG-TAILED NAG.
THE THREE ONE-LEGGED MEN.
THE OLD FLY AND THE YOUNG FLY
TOM AND THE OGRE.

And many other tales.

By J. TEMPLETON LUCAS With numerous Illustrations by Matt Morgan, Barnes, Gordon Thompson, Brunton, and other artists. In small 4to, green and gold, 4s. 6d.

—— Gilt leaves, 5s. 6d.

. This is an entirely new story-book, and one that is likely to become very popular.

Acrostics in Prose and Verse. Edited by A. E. H. 12mo, gilt cloth, gilt edges, 3s.

—— *SECOND SERIES.* 12mo, gilt cloth, gilt edges, 3s.

—— *THIRD SERIES.* 12mo, gilt cloth, gilt edges, 3s.

—— *FOURTH SERIES.* With 8 Pictorial Acrostics. 12mo, gilt cloth, 3s.

—— *FIFTH SERIES.* Easy Double. Historical. Scriptural Acrostics. 12mo, gilt cloth, gilt edges, 3s.

The most popular Acrostics published.

. *Each series sold separately.* These are the best volumes of Acrostics ever issued. They comprise Single, Double, Treble, and every variety of acrostic, and the set would amuse the younger members of a family for an entire winter.

The whole complete in a case, " *The Acrostic Box*," price 15s.

Mark Twain's New Pilgrim's Progress. A delight-

fully fresh and amusing Volume of Travel. Companion to the popular
" INNOCENTS ABROAD." 3s. 6d. ; paper, 1s.

, Readers who approved of this Author's quaint story of "The Jumping
Frog," will be very well satisfied with the "New Pilgrim's Progress:" there has
been no work like it issued here for years.

Mark Twain's Innocents Abroad. *THE VOYAGE*

OUT. Price 3s. 6d. cloth extra ; a paper edition, 1s.

, A delightful, fresh, and amusing volume of travels. Readers who appre-
ciate true wit and humour will be well satisfied with "The Innocents Abroad."

The Luck of Roaring Camp; and other Stories.

By BRET HARTE. Crown 8vo, toned paper, 3s. 6d.; a paper edition, 1s.

, The Work of a new candidate to literary honour. The Publisher of a book
is not perhaps always the most unbiassed person to give an opinion about it ;
but in the present instance the writer has no hesitation in saying that English
readers will be charmed with these inimitable stories of strange life in the Far
West—away on the Pacific slope. The fun, the very humour of the thing, has a
May freshness about it, which smacks not of the Old World.

Champagne: its History, Manufacture, Properties,

&c. By CHARLES TOVEY, Author of "Wine and Wine Countries,"
" British and Foreign Spirits," &c. Crown 8vo, with numerous illustrations, 5s.

, A practical work, by one of the largest champagne merchants in London.

Acrostics. An Entirely New and Original Work,

constituting the FIFTH SERIES of the popular A. E. H. Acrostics.
12mo, cloth elegant, 4s. 6d.

, The authoress is a lady of high position in the North of England, and her
books are very popular amongst the best Families in the country.

John Camden Hotten, 74 and 75, Piccadilly, W.   9

Popular Shilling Books of Humour.

ARTEMUS WARD: HIS BOOK.	HOOD'S VERE VEREKER.
ARTEMUS WARD AMONG THE MORMONS.	HOLMES' WIT AND HUMOUR.
	NEVER CAUGHT.
BIGLOW PAPERS.	CHIPS FROM A ROUGH LOG.
ORPHEUS C. KERR PAPERS.	MR. SPROUTS: HIS OPINIONS.
JOSH BILLINGS.	

Yankee Drolleries. Edited by George Augustus Sala,

Containing Artemus Ward; Biglow Papers; Orpheus C. Kerr; Major Jack Downing; and Nasby Papers. One of the cheapest books ever published. New Edition, on toned paper, cloth extra, 700 pages, 3s. 6d.

Orpheus C. Kerr Papers. The Original American

Edition, Three Series, complete. 3 vols. 8vo, cloth; sells at £1 2s. 6d., now specially offered at 15s.

. A most mirth-provoking work. It was first introduced into this country by the English officers who were quartered during the late war on the Canadian frontier. They found it one of the drollest pieces of composition they had ever met with, and so brought copies over for the delectation of their friends.

A Keepsake for Smokers. — "The Smoker's Text-

Book." By J. HAMER, F.R.S.L. This day, exquisitely printed from "silver-faced" type, cloth, very neat, gilt edges, 2s. 6d., post free.

"A pipe is a great comforter, a pleasant soother. The man who smokes thinks like a sage, and acts like a Samaritan."—*Bulwer*.

"A tiny volume, dedicated to the votaries of the weed; beautifully printed on toned paper in, we believe, the smallest type ever made (cast especially for show at the Great Exhibition in Hyde Park), but very clear notwithstanding its minuteness. . . . The pages sing in various styles the praises of tobacco. Amongst the writers laid under contribution are Bulwer, Kingsley, Charles Lamb, Thackeray, Isaac Browne, Cowper, and Byron."—*The Field*.

Laughing Philosopher (The), consisting of several

Thousand of the best JOKES, WITTICISMS, PUNS, EPIGRAMS, HUMOROUS STORIES, and Witty Compositions in the English Language; intended as "Fun for the Million." Square 12mo, nearly 800 pages, frontispiece, half morocco neat, 5s. 6d.

John Camden Hotten, 74 and 75, Piccadilly, W.

Sets of "Punch," 1841—1860. Mr. Hotten has purchased from the Messrs. Virtue and Co. their ENTIRE REMAINDER of this important set of books, which contains, among its 12,000 Illustrations and Contributions from the most noted Wits of the time, the WHOLE OF LEECH'S SKETCHES, 4 vols.; LEECH'S PENCILLINGS, 2 vols.; TENNIEL'S CARTOONS; DOYLE'S MR. PIPS HIS DIARY; MANNERS AND CUSTOMS OF THE ENGLISH; BROWN, JONES, AND ROBINSON; Punch's Almanacks, 1 vol.; Thackeray's Miscellanies, 4 vols.; The Candle Lectures; Story of a Feather; &c., &c. 39 half-yearly vols. bound in 20 vols., cloth gilt, gilt edges, published at £16 10s., to be obtained of Mr. Hotten for £6 10s. ONLY.

The Standard Work on Diamonds and Precious Stones; their History, Value, and Properties, with Simple Tests for Ascertaining their Reality. By HARRY EMANUEL, F.R.G.S. With numerous Illustrations, tinted and plain. New Edition, Prices brought down to Present Time, full gilt, 12s. 6d.

" Will be acceptable to many readers."—*Times.*

" An invaluable work for buyers and sellers."—*Spectator.*

See the *Times'* Review of three columns.

*** *This new edition is greatly superior to the previous one. It gives the latest market value for Diamonds and Precious Stones of every size.*

The Young Botanist: A Popular Guide to Elementary Botany. By T. S. RALPH, of the Linnæan Society. In 1 vol., with 300 Drawings from Nature, 2s. 6d. plain, 4s. 6d. coloured by hand.

*** An excellent book for the young beginner. The objects selected as illustrations are either easy of access as specimens of wild plants, or are common in gardens.

Gunter's Modern Confectioner. The Best Book on Confectionery and Desserts. An Entirely New Edition of this Standard Work on the Preparation of Confectionery and the Arrangement of Desserts. Adapted for private families or large establishments. By WILLIAM JEANES, Chief Confectioner at Messrs. Gunter's (Confectioners to Her Majesty), Berkeley-square. With Plates, post 8vo, cloth, 6s. 6d.

"All housekeepers should have it."—*Daily Telegraph.*

*** *This work has won for itself the reputation of being the Standard English Book on the preparation of all kinds of Confectionery, and on the arrangement of Desserts.*

John Camden Hotten, 74 and 75, Piccadilly, W.

Original Edition of Blake's Works.

NOTICE.—Mr. Hotten has in preparation a few facsimile copies (*exact as to paper, printing—the water-colour drawings being filled in by an artist*) of the ORIGINAL EDITIONS of the Books written and Illustrated by WILLIAM BLAKE. As it is only intended to produce—with utmost care—a few examples of each work, Mr. Hotten will be glad to hear from any gentleman who may desire to secure copies of these wonderful books. The first volume, "MARRIAGE OF HEAVEN AND HELL," 4to, is now being issued, price 30s., half morocco.

"Blake is a real name, I assure you, and a most extraordinary man he is, if he still be living. He is the Blake whose wild designs accompany a splendid edition of 'Blair's Grave.' *He paints in water-colours marvellous strange pictures—visions of his brain—which he asserts he has seen. They have great merit.* I must look upon him as one of the most extraordinary persons of the age"—CHARLES LAMB.

George Chapman's Plays, from the Original Texts.

Edited, with Notes and an Introduction, by ALGERNON CHARLES SWINBURNE. 4 vols., tastefully printed, uniform with Wm. Pickering's Editions of the "Old Dramatists." [*In preparation.*

UNIFORM WITH MR. SWINBURNE'S POEMS.

Fcap. 8vo, 450 pages. Fine Portrait and Autograph, 7s. 6d.

Walt Whitman's Poems. (Leaves of Grass, Drum-

Taps, &c.) Selected and Edited by WILLIAM MICHAEL ROSSETTI.

"Whitman is a poet who bears and needs to be read as a whole, and then the volume and ?????? of his power carry the disfigurements along with it and away.—He is really a fine fellow."—*Chambers's Journal,* in a very long Notice, July 4th, 1868.

☞ A great deal of prejudice in this country has been shown against this very remarkable author. His work should be read by independent minds, and an opinion formed totally apart from the attacks that have been made upon him.

Rossetti's Criticisms on Swinburne's Poems. Price
3s. 6d.

The Prometheus Bound of Æschylus. Translated in
the Original Metres by C. B. CAYLEY, B.A. Cloth, price 3s. 6d.

SECOND EDITION.—Now ready, 4to, 10s. 6d., on toned paper, very elegant.

Bianca. Poems and Ballads. By Edward Brennan.

MR. SWINBURNE'S NEW BOOK.

. *"A wonderful literary performance."*—*"Splendour of style and majestic beauty of diction never surpassed."*—WILLIAM BLAKE: A CRITICAL ESSAY. With facsimile Paintings, coloured by hand, from the original drawings painted by Blake and his wife. Thick 8vo, pp. 350, 16s.

"An extraordinary work: violent, extravagant, perverse, calculated to startle, to shock, and to alarm many readers, but abounding in beauty, and characterised by intellectual grasp. . . . . His power of word-painting is often truly wonderful—sometimes, it must be admitted, in excess, but always full of matter, form, and colour, and instinct

with a sense of vitality." — *Daily News*, Feb. 12, 1868.

"It is in every way worthy of Mr. Swinburne's high fame. In no prose work can be found passages of keener poetry or more finished grace, or more impressive harmony. Strong, vigorous, and musical, the style sweeps on like a river."—*Sunday Times*, Jan. 12, 1868.

Mr. Swinburne's New Poem. — A Song of Italy.
Fcap. 8vo, toned paper, cloth, price 3s. 6d.
. The *Athenæum* remarks of this poem—"Seldom has such a chant been heard so full of glow, strength, and colour."

Mr. Swinburne's Poems and Ballads. Third Edition.
Price 9s.

Mr. Swinburne's Notes on his Poems, and on the Reviews which have appeared upon them, is now ready, price 1s.

Mr. Swinburne's Atalanta in Calydon. New Edition, fcap. 8vo, price 6s.

Mr. Swinburne's Chastelard. A Tragedy. New Edition. Price 7s.

Mr. Swinburne's Queen Mother and Rosamond. New Edition, fcap. 8vo, price 5s.

Mr. Swinburne's Bothwell. *A NEW POEM.*
[*In preparation.*

Lost Beauties of the English Language. Revived

and Revivable in England and America. An Appeal to Authors, Poets, Clergymen, and Public Speakers. By CHARLES MACKAY, LL.D. In crown 8vo, uniform with the "Slang Dictionary," price 6s. 6d.

[*In preparation.*

Captain Grose's Dictionary of the Vulgar Tongue,

1785. A genuine unmutilated Reprint of the First Edition, price 6s.

₊ Only a small number of copies of this very vulgar, but very curious, book have been printed for the Collectors of " Street Words" and Colloquialisms, on fine toned paper, half-bound morocco, gilt top.

Slang Dictionary; or, the Vulgar Words, Street

PHRASES, and "FAST" EXPRESSIONS OF HIGH AND LOW SOCIETY; many with their Etymology, and a few with their History traced. WITH CURIOUS ILLUSTRATIONS. A New Dictionary of Colloquial English. Pp. 328, in 8vo, price 6s. 6d., by post, 7s.

See TWO UPON TEN, *in the Dictionary, p.* 264.

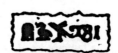

Egyptian Hieroglyphic cork, to be drunk, showing the computation of a man's leg. See under BREAKY LEG *(via. Strong Drink) in the Dictionary, p.* 61.

☞ *One hundred and forty newspapers in this country alone have reviewed with approbation this Dictionary of Colloquial English. "It may be doubted if there exists a more amusing volume in the English language."—*SPECTATOR. *"Valuable as a work of reference."—*SATURDAY REVIEW. *"All classes of society will find amusement and instruction in its pages."—*TIMES.

Original Edition of the Famous Joe Miller's Jests;

or, the Wit's Vade-Mecum; a Collection of the most brilliant Jests, politest Repartees, most elegant Bons-Mots, and most pleasant short Stories in the English Language. London: printed by T. Read, 1739. An interesting specimen of remarkable facsimile, 8vo, half morocco, price 9s. 6d.

₊ *ONLY A VERY FEW COPIES OF THIS HUMOROUS AND RACY OLD BOOK HAVE BEEN REPRODUCED.*

John Camden Hotten, 74 and 75, Piccadilly, W.   21

Hotten's "Golden Library"
OF THE BEST AUTHORS.

⸬ A charming collection of Standard & Favourite Works, elegantly printed in Handy Volumes, uniform with the Tauchnitz Series, & published at exceedingly low prices. ☞ *The New Volumes are:*

HOLMES ——————*AUTOCRAT OF THE BREAKFAST TABLE.* 1s. In cloth, 1s. 6d.

THE CLERGY ——————*THE BOOK OF CLERICAL ANEC-DOTES, and Pulpit Eccentricities.* 1s. 4d. In cloth, 1s. 10d.

CHAS. LAMB ——————*THE ESSAYS OF ELIA.* Complete. *Both Series.* 1s. In cloth, 1s. 6d.

DICKENS——————*SPEECHES UPON LITERARY AND SOCIAL TOPICS.* 2s.

"His Speeches are as good as any of his printed writings."—*The Times.*

A. WARD——————*IN LONDON, with the "PUNCH" LETTERS.* 1s. 6d. In cloth, 2s.

TENNYSON——————*OLD PROSE STORIES OF IDYLLS OF THE KING.* 1s. In cloth, 1s. 6d.

DISRAELI, GLADSTONE, AND BRIGHT'S SPEECHES are issued in separate vols., at 1s. 4d. Cloth, 1s. 10d.

They comprise all the important speeches of these great statesmen during the past 25 years.

CARLYLE——————*ON THE CHOICE OF BOOKS.* 1s. In cloth, 1s. 6d.

Should be read and re-read by every young man in the three kingdoms.

HOLMES ——————*PROFESSOR AT THE BREAKFAST TABLE.* 1s. In cloth, 1s. 6d.

A companion volume to "The Autocrat of the Breakfast Table."

LEIGH HUNT ——————*TALE FOR A CHIMNEY CORNER, AND OTHER ESSAYS.* 1s. 4d. Cloth, 1s. 10d.

A volume of delightful papers, humorous and pathetic.

HOOD ——————*WHIMS AND ODDITIES.* 80 Illustrations. 2 Series, Complete. 1s. Cloth, 1s. 6d.

"The best of all books of humour."—PROFESSOR WILSON.

LELAND ——————*HANS BREITMANN'S BALLADS. COMPLETE.* 1s. In cloth, 1s. 6d.

HAWTHORNE——————*NOTE BOOKS.* English and American. 1s. In cloth, 1s. 6d.

John Camden Hotten, 74 and 75, Piccadilly, W.

CPSIA information can be obtained at www.ICGtesting.com
Printed in the USA
BVOW06s1234190215

388467BV00016B/123/P